A MANNER OF BEING

The Urbana Free Library

A MANNER OF BEING

WRITERS ON THEIR MENTORS

EDITED BY
ANNIE LIONTAS AND JEFF PARKER

UNIVERSITY OF MASSACHUSETTS PRESS
Amherst and Boston

ISBN 978-1-62534-182-2 (paper), 181-5 (hardcover)

Designed by Sally Nichols
Set in Monotype Dante Standard and Adobe Kabel
Printed and bound by Sheridan Books

Library of Congress Cataloging-in-Publication Data

A manner of being : writers on their mentors / edited by Annie Liontas and Jeff Parker.
    pages cm
  ISBN 978-1-62534-182-2 (pbk. : alk. paper) — ISBN 978-1-62534-181-5 (hardcover : alk. paper) 1.
Authors—Biography. 2. Autobiographies. 3. Mentoring of authors. 4. Influence (Literary, artistic,
etc.) I. Liontas, Annie, editor. II. Parker, Jeff, 1974 Jan. 3–
  PN466.M365 2015
  809—dc23

                              2015028019

British Library Cataloguing in Publication Data
A catalogue record for this book is available from the British Library.

The following essays were published earlier in slightly different form;
copyright permission acquired and acknowledged:

    Nick Flynn on Philip Levine as the introduction to an anthology of
        writings dedicated to Levine.
    Anya Groner on Beth Ann Fennelly on *Literary Mothers*, the online
        blog celebrating female literary influence.
    Michael Martone on John Barth in the *Northwest Review* and in the
        book *Michael Martone*.
    Edie Meidav on Peter Matthiessen on 2paragraphs.com.
    Lee Montgomery on Five Mentors in the *Glimmer Train* newsletter.
    Padgett Powell on Donald Barthelme was delivered as a speech honoring the
        University of Houston Library's acquisition of the Barthelme papers.
    Rodrigo Rey Rosa on Paul Bowles (in Spanish) in *Lentra Internacional*, 2006.
    Tobias Wolff on John L'Heureux as the introduction to *Conversations with
        John L'Heureux* (CSLI Publications, 2011).

CONTENTS

OUTLIERS

LINEAGE II

TOUGH LOVE

NO MENTOR HERE

INTERVENTIONS

LINEAGE III

A MANNER OF BEING

INTRODUCTION

JEFF PARKER

I knocked on Arthur Flowers's office door in the Hall of Languages. I knocked again. We had a meeting scheduled—though I don't recall how we might have set that up. This was 1996, just pre-email era. There was a shuffling, unmistakably the sound of someone stirring from sleep. "Parker?" he said. "Hang on." He opened the door and told me to give him a minute. He walked down the hall to the bathroom, toothbrush in hand, and I stepped into his office. There was a makeshift bed of sheets on the floor, boxes of books, the smell of incense coming from some kind of shrine over the desk, clothes strewn around—clearly he was living here.

I have to admit, this was something of a surprise. It hadn't occurred to me that professors could be living in their offices. Then again a lot of things didn't occur to me. I was twenty-two years old and dumber than a stump, also less worldly than a stump. He came back down the hall, a lot more spry now, and instead of trying to hide the fact that he was living in his office, he told me straight up: he hadn't paid taxes on a grant, and the IRS was garnishing his wages. He didn't yet have enough for rent.

This was pure Flowers: I hadn't known him for five minutes. I was some idiot incoming MFA student. But he was unflinchingly honest and generous and real with me, as he is with everyone, before we even properly knew one another.

We talked for a long time that day. And we talked a lot after that. In his office and later at his apartment. (He moved out of the schoolhouse a couple weeks into the term.) I took an experimental fiction class with him in which he said one day: "I'm an experimental writer because I write about love, and what's more experimental than love?" We geeked out on hypertext. I read his books, which blew me away. I had never read anything like them. *De Mojo Blues* was a hardcore Vietnam novel about black soldiers from the Delta who were into Hoodoo. And his second novel, *Another Good Lovin' Blues,* was as close as a modern novel gets to pure song—this one about the tumultuous love affair between an old blues singer and a conjure. He explained to me what Hoodoo meant to him—it's a way of talking about the magic that great art, that great literature, that great mentoring makes—and he gave me a sacred book of something like spells. He introduced me to Clarence Major and Ishmael Reed and the Afro-spiritual literary tradition, which was about as far away as could be from what I knew of literature then. He told me about the tradition of the griot, the storyteller. He gave me a highjohn the conqueror root with a clear marble embedded in it. He told me that if he'd met me ten years ago he likely wouldn't have talked to me, some white guy. We couldn't have been more different; we couldn't have come from more different places and times, and those facts made his generosity of spirit toward me all the more meaningful. We shot pool. Went to Outback Steakhouse (though we were both vegetarians). He tried to teach me how to play blues harp. (I was hopeless, but he never let on.) He read early drafts of my novel *Ovenman* more times than I can count and I'm sure more times than he would care to remember. He was bringing me up without my even knowing it. When I graduated he gave me a kalimba, a thumb piano.

He wasn't the only important figure for me in the Syracuse University MFA program. Two fiction folk had been hired my first year. One of them was Flowers and the other was George Saunders. George is now sometimes known (rightly) as the "greatest living American short story writer," but back then he was just some dude who'd graduated from the program himself and recently had his first book of stories published.

George taught my first graduate workshop. Before arriving, George had requested all our manuscripts from our applications, and he would often refer back to them throughout the term. Here was a guy who was on his way to stratospheric, and it seemed like we—like I (though I know George makes everyone feel this way somehow) was the most important thing going. He marked up my manuscripts and made more time than seemed reasonable to sit in his office and break my writerly heart, to tell me what I needed to hear. In editing this book, I learned where he got this: from Doug Unger, who showed George respect by not telling him that the shit *he* wrote back-when was good when it wasn't.

George was so nice and giving that it mystified me a little bit. While I burned to write, I didn't have the slightest notion what it meant to be a writer or how one did it or really what the hell a writer was. I had already had a couple of mentors before I got there. I had already been infused with a kind of skepticism of the usual by Padgett Powell and caught a bit of redneck wild man from Harry Crews; but while those two have many strengths, "nice" and "giving" would not be the words you'd use. Back then if I was asked to describe what it meant to be an artist in the world, I would have said: be a maniac. Be Hunter S. Thompson or Charles Bukowski or Henry Miller. George was a completely different animal.

Saunders describes in his mentor essay having almost the exact same realization about Tobias Wolff that I had about him fifteen years later. George was watching Wolff with his family and realized that Wolff adored them, doted on them, even, and that conflicted with George's vision of what a writer was: "I [had] always thought great writers had to be dysfunctional and difficult, incapable of truly loving anything, too insane and unpredictable and tortured to cherish anyone, or honor them, or find them beloved."

In turn I watched George doting on his daughters or helping his wife Paula clean up the house at the end of a party they hosted for a bunch of dopey twenty-somethings, and it was, as hokey as this sounds, to bear witness to love, pure and simple.

I don't have much patience for arguments against MFA programs, especially when the program in question is one that students don't pay to attend. Whether one chooses MFA or NYC is beside the point. It is difficult to find a writer who did not study deeply at some point with another writer—and this almost universal relationship is all the more important for those like me, who come from places (the Redneck Riviera) and backgrounds (nonliterary, to say the least) that don't provide the stuff you need to know what it is or what it means to be an artist. It's not that one has to go to an MFA to learn to write or to find a mentor. One most certainly does not. But could there have been another context that might've drawn me into contact with Flowers and Saunders at one of the most impressionable moments of my life? When I was molding myself toward some as-yet unconceived manner of being?

In 2011, I started soliciting writers for the pieces in this book. I didn't know at the time exactly what I would do with them, but I knew that I had been trying to say for some time what it meant for me to know Flowers and George. And I was teaching more and more, trying to be some version of what they were to me but unable myself to say exactly what that was.

In the middle of assembling this book, Flowers brought me and about twenty other MFA alumni back to Syracuse for a panel on literary success and significance. Rather than using his own research fund for "research" in the Bahamas, he spent it all on bringing us up there. At this event I met a young writer named Annie Liontas, a graduating MFA student, and we hit it off. She signed on to co-edit *A Manner of Being*, and many of the fine pieces here are the result of her good work. Annie and I are completely different in so many ways, but we've both found something absolutely necessary in the same two mentors. After me, she is the next generation in the line of Flowers, as he might say.

As contributions for the anthology rolled in, I was surprised at the commonalities that emerged in folks' experiences. I was impressed by the unexpected mentors that some writers claimed (Fabian Cancellara's legs for Richard Poplak, an Ann Arbor bookstore clerk for Mary Gaitskill, a Random House publicist for Sheila Heti). And the advice, on writing and life—the advice! Before I knew it, the manuscript had become a testament to studying art deeply with someone, a handbook for those who wish to teach and mentor, and a compendium of the most essential advice passed down through one line or another.

One of the resounding messages here is that mentors give permission. As Peter Meinke says, "poets don't need a lot of encouragement, but they need some." Aimee Bender calls Judith Grossman "a gate opener, a wing maker." James Franco says that teachers open doors. "Teachers say, 'yes,'" he writes. Hubert Selby, Jr., told a young Henry Rollins, "You're a real %$#%! great writer!" Mentors gave Alissa Nutting and George Saunders permission to be themselves in their writing: whenever Nutting resisted her impulses to write the weirder stuff that came naturally but didn't seem like "serious fiction," Kate Bernheimer told her, "Whatever you're doing, don't stop"; and Tobias Wolff kept reminding Saunders throughout his Hemingway-impersonation period not to lose the magic.

Another thing mentors do is to take you seriously, often when, as in my case, there is no good reason to do so. With every interaction, John Hawkes had the ability to make Mary Caponegro feel like she was the most important writer in the world. Ron Carlson, in fondly recalling his drama teacher, writes that the man's "responses took my work with such engagement that I had to recommit." Jon Paul Fiorentino remembers Robert Kroetsch as someone who constantly implored, "It's your turn to talk . . ." John L'Heureux was "dead serious" in reading the work of a young Tobias Wolff and "absolutely honest in his response; after which, for those with ears to hear, he generously helped us imagine the possibilities for successful revision." Douglas Unger writes that Raymond Carver gave to his best students the message that all writers need to hear: they've got a chance; they've *got a shot.* "Keep going, just this way," Carver would say. "With luck, you're going to make it." As Sheila Heti writes, "a person needs only one figure of understanding in order to not feel she is a random, spinning particle in the universe, without destiny or care."

These essays contain more nuggets of good advice and invaluable lessons learned than I can count. Kevin Canty writes that he never embarks on a rewrite without hearing Harry Crews's voice asking, "Son, what's this story *about?*" and saying, "Nothing will happen to a reader unless it happens to a character first." Gordon Lish taught Sam Lipsyte that there's no getting to the good part; rather, "it all has to be the good part." Ron Carlson told Tayari Jones that "being a writer is all about making mistakes and managing disappointment. . . . You have to recover and move on." Megan Mayhew Bergman's friend Tammy encouraged her to "leap and don't look" and to "make yourself vulnerable and have at it." Hubert Selby, Jr., ripped a young Henry Rollins for letting his ego get in the way of his writing and preached smallness of self: "The writer must do all he or she can to get out of the way of the story." Terrence Malick urged Josip Novakovich to write to his strengths, to create lengthy dialogues like the ones the two of them had engaged in as they walked around Austin together. Beth Ann Fennelly's tough love taught Anya Groner that brutal edits make beautiful poems: "If you break up," Fennelly said, "do it fast. It'll hurt, but if you let unhappiness linger, it'll only hurt more." Jay Parini asked Gore Vidal whether or not he could get away with twenty to thirty pages in which characters discuss the philosophy of Kierkegaard. Vidal squinted into the sun, scratched his forehead, and said, "You can do that. But only if these two characters are sitting in a railway car, and the reader knows there is a bomb under the seat."

Sometimes a mentor just tells you the simple thing that you need to hear, as Fred Chappell said to George Singleton: "Sit down and get your work done."

Arthur Flowers, in remembering John Oliver Killens, chalks mentorship up to this: "At a critical moment in my aspiration to the literary life I had somebody in my life who cared. A traveler who knew the road. Giving me guidance every step of the way."

The pronouncement that reverberates loudest through the selections in this book is exemplified in Unger's piece, "A Manner of Being." Unger explains that "it's not so much what [a mentor] *tells* a developing writer as what [a mentor] *does* to the writer that changes everything." A manner of being, then. U.S. army sergeant Martha Washington taught Pam Houston to "be helpful, tell the truth, do unto others. . . . Take your dishes to the sink, clean up your Legos, think about the other person as often as you think of yourself." Even in rejecting potential mentors, Paisley Rekdal found herself moving into a certain state of being, a place where she could come into her own as an artist and a person. Stephen Elliott, without naming any one mentor, taps into this notion: "in the moments when I've been ready to let someone in, a saint has always arrived in my life"—and he surrounds himself with the people he most wishes to become.

I'm biased, of course, but I think that Saunders describes it best: he remembers an uncomfortable moment after a reading in Las Vegas when one of Unger's students approached and confessed a personal tragedy to the two of them. Saunders watched Unger throughout the exchange:

> What I see Doug doing gets inside my head and heart and has stayed there ever since, as a lesson and an admonition: what Doug is doing is staring at his student with complete attention, affection, focus, love—whatever you want to call it. He is, with his attention, making a place for her to tell her story—giving her permission to tell it, blessing her telling of it. What do I do? I do what I have done so many times and so profitably during my writing apprenticeship: I do my best to emulate Doug. I turn to her and try to put aside my discomfort and do my best to listen as intently as Doug is listening. I remember this moment as an object lesson in what I take to be Doug's ethos: be kind, pay attention, err on the side of generosity.

When I finished a novel draft in 1999, my final year at Syracuse, Flowers invited me to New York City—he wanted to hand-deliver my manuscript to his agent and introduce me to her. I could stay at his girlfriend's apartment with the two of them. They brought me to an Ethiopian restaurant in Harlem. He took me aside and told me to be sure to wash my hands before we ate because in an Ethiopian restaurant you eat communally with your hands. I had never eaten Ethiopian food before; and while I would like to think that, at the age of twenty-five, I didn't need to be told to wash my hands before eating, I probably did. The next day we got on the bus. I don't remember what part of the city we were coming from or what part of the city we were going to. But I remember

Flowers explaining to me what a transfer was, telling me that no matter what I did in life, I should always take my transfer.

We got off the bus. He walked purposefully ahead of me. We entered a swanky building and took the elevator up to his agent's office. I was nervous as hell, and I breathed a huge sigh of relief when she wasn't there. He turned the first page of my novel manuscript over and scribbled a note to her in his handwriting that looked more like Chinese than English, and he left it with her assistant.

About a month later, his agent called me up and took me on. The story from there is a long one, full of ups and downs, but that's pretty much the beginning of my literary life. I couldn't then and I still can't believe he did all that for me. But that's how to be, isn't it?

Working with Saunders and Flowers, I learned a lot about a manner of being, one that's informed everything, that's made and remade me. I don't mean to say that I'm perfect. Far from it. I've done a stint or two living out of my office. I've had failures of kindness and respect. I've fucked up big—in life and in my work, and I will again.

Saunders writes that knowing Unger and Wolff has helped him grow into a better version of himself, more dignified and less selfish. I was all brash and posture back then. I didn't know who or what I was, and I was imitating all the wrong things. I can only imagine the version of myself (as writer and as dude) I could've grown into with different mentors or none. How much more and how much more severely I would have fucked up, how much crappier I'd have written. In the ways that I can, I try to do what they did for me for the young writers I'm fortunate enough to cross paths with: to go above and beyond the call.

But here's the most profound thing that I realized while editing this book: to some degree the process of coming into a new manner of being under a great mentor is, for me, very much like the process of writing fiction. On some level, sure, there's empathy, a quality central to spoiling paper with ink by writing lies about fake beings. But even beyond that, the identity of your writing is forged from your experience and obsessions, which you allow to develop organically. You never force it, you remain open to possibility, you want your work to surprise you, and you want to make of it (and of yourself) something greater than you ever could have imagined possible when you started. You revise you revise you revise, and then, if you're lucky, when all is said and done, you have a bruised and broken text that means something to you and is capable of speaking to others, and only then have you written something, and only then have you begun to be.

Jeff Parker, George Saunders, and Arthur Flowers, 1998

LINEAGE I

TOBIAS WOLFF

ON JOHN L'HEUREUX

In the summer of 1974, my brother, knowing my interest in short stories, gave me a collection he had recently read and thought I'd like—*Family Affairs*, by John L'Heureux. I loved it. What kind of man could write a sentence like this, describing a nun's self-destruction by car and bovine: "Mother Humiliata took the cow at sixty . . ."?

My kind of man.

I had been writing in isolation since I was fifteen, and managed to publish a novel in my late twenties, but when the actual book arrived, and I cracked a beer in lieu of champagne, and began to read it, I discovered that I hated it. Hated the writing, the too-purposeful "plot," the protagonist. I had to make a new beginning, that was clear, but how? And then, in a great stroke of fortune, I received a Wallace Stegner Fellowship to enter the Stanford writing workshop led by John L'Heureux—this just months after reading his book.

While at Stanford I had the benefit of meeting with other fine writers and teachers, but it was John who affected me most profoundly: the rigor of his reading, the invention and boldness of his editing, and the humanity and wit of his personal presence. It was a truculent workshop in many ways, skirmishes flaring constantly along the borders of gender, politics, sexual identity, and failed romances, but John could make us laugh pretty much at will, and did. Nor did he bestow this gift on us alone: I once happened to meet a man who'd been a student of his years earlier at a Jesuit high school back east. He told me that another priest had been needling John with snide messages left on the blackboard. When

displeasure with a terribly overwritten story, as if hoping to talk about any-thing *but* its failings, which were apparently so obvious they deserved little comment from him. To earn his approval—at least for *one* story!—I changed everything about my writing, stripping it down to a harder core of honesty, which I define not as realism as much as making sure each sentence contrib-utes to a significant emotional truth or crucial idea in a fictive world. I remem-ber pacing back and forth outside his office, waiting until he finished that one story I had worked so hard on, draft after draft. Finally, he opened the door, and with an obvious, cheery enthusiasm, he said: "It's marvelous. Almost there. Are you busy now, or can you spend some time?"

In this manner, Stern taught me an invaluable lesson about teaching. Not unlike the way a theater director pulls the performance from a struggling actor on a stage, it's not so much what one *tells* a developing writer as what one *does* to the writer that changes everything. He worked with my fiction for two years until I had pieced together a book, and it earned a trip to New York and an option from Random House. Later, when that fledgling, apprentice novel wrote itself into a failed mess, Stern pulled strings to help me get into the Iowa Writers' Workshop, long past the application deadline. He kept checking in, as he did with dozens of former students, for years and years. He even saved me from an impending eviction once by sending me a check for a hundred dollars. His acceptance and encouragement we celebrated that day in his office "with cheery knowledge," as he put it, is a major reason that I decided to pursue writing as a vocation, and our friendship continued for more than forty years until his death in 2013, at age eighty-four. In the lengthy feature-obituary by Bruce Weber that ran in the *New York Times,* Philip Roth speaks of Stern as "a writer's writer" for the effusive erudition of his writing style and his generosity to characters. Add to this his generosity to young writers, holding back his encouragement until just the right moment, then cheering them on for the rest of their lives.

At Iowa, I worked with John Irving, who served as my thesis adviser. I still run workshops according to John's model: requiring students to read each manuscript twice, the first time straight through, without critical judgment; followed by a second reading with a pencil in hand, marking the pages, then writing a brief, thoughtful critique so that the writer who submits can better absorb and de-program from the intense hothouse atmosphere of a workshop by going over the written responses. John Irving has a wonderful eye for what's strongest in a manuscript—like a precise tool for literary navigation. Developing writers need this guidance, a story-sense kind of geolocation.

John would note in a margin: "Good. Strongest here." Or: "Develop this." In conference, often fresh from a workout in the gym, still in his wrestling sweats, he would push me to move a story in a certain direction to develop a strength he perceived. Irving also showed his courage and generosity by workshopping some of his own writing with us, reinforcing a community sense that *we're all in this together.* He workshopped an early draft beginning to his landmark novel, *The World According to Garp* (about forty pages or so); then he kept us informed of its progress as he cut all but the last few pages, which he developed into the opening of the published book a few years later. This breaking through the master-student authority relationship was a wonderful feeling— the respect he showed for us by letting us critique his own rough-draft work, like co-conspirators in a common enterprise of making art, which we certainly were and are still. When it feels right for the chemistry of a workshop, I do the same.

Overall, though, the most impactful influence on my teaching comes from my close friendship with Raymond Carver. Through a strange, coincidental series of turns on life's journey, Ray and I ended up as shirt-tail in-laws—brothers-in law through the Burk sisters: my late wife, Amy, and Ray's first wife, Maryann. We became best friends, beginning with that time Ray called his "hardscrabble years" of alcoholism and even harder living right at the edge. We shared multiple, low-rent living situations: in San Francisco and the Bay Area, in Iowa, in New York. During his worst years, he was my homeless guest, a time filled with dramatic scrapes and shocks, chaos in our families, and personal destructions caused by way too much drinking powered at least in part by what I believe to have been a deliberately bohemian embrace of the false myth of a rebellious, decadent life that the creative artist should be living. "These are mythic times," we used to say, drunk and stoned, blinded by ego and selfishness.

Later, after Ray quit drinking, we shared much better years—times of sincerest, heartfelt generosity to his students and friends. He taught at El Paso, then at Syracuse. Applause and fame visited Ray and his work with a truly mythic reversal and suddenness like no other writer I've known before or since. When Ray won the Harold and Muriel Strauss Living Award from the American Academy of Arts and Letters, I was among the first people he called to share the news, with an ecstatic, triumphant celebration. "I'm never going to have to teach again!" he said. Then: "Are you interested in my job?"—which is how Syracuse University invited me to try out two semesters as visiting faculty, which turned into a tenure-track position.

Over the years, bad and good, Ray shared a lot of his thoughts about writing with me. I saw both sides—the man and the artist—sitting next to him as we read manuscripts, taking coffee breaks together, and we spent hundreds of hours on the telephone, talking about writing, our student writers, and *how to be a writer in the world,* which he spoke about with full-throated generosity, wanting, I believe, what John Gardner pointed out that all writers really want, deep down—to be loved and admired, especially by other writers, not only for our words but for who we are as artists and as people, or for our *characters,* as Gardner put it, both real and fictional. To be a "good fellow" was, in Ray's worldview, a term of highest praise.

In the "bad old days," Ray and I would get together with other writers and read from our works to each other through a boozy haze. If a passage were good, Ray would say so mainly by repeating a line or two right back at the writer. At a weak passage, he'd scoff, or laugh, or just say, "Oh, no," with an expression of having suffered some irritating indignity. On the ride back to his house in Cupertino, or later, to whatever cheap apartment where we were living, passing a half pint of vodka back and forth, Ray might say, "Just bag that one," if he didn't like what I'd read. And I recall two important lessons he taught about stories during those drunken rides: "First, you have to set the scene or situation. Give it at least a page and a half before cutting away or flashing back." Then: "Never get chi-chi or pretentious. Don't get carried off by the sound of your words. For sure don't do it in the first paragraphs."

Those were my early workshops with Ray: in the front seats of cars, or on shabby sofas in rented rooms or cheap motels, during those harsh "bad old days." During his later, sober, "good years," visiting each other in our homes in Syracuse or in Washington State, he taught me many more lessons: "When you think you're finished with a story, set it aside for a while. Pick it up again and write the two pages that come before the beginning to make sure you've begun in the right place. Then do the same with the ending—try writing two pages after it to make sure it's right." As in his essay, "On Writing," he'd say, "at any point in a story, anything can happen. Stay open to suggestion, no matter where it comes from." Ray believed that only by the rarest of accidents could good writing happen without extensive revisions: "Fifteen drafts might be enough," he would say. "Or sixteen." Or: "I can't understand writers who say, 'if I'd only taken the time to go at that passage once more.' Remember: never let go of any story too soon. With some stories, well, if you can't just bag it, best never let it go," he said, and then he laughed.

Looking back at my own teaching, I couldn't be more grateful for the privilege of Ray's mentoring. He gave to his best student writers what I think all young writers need: that sense that they've got a chance, they've *got a shot*. "Keep going, just this way," he'd say. "With luck, you're going to make it." If not in person, he could communicate this by a phone call, or by just the right scribbled note at the bottom of a manuscript page. He made the young writer whose work he liked feel anointed and embraced by the literary world. Ray showed reticence to some students, yes, those whose work he didn't like, in which case he simply didn't have the time for them. But for writers he liked, he'd do almost anything. Need a job? He'd talk a writer up on the phone. Need an editor or an agent? He made calls right away, or he'd write a note: *pay attention to this one*. Above all, Ray Carver passed on his total commitment to artistic generosity toward young writers, so crucial in their lives, which is one of the reasons he's still so loved and admired, and surely one of the least "dead" dead writers of the twentieth century.

Good teaching lives on in ways we can't know or predict, and more than specific content, it's a *manner of being* in our mentors that I believe we keep tapping into as a vital source for our students. I can never express enough how grateful I am to the three ingenious, generous writers who taught me— Richard Stern, John Irving, and Ray Carver. These days, more and more, it's their *manners of being* that I aspire to keep passing on, adding some sense and spirit of my own, with cheery knowledge, as Stern would put it, at how *lucky* we are to be doing this. Thanks to them! Thanks to the writers who follow us into teaching!

Raymond Carver and Douglas Unger, Christmas 1977

GEORGE SAUNDERS

ON DOUGLAS UNGER AND TOBIAS WOLFF

MY WRITING EDUCATION: A TIMELINE

February 1986

Tobias Wolff calls my parents' house in Amarillo, Texas, leaves a message: I've been admitted to the Syracuse Creative Writing Program. I call back, holding *Back in the World* in my hands. For what seems, in chagrined memory, like eighteen hours, I tell him all of my ideas about Art and list all the things that have been holding me back artistic-development-wise and possibly (God! Yikes!) ask if he ever listens to music while he writes. He's kind and patient and doesn't make me feel like an idiot. I do that myself, once I hang up.

Mid-August 1986

I arrive in Syracuse with 300 dollars, in a 1966 Ford pickup with a camper on the back. Turns out, here in the east, they have this thing called "a security deposit." For the next two weeks I live out of my truck, showering in the Syracuse gym, moving the Ford around town at night so as not to get nabbed for vagrancy, thinking it might reflect badly on me if I have to call Toby, or Doug Unger, my other future teacher at Syracuse, and request bail money.

One day I walk up to campus. I stand outside the door of Doug's office, ogling his nameplate, thinking: "Man, he sometimes *sits* in there, the guy who wrote *Leaving the Land*." At this point in my life, I've never actually set eyes on a person who has published a book. It is somehow mind-blowing, this notion that the people who write books also, you know, *live:* go to the store and walk around campus and sit in a particular office and so on. Doug shows up and invites me in. We chat a while, as if we are peers, as if I am a real writer too. I suddenly feel like a real writer. I'm talking to a guy who's been in *People* magazine. And he's asking me about my process. Heck, I *must be* a real writer.

Only out on the quad do I remember: oh crap, I still have to write a *book*.

Late August 1986

After the orientation meeting, the program goes dancing. Afterward, Toby and I agree we are too drunk to let either him or me drive the car home, that car, which we are pretty sure is his car, if there is a sweater in the back. There is! We walk home, singing, probably, "Helplessly Hoping." In his kitchen, we eat some chicken that his wife Catherine has prepared for something very important tomorrow, something for which there will be no time to make something else.

I leave, happy to have made a new best friend.

The Next Day

I wake, chagrined at my over-familiarity, and vow to thereafter keep a respectful distance from Professor Wolff and his refrigerator.

For the rest of the semester, I do.

Classes Begin

I put my copy of *Leaving the Land* on my writing desk so that, if anyone happens to walk in, he or she will ask why that book is there, and I will be able to off-handedly say: "Oh, that guy's my teacher. I sometimes go into his office and we just, you know, talk about my work."

And then I'll yawn, as if this is no big deal to me at all.

September–October 1986

I start dating a beautiful fellow writer named Paula Redick, who is in the year ahead of me. Things move quickly. We get engaged in three weeks, a Syracuse Creative Writing Program record that, I believe, still stands. Toby takes Paula to lunch, asks if she is sure about this, the implication being, she might want to give this a little additional thought.

Later That Semester

At a party, I go up to Toby and assure him that I am no longer writing the silly humorous crap I applied to the program with, i.e., the stuff that had gotten

Toby read Chekhov aloud: they are simply tools with which to make your audience feel more deeply—methods of creating higher-order meaning. The stories and Toby's reading of them convey a notion new to me, or one that, in the somber cathedral of academia, I'd forgotten: literature is a form of fondness-for-life. It is love for life taking verbal form.

May 1987

Paula and I are married in Rapid City. We get a nice chunk of money at the wedding. We honeymoon on the island of Saint Bart's, in a madly expensive villa, which happens to be right next to an even more madly expensive villa being rented by Cheech, of Cheech and Chong fame. We spend all of our wedding money. Why not? Soon we will be rich and famous writers and money will mean nothing to us.

September 1987

I am in a workshop with Toby. One night, our workshop is being disrupted by the Syracuse University cheerleading squad practicing loudly in the room above. Toby grows increasingly annoyed. Finally he excuses himself. We're worried. In Syracuse, the cheerleading squad is about equal in status to the mayor. We think of how we might console Professor Wolff if he returns with an S.U. megaphone squashed down on his head.

But no: instead, here come the chastened cheerleaders, humbly toting their boom box, muttering obscenities.

Toby sits down.

"Let's continue," he says.

We feel that the importance of what we are doing has been defended. We feel that, even if we are members of a marginalized cult, our cult is tougher and more resilient than theirs, and has cooler leadership.

Later That Semester

Toby is a generous reader and a Zen-like teacher. The virtues I feel being modeled—in his in-class comments and demeanor, in his notes, and during our after-workshop meetings—are subtle and profound. A story's positive virtues are not different from the positive virtues of its writer. A story should be honest, direct, loving, restrained. It can, by being worked and reworked, come to have more power than its length should allow. A story can be a compressed bundle of energy, and, in fact, the more it is thoughtfully compressed, the more power it will have.

His brilliant story "The Other Miller" appears in the *Atlantic*. I read it, love it. I can't believe I know the person who wrote it, and that he knows me. I walk over to the Hall of Languages and there he is, the guy who wrote that story. What's he doing? Talking to a student? Photocopying a story for next day's class? I don't remember. But there he is: both writer and citizen. I don't know why this makes such an impression on me—maybe because I somehow have the idea that a writer walks around in a trance, being rude, moved to misbehavior by the power of his own words. But here is the author of this great story, walking around, being nice. It makes me think of the Flaubert quote, "live like a bourgeoisie and think like a demigod." At the time, I am not sure what a bourgeoisie is, exactly, or a demigod, but I understand this to mean: "live like a normal person, write like a maniac." Toby manifests as an example of suppressed power, or, rather: *directed* power. No silliness necessary, no dramatics, all of his considerable personal power directed, at the appropriate time, to a worthy goal.

December 1987

Paula is four months pregnant with our first child. We are still not rich and famous. While we are out in South Dakota visiting Paula's family, she goes into early labor. Her doctor says he has good news / bad news. Good news: he thinks he can save the baby. Bad news: she's going to have to go to bed, and won't be able to get up until the baby is born in March.

I write to my teachers at Syracuse about this, promise to do the work by mail. I try to do so. I read and write like a fiend. I'm worried and distracted, schlepping back and forth from the Rapid City library and home and the post office. Finally I get a call from Doug. I'm afraid he might be calling to say that this method just isn't working: I'm going to have to drop out, forfeit my fellowship checks. But no. He's calling to say he thinks I'm worrying about his class too much. You've done enough, he says, you pass, knock it off, go spend more time with Paula, that's what's important, that's what you'll remember years from now.

So that's what I do.

March 1988

Our first daughter is born. Life goes crazy, in a good way. Artistically, I continue to lose the magic, writing stories in which I am sort of like Nick Adams, but in Sumatra, Indonesia. The guy in the story is a thinly veiled version of me, when I was in the oil business, if I had been more like Nick Adams. Get it? I am not so crass as to name myself "Nick." Instead I name myself "Casey." Or, sometimes, when I am really off my game, "Vic." Once, in a very confused moment, I am "Bernard Casey." Casey / Vic / Bernard Casey is always silently witnessing petty and/or decadent cruelties, then eventually participating in them himself, because our times are so rotten and we are such a—well, not a "lost" generation, but more like a sort of "drifty" generation. Anyway, at the end of my stories, Casey / Vic / Bernard Casey, having done something naughty, will often broodingly go off to stand by a river, to feel miserable and think a line that is like an epiphany. Sometimes something in the natural world might metaphorically mimic Vic's mental state:

> Vic thought of the Indonesian village he had just accidentally burned down while goofing around. He felt bad. His spirits drooped, there on the banks of the river.
> In the river an elephant's trunk drooped.

This story might be called, for example: "On the Dark Banks of the Tragic Sad River."

May 1988

I have my final thesis meeting with Doug. My thesis, with its revised title, "On the Tragic Banks of the Dark Sad River: Stories," is crap. We meet in the student cafeteria. Had there been an elephant in there, his trunk would have been very droopy indeed. I've tried my hardest during my two years at Syracuse, but somehow, under the pressure of suddenly being surrounded by good writers, I went timid and all the energy disappeared from my work—I've lost the magic indeed, have somehow become a plodding, timid, bad realist. I'm terrified before the meeting. I know I haven't done good work, but don't want to hear that. But I also don't want to hear that what I know is bad, is good.

What Doug does for me in this meeting is respect me, by declining to hyperbolize my crap thesis. I don't remember what he said about it, but what he did *not* say was, you know: "Amazing, you did a great job, this is publishable, you rocked our world with this! Loved the elephant." There's this theory that self-esteem has to do with getting confirmation from the outside world that our perceptions are fundamentally accurate. What Doug does at this meeting is increase my self-esteem by confirming that my perception of the work I'd been doing is fundamentally accurate. The work I've been doing is bad. Or, worse: it's blah. This is uplifting—liberating, even—to have my unspoken opinion of my work confirmed. I don't have to pretend bad is good. This frees me to leave it behind and move on and try to do something better. The main thing I feel: respected. Doug conveys a sense that I am a good-enough writer and person to take this not-great news in stride and move on. One bad set of pages isn't the end of the world.

August 1988

I graduate and get a job as a tech writer at a pharmaceutical company. At night I leave through the downstairs labs, where the animal tests are done. One night I see a bunch of beagles in slings, awaiting morning surgery. They are in the slings so that their heart rates will stay low. To me, it seems that being suspended in a sling in a dark lab overnight would have the opposite effect. But mine is not to question why: I have a young family to support.

Goodnight, dogs, so sorry.

1988 or so

On a visit to Syracuse, I hear Toby saying goodbye to one of his sons. "Goodbye, dear," he says.

I never forget this powerful man calling his son "dear."

All kinds of windows fly open in my mind. It is powerful to call your son "dear," it is powerful to feel that the world is dear, it is powerful to always strive to see everything as dear. Toby is a powerful man: in his physicality, in his experiences, in his charisma. But all that power has culminated in gentleness. It is as if that is the point of power: to allow one to access the higher registers of gentleness.

August 1990

Our second daughter is born. We are happier than ever, poorer than ever, busier than ever. Officially I am still a tech writer, but I work for an environmental company now. Really what I do is not so much tech-write but make copies of reports. My special area of expertise is: doing the covers. I am trying to write at work but have begun to realize that, not only will the world not mourn if I never write again, it would actually prefer it.

September 1990

I finally break out of Nick Adams mode and write what I think might be a good story. When I finish it, as in a movie, I hear Toby's voice in my head: "Don't lose the magic." Of course, of course, I finally get it! All these years I've been losing the magic! Toby's comment at that party all those years ago suddenly presents as a sort of hidden teaching moment, a confirmation that this leap I have made is real.

Seeking confirmation, I send the story to Toby. Is he busy, does he have three kids, is he teaching a full course load, is he in the middle of a new book? Yes. Does he read it and send me a generous letter, confirming that I'm on the right track, in less than a week?

Yes.

1996

My first book comes out. Please note that, between this entry and the previous one, six years have passed. I have been working as a technical writer all this time. One of the bosses, all these long years, keeps calling me "GeorgeMan."

Ugh.

1997

I am teaching at Syracuse myself now. Toby, Arthur Flowers, and I are reading that year's admissions materials. Toby reads every page of every applicant's story, even the ones we are almost certainly rejecting, and never fails to find a nice moment, even when it occurs on the last page of the last story of a doomed application. "Remember that beautiful description of a sailboat on around page 29 of the third piece?" he'll say. And Arthur and I will say: "Uh, yeah . . . that was . . . a really cool sailboat." Toby has a kind of photographic memory re stories, and such a love for the form that goodness, no matter where it's found or what it's surrounded by, seems to excite his enthusiasm. Again, that same lesson: good teaching is grounded in generosity of spirit.

1998

Toby has moved to Stanford. Paula and I buy Toby and Catherine's house on Scott Avenue. In the garage is the sled that is the real-life corollary of the sled in "The Chain." On a section of molding is a penciled chart of the heights of his kids. In the basement, on a workbench, in a childish scrawl, in crayon, is written: DOWN WITH THE REPUBLICANS!

One night I'm sitting on the darkened front porch of our new house. A couple walks by. They don't see me sitting there in the shadows.

"Oh, Toby," the woman says. "Such a wonderful man."

Note to self, I think: Live in such a way that, when neighbors walk by your house months after you're gone, they can't help but blurt out something affectionate.

1999

I do a reading at the university where Doug now teaches. During the after-reading party, I notice one of the grad writers sort of hovering, looking like she wants to say something to me. Finally, as I'm leaving, she comes forward and says she wants to tell me about something that happened to her. What happened is horrible and violent and recent, and it's clear she's still in shock from it. I don't know how to respond. As the details mount, I find myself looking to Doug, sort of like: Can you get me out of this? What I see Doug doing gets inside my head and heart and has stayed there ever since, as a lesson and an admonition: what Doug is doing is staring at his student with complete attention, affection, focus, love—whatever you want to call it. He is, with his attention, making a place for her to tell her story—giving her permission to tell it, blessing her telling of it. What do I do? I do what I have done so many times and so profitably during my writing apprenticeship: I do my best to emulate Doug. I turn to her and try to put aside my discomfort and do my best to listen as intently as Doug is listening. I remember this moment as an object lesson in what I take to be Doug's ethos: be kind, pay attention, err on the side of generosity.

2000

Toby comes back to do a reading at Syracuse. He reads "Bullet in the Brain" to a standing-room-only crowd. Afterwards, there is a stunned, appreciative silence—a little like that moment after fireworks just before the yelling starts. I look at Paula. There are tears in her eyes. Mine too. These, we later agree, are tears of gratitude. How lucky we are, we feel, that such a person exists in this world, and that we had the good fortune to cross paths with him, and be his students. Knowing him has helped us grow into better versions of ourselves: more dignified, less selfish. This, of course, is what a "role model" is: someone who, by gracefully embodying positive virtues, causes you to aspire to them yourself.

During the Q&A someone asks what Toby would do if he couldn't be a writer.

A long, perplexed pause.

"I would be very sad," he finally says.

The room makes a sound that means "Us too."

AND IN SUMMARY

Why do we love our writing teachers so much? Why, years later, do we think of them with such gratitude? I think it's because they come along when we need them most, when we are young and vulnerable and are tentatively approaching this craft that our culture doesn't have much respect for, but which we are beginning to love. They have so much power. They could mock us, disregard us, use us to prop themselves up. But our teachers, if they are good, instead do something almost holy, that we never forget: they take us seriously. They accept us as new members of the guild. They tolerate the under-wonderful stories we write, the dopey things we say, our shaky-legged aesthetic theories, our posturing, because they have been there themselves.

We say: I think I might be a writer.

They say: Good for you. Proceed.

ADAM LEVIN

ON GEORGE SAUNDERS

Early in my first semester at Syracuse, I was pissing into a urinal while Christian TeBordo, my new best friend and fellow MFA student, was also pissing into a urinal. We were talking about something I don't remember—probably a book or a girl with red hair—when George Saunders came in, and we clammed up fast. We had both come to Syracuse to study with George but didn't know him very well yet. He hadn't yet taught us the ways in which good fiction resembled good flirting. He hadn't yet explained to us how the world wanted us to fail, to break, to sell convenience and opinions—and how that was a blessing, how that had made us who we were and would make us who we'd be. We didn't yet know how good he was at family and friendship, how generous and decent a human being he was—we'd heard things, but still had yet to see them firsthand, and I, at least, had trouble believing them, having long since consumed more than a few haunting facts about certain other writer heroes of mine. We had no idea how hard he worked. We didn't yet even really believe we could be taught. Also we were young, and prone to getting starstruck. Beyond all of that, our dicks were out. What to do was unclear. Did one with his dick out say hello to his favorite writer? If one with his dick were to say hello to his favorite writer, did he follow with a dick joke? If I were the living master of the twentieth- and twenty-first-century short story and some student with his dick out were to say hello to me, would I think less of that student? And what if the student *didn't* say hello to me? Would I think he was snubbing me? That he was ashamed of his dick? That he was snubbing me *because* he was ashamed of his dick?

"You know, I was just thinking," George Saunders said—he was washing his hands. "If a bomb went off in this bathroom, killing us all, how fucken crazy would that be?"

"Very," said TeBordo.

"I know!" I said. "That would be *so* fucken crazy!"

"I mean, the progress of American letters," George said. "It could be set back as much as fifteen seconds."

SCHOOLHOUSE

Here's where you get good bread in Irvine, she told us. She liked to think about the work. She liked to run it through her mind and give it depth that way. Her intellect was rebellious and playful and wide ranging and incisive. She told me about the idea of mythic versus public language—and that a story with a voice could be helped by being grounded in a real place or else lifted into the magical. When asked what she was reading once, she proudly said, *"Love and Rockets,"* which I later discovered was a graphic novel. I had not known that was an allowable answer. She did not fit what I imagined an MFA interim director would do and say, and in this way she was a gate opener, a wing-maker.

MARY CAPONEGRO

ON JOHN HAWKES

I feel that nearly everything good in my life originated with or intersected the fact of Jack. He was the closest thing to a guardian angel one could have in this mortal realm, but his angelic nature was beautifully shot through with mischief. The day I met him, the first day of the term at Brown in 1981, he talked with me extensively about my fiction, assuring me among other things that everything I wanted to do in poetry I could do in prose, and stood with me beside the soda machine in some building on the university quad, hesitating before the illuminated square buttons, smiling and asking in charming neurotic sincerity, "Which do I *really* want?" We were kindred neurotics from the start.

As to what was right for someone other than himself, he seldom hesitated. He knew exactly what he wanted on my behalf, was often adamant. He probably advised me on almost every category in life: literature, writing, employment, academia, romance, health, cuisine, travel, you name it. How to eat a baked potato daily to gain weight. Which of his good friends to stay with in Vienna or Wurtzburg. Whether or not and when to trade adjunct teaching for a tenure-track job. Whether or not to take a fellowship in Rome, a residency in Santa Fe. Even whether to change a reservation in order to expand or contract a brief visit to Providence. And the most charming part was the active role he took once the decision was made. I will never forget the relish he took in calling the airline to change the reservation for me. He loved to take charge that way, to improve a situation, to make something happen. He was a force of generosity. I believe that one of my earliest publications took place because he strong-armed someone on the editorial staff to take a chance on a story he believed in. And his belief was a good-luck charm. He was fierce in his assumptions about what one's work merited—that it should be graced with the best publisher, the best agent, etc. Accept nothing less.

But who needed anything outside the sphere of Providence, when you could have John Hawkes introduce you for your master's thesis reading—they were held in those days at the extremely classy Spanish House—and make you feel you were the most important writer in the world, in his eyes? As if that weren't gift enough, there was the sharing of a beautiful, serene, domestic environment. To dine with Jack and Sophie in their Everett Avenue home was such a lovely thing: to visit in the afternoon and view Sophie's garden out back behind the dining room, to eat her delectable, elegantly prepared meals as light poured in, to visit in the evening and watch Jack, apron-clad, prepare his favorite pasta puttanesca, to drink French wine, and listen, until the wee hours, to the infinitely entertaining anecdotes about Vaucluse and Provence, about Sade's castle, about horseback riding, about crazy literary festivals, about creative ways to sneak benign substances through customs. Every member of a dinner party at the Hawkeses' was the recipient of delightful hospitality and storytelling nonpareil. I'm afraid that my reciprocation couldn't possibly live up to its intention, and the brownies I would bake for the workshop that was regularly held in my apartment (which had the literary blessing of having as its prior tenant Angela Carter) were a sorry substitute for the elegant fruited concoctions that would grace their table for dessert. I think Jack would have been quite happy if those brownies had transformed themselves to chocolate torte or apple pie or tiramisu, but there was wine and cheese and probably that mattered more. A workshop without wine in Providence was unthinkable.

There was so much that went above and beyond the call in John Hawkes's mentorship. He was 100 percent Jack, not one ounce of pretentiousness, the most authentic human on the planet—though some people, alas, misread his deep sincerity as posturing. He responded emotionally to narrative, not just intellectually; some thought him too sentimental, but he wasn't. So many of the novels that I came to love and teach were first suggested to me by Jack: *Nightwood*, *The Ogre*, *The Good Soldier*, *The Heart of the Matter*, *Waiting for the Barbarians*. I remember with shame his disappointment when he brought Nabokov's story "Symbols and Signs" to our graduate workshop and I couldn't yet appreciate its manipulative magic, instead claiming that it paled against the mastery in Nabokov's novels. Jack couldn't bear that I didn't instantly share his adoration for it. My epiphany came soon after; and of course by now, I've taught that story more often than any other. I learned from him how to read, to write, to critique, to teach. It seemed so natural to teach, so ineluctable, when one had known the miracle of such devoted mentoring. Auspiciously, as I write this, I prepare to teach *The Passion Artist*—fortunately back in print. My students are already relishing it. The class is called "Le Mot Juste" and it features stylists. Who belongs on such a syllabus more than Jack? He modeled in every sentence the relation of eros to language.

One of the earliest stories I ever wrote, "The Star Café," was guided through its many, many drafts by Jack, who never ceased to nurture it and then to champion it. Decades later, it remains my best-known story. When its erotic nature garnered labels of pornography from some, he wouldn't let me for a minute give the allegation credibility. He told me how his mother had fended off the prudery of those who found his fiction inappropriate and offensive. When my father died while I was in the middle of working on a comic novella called *Sebastian,* and I didn't know how in grief to reconnect to comedy, Jack and Sophie brought me gorgeous peonies, and he bequeathed his secrets about writing through the most phantasmagoric manifestations of grief after his own father had died. That was his most useful advice of all, I suppose, because no grief can accommodate the magnitude of loss that represents Jack's passing from this world.

Postcard from John Hawkes to Mary Caponegro

JAMES FRANCO

ON SCHOOL

Mentors. I've had a few. I've been to too many schools. I've been at some schools for too much time. I've been a mentor to some. But I haven't given enough time to being a mentor; this is why I teach at two universities, one art school, and have a bicoastal acting and filmmaking school of my own.

The teachers I loved—acting teachers, writing teachers, directing teachers— were the ones who were completely focused on their students. There were some teachers who had their own careers, and you knew that they were only doing it for the money. Some teachers had their own careers and didn't need the money, but they were doing it to meet young actresses, and to feed off the students' energy.

Even though I teach, I know that I'm still wrapped up in my own work. The teaching pulls me out of myself. I have been teaching for four years now, and I usually schedule a single day for all of my Los Angeles classes so that if I'm working out of town—for example, when I was in *Of Mice and Men* on Broadway—I can fly into Los Angeles, teach, and then fly back out within twenty hours. But even though I'm killing myself, and spending tons of my own money, and having to fight to carve out that time from my professional schedule, I still feel like it's not enough.

When I was a freshman at UCLA I wasn't in the theater school, and I wasn't in the film school, and I was jealous of all the creative students that had been admitted to those selective programs. I had wanted to go to art school, but my parents wouldn't pay for it, so we compromised: I was an English major. There were creative writing classes in the English department, but students were admitted by selection, and I was so worried that my freshman-level creative writing wouldn't get me in that I didn't even try. I felt locked out of all these creative programs. I wanted to write, I wanted to make art, I wanted to direct, I wanted to act. So instead of trying to jump through the hoops at UCLA, I left after my first year and went to acting school.

Acting school was a place where my creative desires were accepted and supported; I was surrounded by students with similar interests, and dedicated teachers. In that environment I could work hard, as hard as I wanted, and I could see dividends. I worked my ass off. I did acting exercises and rehearsed scenes with whomever I could, from morning to night; I drove as far east as Eagle Rock, and as far west as the beach at Santa Monica. I rehearsed in generic actor apartments, in parks—the police were called more than a few times for what concerned citizens thought were real altercations—and in restaurants. I couldn't stop rehearsing.

Even when I started getting professional work, I stayed at school. I couldn't train enough; I wanted to be the best. I stayed at acting school for *eight years*. By the time I left I had won a Golden Globe, been nominated for a Sag Award, an Emmy, and been in some of the biggest movies ever made, but I was still interested in finding a way to be *great,* truly great, to stand alongside DeNiro, Brando, Dean, and Montgomery Clift. I wanted to be River Phoenix, but I thought I wasn't odd enough to be the next River, so I had to supplement my emptiness with diligence.

After eight years, the amount of time it takes to become a doctor, when my twenties were three-quarters over, I left acting school because I realized that it had become too tightly entwined with my life. I didn't know how to socialize because I spent all my time rehearsing. I didn't know how to choose which movies to be in because I only chose films that my teachers would approve of. I didn't know how to relax because I filled every free moment reading the books I would have read if I had stayed an English major at UCLA—except that I read even more than I would have read had I stayed, because I was overcompensating for dropping out.

It's weird to say, but I went through a depression. I don't say this for pity, and I certainly didn't talk about it much when I was in the middle of it because how would it look if the guy who was cast as Spider-Man's best friend in a billion-dollar franchise was sad because he didn't like most of the work he was doing? And I got even more depressed because I couldn't talk about it with anyone. I mean, I woke up crying. I searched for ways out of the slump: religion, volunteering, Italian vacations. Finally, my girlfriend—the person who witnessed the middle-of-the-night crying and slumped around Italy with the wet-noodle boyfriend—suggested I take a class at UCLA Extension, opening the idea that education could be the answer.

After taking a writing class with my now-friend and poetry publisher Ian R. Wilson and a Bible-as-literature class with Lynn Batten, I was hooked on school. Before, such classes had felt like a distraction to my budding acting career: now they were the most interesting things I had going because they were learning environments unburdened by the professional pressures of my acting life. I then learned that the UC system allows students to reenroll at any time, that an eighty-year-old actor had recently gotten his bachelor's degree after leaving school for a career when he was eighteen. I didn't want to wait sixty years to come back; I was ready to actually put my career on hold for the education I had put aside years before.

After reenrolling, I had some legends of English academia as teachers: A. R. Braunmuller for Shakespeare, N. Katherine Hales for experimental fiction, Mark McGurl for early twentieth-century American literature, and Eric Sundquist for Holocaust literature. I put my head down and humbled myself because I was eight years older than most of the other students. I felt like an intruder, but I wanted to be there so badly, I endured. There were some odd reactions to my presence, but they didn't deter me from my work with my professors. I took too many classes because I couldn't get enough learning. My attitude was completely different from when I was eighteen: now I was there because I wanted to be.

I also got into the creative writing classes that had intimidated me when I was eighteen, and Mona Simpson became the first reader of my first book, *Palo Alto.*

After I got my bachelor's degree, I signed up for more school. I went to four graduate schools at the same time because I realized that in grad school you get to study exactly what you want, and in the writing programs your teachers are often the best writers alive. Going to school with Gary Shteyngart, Tony Hoagland, Robert Boswell, James Wood, Jonathan Lethem, Michael Cunningham, David Shields, Amy Hempel, and so many others was as good as working as an actor under Marty Scorsese, Francis Coppola, or Steven Spielberg.

After a while the press heard about all my schooling and it became a thing to criticize, as if I were doing it all for the attention or not taking it seriously. This is fine, they can read into it whatever they want; I still got the education and the guidance from some of the best mentors in my fields of interest. And it also warms my insecure heart a little to know that in the future I'll be able to say to any snarky critic, "That's Doctor Franco to you, bitch."

As a teacher of film directing, writing, acting, and art, I try to open the doors of opportunity and ability for my students. I try to give them what I felt like I was missing for so long, a way *in;* and I try to guide them down their individual paths so they can walk with confidence.

For so long, I felt shut out of everything I was interested in. Sometimes I still feel that way. My gluttonous engagement with education was pricked by a need to break through to the other side. My overextended efforts were part of a personal battle to run beyond the pressures and the naysayers that might hold me back or imprison me in the boxes they had fashioned for me: "privileged straight white male," "stupid actor," "dilettante," "attention seeker," "no talent."

What I found on the other side, once I had broken through, was a bunch of artists, and now I was one of them, having a conversation with them. With my students I *open* the doors. As a teacher I say *yes.* As a teacher I give them everything I would have wanted as a student.

Recently, Harmony Korine gave me some advice because I was still worried about how some of my work was being perceived.

THE WISDOM OF HARMONY

- Roll with it. You'll be free when you realize that none of this really means anything. Just keep doing your thing.
- It all goes by in a blink.
- Just keep having fun.
- Artists have become very tactical because of the money.
- Always remember you are inventing your own game . . . it takes a while for people to figure out what's goin' on.

Peace.

LEE MONTGOMERY

ON FIVE MENTORS

"Take my hand," Los Angeles novelist and poet Jim Krusoe said, laughing, "and I will lead you . . . into obscurity." This was the mid-nineties, a brilliant sunny Los Angeles afternoon. Jim and I were walking across Santa Monica College's campus to grab a coffee. We met weekly in those days; Jim had just hired me as the new editor for the *Santa Monica Review.*

The hilarity of his statement is unforgettable, and oddly prescient, but the inspiration remains foggy. Since I had just returned from a rollicking two-year ride as a student at the Iowa Writers' Workshop, I was probably thanking him for our friendship, for trusting me as the new editor, and for being steadfastly supportive of my work during its long and awkward infancy. After all, only three years earlier, Jim, who was my first creative writing teacher, had started me on the road that led to one of the most intense writing workshops in the country. As a new creative writer, and naïve to this world, I endured many dark days during that first year in Iowa. If it hadn't been for Jim, who was always available to offer up some zany wisdom, and other kind souls who lent their shoulders, I might have taken a Woolfian plunge into the Iowa River.

In Los Angeles everyone knew about Jim Krusoe because he ran the *Santa Monica Review.* He also directed the Santa Monica Writers' Conference, led workshops at Beyond Baroque in Venice, and held Wednesday night creative writing classes at Santa Monica College. As a novice writer, I applied to them all; and although he said no, he did invite me to take a beginning creative writing class on Mondays. Since I had been writing for newspapers for almost ten years and was then writing a weekly art column and monthly cover features about Los Angeles artists for one of the biggest dailies in the area, I was humbled. Very. And fiercely determined to crack out of my beginning phase and find a path into the fictional universe.

I did. Slowly. Week after week in Jim's Monday night class, I began to learn about creative writing. He gave prompts for in-class assignments that were often whacky. *Write about something completely unexpected in a room, like a car behind a couch. A pool in the kitchen. Include sentences that have the following number of words. One. Twenty. Ninety-eight words. Four.*

Beyond smart, beyond hilarious, Jim possessed another quality that I can only describe as magical—a little like the good part of the Pied Piper, before he led the children off the cliff. He was expert at creating a sense of discovery and adventure within the process of writing. There were no rules. The point was not to write a prize-winning story. Or even a linear one. The point was to find something new, surprising, and then turn it on its ear. Again.

Jim Krusoe is a legendary teacher, I think, because he has an almost mystical way of opening creative windows by creating absence or, more succinctly, blowing holes in narrative. His line-to-line comments are typically minimal; he is a man committed to the solemn beauty of the bracket—one at the beginning of the recommended deletion and one at the end. Invariably the recommended incision isn't clean but leaves scraggly ends, like severed organs in need of mending. On larger pieces, I often found little x's in the righthand corner of the page, page after page after page, no apologies, no explanation, just full-on mayhem: cut, cut, cut. Once, he deleted everything in a twenty-five-page story *but* the first paragraph.

After I recovered from the shock of the slaughter, I often sat in bewildered wonder, overwhelmed by blank fury, staring into craters of nothingness. I didn't know it at first, but I eventually learned that if I sat long enough and endured the horror and pain of failing (again), not knowing the answer (again), writing poorly (again), something might flower. And if it did, that something was always better. Much better. *Way better.*

Whereas Jim Krusoe pushed out, encouraging wild leaps of imagination, Deborah Eisenberg, more of a realist and traditionalist, pushed in, leading me toward the power of crystalline language and the constructs of the traditional narrative. Sometimes I saw (or maybe I dreamed) the process as this: Deborah and I sitting together in a teeny-tiny room and splitting hairs with teeny-tiny tweezers. *No, not that hair. This one.*

Deborah's teaching strategy was subtle, full of whispers, and never directive, as if she were trying to blow me in the right direction, like a piece of paper across the room. Her comments on manuscripts were lightly penciled in tiny, tiny letters, encouraging precision, precision. Her stories are often like little plays and, to my mind, so perfectly executed, I can't begin to discern the scaffolding. We were doing intricate work, not brain surgery, certainly, but almost, braiding stories with silk threads. When we sat to review a story, I'd follow her long, slender, white finger as it traipsed across the page, sentence after sentence. *Here,* she pointed, her voice deep and dramatic and slow, *here, going along. Okay, good, good, and then? And chaos. It's as if you just gave up and said, oh, hell, . . . you know what I mean.*

Deborah, who said she took years to write a story, taught me that writing is a long, long process of discovering clarity. You first write this, for example, but it will take many, many drafts to begin to understand where you're headed. And then sometimes you have to be able to accept that you're headed nowhere.

In my first semester at Iowa, Deborah's workshop was full of All-Stars, second-year students, all big fellowship holders, with talent and book deals and agents and swinging egos, who were versed and savvy in the ways of this peculiar world. I was one of only two first-year students in the class. (The other had been studying writing since kindergarten, when he began reading Dickens, and was best friends with Annie Dillard and another famous author.) With one year of creative writing classes at a community junior college under my belt, I knew no one. Plus, I had just left a summer writing workshop in Topanga Canyon, where people actually *sang* their novels.

At Iowa, at least in my first year, workshops were discouraging and overwhelming because I didn't get what it was that I was after. Or why it seemed so impossible to attain. I felt that whatever glory was waiting in the publishing world wasn't meant for me. That is why Jim McPherson's complete lack of interest in anything but books was such a relief. Though he was a man of very few words, my meetings with him eventually helped me to define my work. Despite its failings, which were many, he was able to intuit where the work might have originated—what impulse, what interest—and spent most of our meetings going through bookshelves and delivering books by authors he thought might help me do whatever I was trying to do.

Marilynne Robinson was also seminal for a variety reasons. For instance, she rarely minced words. "Some people can never be writers because they lack the character," she said during one of our seminars. Though I am paraphrasing, I never forgot the essence of her remark because I feared she was talking about me. (I swear she was looking right at me.)

Because life and consciousness are experienced and remembered differently, they are not always malleable enough to be crammed into a linear composition. I was trying to write like a regular person, but I couldn't seem to compose stories in a normal way. I really wanted to write like Alice Munro, but to do the engineering, to invent the contrivances to make that sort of marvel of a story, bored the hell out of me. I was interested in language and expression. My brain did not work in a realist way.

The early nineties were the heyday of Ann Beattie and Raymond Carver, both masterful realists, and I began to believe there was a conspiracy favoring narrative prose. I felt confused about why stories had to be composed using techniques of linear narrative. For whatever reason—brain wiring, too much LSD as a teenager, bad chemistry—I took a long time to understand how the experience and consciousness I was interested in writing about could be accurately reflected in dialogue and scene.

At Iowa, I took refuge in reading the experimentalists and was mildly annoyed when sitting around seminar tables listening to twenty-two-year-olds criticize the work of John Barth, Robert Coover, and William Gass. I was working as a reader for the *Iowa Review* and often retreated to its offices to talk to David Hamilton about this. "Where did the experimentalists go? Who were their protégés? Were they being published and if so by whom?"

David Hamilton, the consummate professor, down to the leather elbow patches on his tweed blazer, was intrigued enough to keep the conversation going. Eventually he suggested I help him edit a special issue about experimentalists for the *Iowa Review*. The University of Iowa Press turned the issue into a book, and William Gass wrote the introduction, which appeared in the *New York Times Book Review*.

The experience changed my life. For one, it started my career as an editor. It was also another step toward becoming the writer I have become, which, it seems even after twenty years, means "the writer I am still becoming" as I mostly bump along as if following crumbs through the forest, looking to the sky, awaiting my instructions.

CARMEN MARIA MACHADO
ON KEVIN BROCKMEIER AND MICHELLE HUNEVEN

My final term at the Iowa Writers' Workshop did not so much resemble a semester of school as it did a woman scrabbling to hold onto a boat that is rapidly tipping sideways. I was at the end of an abusive relationship and had spent the semester manically tearing through no fewer than six brand-new stories—one of them an eighty-page novella of fever-dream provenance—simply because if I stopped moving long enough to think about my life, I was certain I'd drown.

I'd signed up for two workshops that semester—one with Michelle Huneven, one with Kevin Brockmeier. Michelle's was all-genre, and Kevin's had a science fiction / fantasy focus, but I loved them both with equal measure. Kevin was a serene, generous, and thorough reader. Michelle was brilliant and funny, thoughtful and no-nonsense. By contrast, all semester I showed up to workshops looking like I'd been keelhauled. I spent more than one class with my head tipped slightly back to keep the tingling behind my nose from becoming tears. And I turned in uncontrolled and unedited stories, things that felt less composed than cut out of me.

In workshop, Michelle was kind but firm. "These stories have great imagination," she said. "But you need to be tougher with yourself. Your writing gets away from you and you need to sit harder on your prose. Examine these stories more. Go deeper." I was embarrassed. Maybe I didn't have the discipline to be a writer. Here I was at the end of my MFA, I thought, and I am the worst kind of fraud.

A few days later, I opened up my card-catalogue mailbox and found inside a tiny Schleich lamb figurine with stippled plastic wool. It was the size of a black walnut but solid—satisfying to hold. I didn't know who'd left it there, but I carried it around with me for days before setting it on my nightstand.

When I met with Kevin to talk about my thesis, I apologized for everything I was writing. "I feel like I'm a mess," I confessed. "And these stories are really weird and broken." He took out his copy of my manuscript and went through each story individually, talking about its strengths and weaknesses. He tapped the novella with his finger, the one I was worried about the most. "This one is special," he said. Later, he gave me a workshop letter reminding me that every reader is not my reader and encouraging my experimental impulses.

At the end of the semester, Kevin presented our entire class with a box of vintage robot wind-up toys. "It's tradition," he said, "to give these out to every science fiction and fantasy class at the workshop." (A joke—we were the first.) I chose one made of gold and pea-green hammered tin. It had wide red feet and a key jutting from its torso. When I turned the key and released the lever, the robot lurched toward me in a guileless way that made me smile despite myself.

When the semester ended, so did my relationship. I invited Michelle to coffee and asked for her advice. Love advice, for once. She talked about knowing when something is worth saving—more accurately, when it's worth working hard for—and when you need to let go. Afterwards, she asked, "Did you get my lamb?"

I looked up from my mug. "That was you?" I said. "Why?"

"I just saw it and thought it was something you needed," she said.

The artifacts of Michelle's and Kevin's wisdom—the lamb and the robot—now sit on my desk; my mentors and their advice staring me down every time I open my computer to write. Imagination and discipline: lessons from a sinking ship.

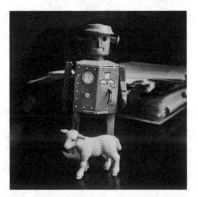

Gifts from Kevin Brockmeier and Michelle
Huneven to Carmen Maria Machado

LEONID KOSTYUKOV

ON ANATOLY KIM

When I enrolled at the Moscow Literary Institute, which was essentially a constellation of writing workshops, I was assigned to the seminar taught by Vyacheslav Maksimovich Shugayev. The bond between the two of us had three—if I can put it this way—birth defects: I didn't know Shugayev as a writer, I didn't choose him, and he, in truth, did not choose me. We didn't get along so well. To be quite fair, I must say that Vyacheslav Maksimovich was a decent and well-intentioned man, and years later I found some benefit in his advice. That is a different story, though.

At that time, in the 1980s, one of the growing literary schools in Moscow was the Urban School (*Gorodskaya Shkola*): Anatoly Kim, Vladimir Makanin, Ruslan Kireev. I liked their writing. To be precise, I liked Kireev a lot or not at all, which put me on guard because I felt that he himself could not differentiate a success from a failure. I liked Makanin, but we were both graduates of the Department of Mechanics and Mathematics at the Moscow State University, and I could see some of the common patterns that we shared. I would say that I liked Kim's writing without reservation. An ethnic Korean, he added something special to the matter of Russian prose, something that I could roughly call meditativeness.

Here I should probably add that of the two writers I admired—Makanin and Kim—I had more admiration for the one who was less accessible for me, less easy to understand. I am not sure whether many would agree, but I feel admiration is closely connected with a sense of wonder.

And so, having written a big original work in my second year, I nervously brought it to Kim to read—with the request to join his seminar. This way, I chose a teacher for myself. Kim had closed his seminar and didn't plan to teach again or take on new students, but he did agree to read my work and happened to like it so much that he allowed me to transfer in. This way, our choice became a mutual one, and our teacher-student relationship grew.

The people we meet, the things we do, the things that happen to us, our successes and failures all form experience, and any kind of experience has benefits. When talking about the value of mentorship in writing, it clearly would be best to find some benefit that's more direct and immediate in nature.

During my student years, there were two valuable qualities that Kim showed: first, he was always sincere and firm in estimating successes and failures; and, second, when he praised, he praised with generosity and passion, which gave me confidence.

In 1987, I wrote about sixty stories and five or six novellas—a lot of fiction, and Kim liked it. He helped me to compile a book and escorted me to the publishing house. I was held up a bit inside, and when I came out, my teacher was waiting for me. It turned out that he also wanted to take me out for dinner. We went to the legendary restaurant at the Central House of Writers (*Tsentralny Dom Literatorov*), which, at the time, was not open to the general public and where I saw Yevgeny Yevtushenko at the table next to us. As I was digesting the delicious meat, an idea dawned on me: I had written four hundred pages' worth of stories and novellas when I could actually have written a novel . . .

"You think now that you could have written a novel," Kim said. "But it isn't true. You need a longer breath to write a novel, which you don't have yet."

You know, if this had happened to someone else and not to me, I probably wouldn't believe it. But by that time, my teacher knew me so well that he just literally read my mind. It's hardly surprising, but after that I trusted 100 percent in this idea of a long breath and didn't try to write a novel for another couple of years. When I eventually did, I breathed a long breath and completed a novel, if not a good one. This is how Kim saved me a whole year of life that I could easily have wasted on fruitless efforts.

Translated from the Russian by Alina Ryabovolova

SCOTT LAUGHLIN
ON ALBERTO DE LACERDA

I met Alberto de Lacerda (1928–2007) in the fall of 1991 at Boston University as a student in his class "Poetry from Baudelaire to Surrealism." After one dazzling class midsemester, he asked whether any of us wanted to have coffee. No other professor had issued such an invitation to me, and I was totally intimidated. A week later, however, I saw Alberto limping along Commonwealth Avenue, and an impulse prompted me to approach him. He announced we could meet that Friday at 9 a.m. "Don't be late!" he scolded in advance.

I was not late, and a friendship was born. It was, of course, more of a mentorship (he had no children, and I, no father), but he always treated me as an equal, which is perhaps one key to the mentor relationship. "I don't play guru," he used to say, but then he played exactly that. I soon learned that his poetry, which he wrote in his native Portuguese, was not just admired but had been praised by some of the major figures of the twentieth century: Elizabeth Bishop, Edith Sitwell, Sofia de Mello Breyner, T. S. Eliot, John Ashbery, Octavio Paz, Anne Sexton, and Robert Duncan, to name a few. He had read with, corresponded, or dined with them all.

As I was initiated into the details of Alberto's life, I learned that people universally considered him the most cultured person they knew, and I was lucky enough to come under his wing. He sent me countless books and catalogues, always inscribed "With Love" in his neat hand. He introduced me to the work of the best, but not necessarily the most well known, writers from many cultures and eras: Cavafy, Saint John of the Cross, Machado de Assis,

Fernando Pessoa, Frank O'Hara. He sent me compact discs, everything from his beloved Mozart to Bill Evans. I was lucky enough to walk next to him through some of the best museums of the world. His passion for the Bellinis—Jacopo, Gentile, and especially Giovanni—became mine, as did his adoration for the three giants, as he called them, of twentieth-century art: Picasso, Matisse, and Klee. The bar was set very high, and, of course, I've failed to meet it—but mentors naturally have high, often unattainable, expectations.

Alberto gave me my first work of art, a serigraph by Vieira da Silva, signed, which she had created specifically to illustrate his long poem "Lisbon." He arranged for the most famous living Portuguese painter, Paula Rego, one of his closest friends, to draw me one afternoon in London. Immediately after finishing it, she handed me the drawing, along with an etching. I've kept acquiring such pieces and now have a modest collection. Alberto was adamant about the necessity of experiencing art when given the opportunity, whether a play, concert, gallery, or museum show. When the Vermeer exhibition came to Washington, D.C., in 1995, he insisted I travel from New York to see it. "These paintings won't be together again in your lifetime," he said.

Today I still heed this creed. In 2012, I flew to New York specifically to see Phillip Seymour Hoffman in "Death of a Salesman." When Hoffman tragically died a couple of years later, I heard Alberto say from beyond the grave, "I told you!"

I first visited Portugal because of Alberto, an experience that led me to cofound the DISQUIET International Literary Program, a big part of my life that has introduced hundreds of other writers, famous and unknown, to Portugal and its heritage and culture. The program is dedicated to his spirit and memory.

But above all what I cherish most are his letters. We wrote more than three hundred letters back and forth during our sixteen years of friendship. I keep his letters next to my bed, but it took a miracle to find my letters to him. After his death in 2007 of a stroke, his flat was revealed as a wasteland of trash, newspapers, plastic bags, and other detritus. It was impossible even to walk through the halls. Mice were living under his bed. It was a very sad discovery for his friends, none of whom had been inside his apartment for a number of years. But more importantly, inside that apartment was a treasure trove: 24,000 books and publications (many signed), 9,000 LP recordings, 13,000 literary documents, 12,000 photographs, and close to 1,000 works of art. His estate, weighing sixteen tons, was sent to be scanned and digitized at the Mario Soares Foundation in Lisbon, at the behest of Soares himself—

one of Portugal's most important political figures and a big fan of Alberto's poetry.

On a visit to Portugal after the estate materials had arrived there, I went to the foundation and was promptly handed a box. My letters to him had been found, and now they were being returned to me. It was a sad but beautiful feeling to hold a part of myself I thought I had given away forever. It was, in many respects, my past self, some part of me I never thought I'd know or see again, were it not for Alberto. Yes, he was right, "guru" isn't quite the right word for what he played; in fact, it was something well beyond.

JEDEDIAH BERRY

ON WILLIAM WEAVER

To teach at a college you once attended as a student is to lead a double life. In one, you are a mature adult with vast stores of experience, respectable shoes, office hours. You have the answers to important questions, or you know how to deflect them with questions of your own. Sometimes you find yourself saying something inspiring, and pen points scurry over notebook pages. When young people come to you for guidance, your advice seems reasonably sound, even to you. You learn from your students, because it's impossible not to.

Meanwhile, in your other life, you are eighteen years old and wondering how you're getting away with this charade. At faculty meetings you wait for your colleagues to realize that a student has infiltrated their ranks. In the classroom, when you write on the blackboard, your handwriting looks awkward and childish. Yes, you want to push your students to work beyond the limits they've imagined for themselves, to get them thinking deeply, critically, creatively—but you also want to talk about the bands playing on campus next weekend. This other life is not unlike those dreams in which you travel back in time, your old brain transported to a place that knew you when. Everything feels familiar, but nothing's quite the way you remembered it to be.

In 2013, nearly fifteen years after I'd graduated from Bard College in upstate New York, I was back with an office of my own and a title with the word "professor" buried in it somewhere. My old student ID number was now my faculty ID number. Some of my former teachers were now colleagues.

Those first weeks, my body remembered things about the campus which I thought I'd forgotten. It knew exactly how many steps to take in the library stairwell before grabbing the newel post to swing toward the door. I once caught myself walking toward my old dormitory instead of toward the building where the Written Arts program was housed. And every time I passed it, I checked to see if the lights were on in William Weaver's house, close to the center of campus on Annandale Road, a house that had once belonged to Mary McCarthy. Then, a moment later, I would remember that William Weaver, like Mary McCarthy, didn't live there anymore.

Before I knew William Weaver, I knew the work of Italo Calvino. The eighteen-year-old I'd been had encountered an excerpt from one of his books in an essay assigned for a course on critical theory. I don't remember the essay, but I remember the passage from Calvino. *Men of various nations had an identical dream. They saw a woman running at night through an unknown city.* . . . I tracked down a copy of *Invisible Cities* in Kingston, New York, and read it over Thanksgiving break in something like a state of intoxication.

Later, I realized that the name of the translator was familiar. Hadn't I seen William Weaver's offerings in Bard's own course catalogues? Yes, but he taught classes on Italian literature and translation, and I knew almost nothing of the language. Undeterred—and accompanied by a friend who shared my interest in Calvino's work—I approached Professor Weaver about sponsoring an independent study. I was grateful to learn that he'd been waiting for someone to make this very request.

Professor Weaver was soon Bill. Each week, we met for several hours at his house, in the cluttered but cozy study there. When my friend and I arrived, Bill would either be building a fire in the fireplace or making espresso on his stovetop. I didn't drink coffee, so when he offered me a cup, I declined. He made the same offer every week, and I kept turning him down. Eventually, though, I saw how much this disappointed him, so on the fourth or fifth week, I accepted. Hospitality was important to him, and I was expected to perform my part in the ritual.

A ritual which, in this case, left my head buzzing from the unprecedented rush of caffeine. I remember feeling as though I had floated up to the ceiling, my eyes losing focus, while Bill told stories about his life and work. It was through stories that Bill did most of his teaching. He told us about serving as an ambulance driver in Italy during the Second World War. And with great humor, he described some of his earliest jobs as a translator, writing Italian subtitles for American B movies. I felt the thrill of the young idolater when he spoke of meeting Calvino in his study: "blank white walls, no pictures, no distractions." When Bill had asked Calvino what he was working on, he'd gestured vaguely and said, "A little something about cities."

We did not read all of Calvino's work that semester—Bill told us from the start that we would discuss only the books he himself had translated. But this left us with no lack of material. *Cosmicomics, The Castle of Crossed Destinies, If On a Winter's Night a Traveler,* each a puzzle, a revelation, a journey to the beginning of the universe or to the moon, stories within stories, books within books. Bill's respect for and love of language were evident in all his lessons. He spoke of cadence and tone, of the musical qualities of the prose. We read aloud together, his English and Calvino's Italian, so we could hear the rhythms of each.

And he circled back again and again to one point in particular. Though Calvino experimented with many styles and structures, he said, one could always identify him in his sentences, and in the consistency of his vision. Like the pre-big-bang universe depicted in his story "All at One Point," the whole was contained in the smallest part.

Calvino died when I was eight years old. I'd gone into this study thinking that William Weaver was the closest I would ever get to him. And maybe this was true, but I quickly realized that what Weaver could give us of Calvino was no more important than what he gave of himself.

Calvino, he said, had for some years fallen out of fashion in Italy. "Over there," he said, "they think he is cold." To me, his blend of the mythic and the humorous was anything but cold, and even the scientific qualities of the fiction were expressed playfully. This was true of the original, but I knew it only because Bill's own warmth and humor were part of the equation. The man who built fires and made espresso for his undergraduate pupils was, in the corridors of the written word, among the finest of hosts.

He and Calvino did not always see eye to eye. To hear Bill describe it, their relationship was occasionally tempestuous, but the two clearly respected one another. Italo had once presented him with a print of Saint Jerome, inscribed: *To Bill, the translator as saint.*

Sometime between my last day as a Bard student and my first as a teacher there, I published my first novel. As soon as I received a few copies from the publisher, I sent one to William Weaver at his address on campus. But the package was returned, stamped NO SUCH ADDRESSEE. When I asked around, I learned that Bill had suffered a stroke years before, and that his language skills and memory were deeply impaired. This was heartbreaking. I thought again of Calvino's cities, organized like the spiral of Dante's hell: Cities & Signs, Cities & Memory. Where was William Weaver, if not in language and in his stories?

In November of 2013, I was teaching on the day Bill Weaver died. I'd been thinking of him for months, and now he was gone again.

In class the following week, I told my students about studying with Bill. We had read some of his translations earlier in the semester; they were eager to hear more.

Soon after that, the boundaries of my double life began to erode. Every teacher must feel sometimes unsure of how to play the role of mentor. But there was room for us in the classroom. I taught. We read aloud. We talked about music, art, and writing. We talked about what bands were coming to campus, and sometimes I wore sneakers. Our classroom had no fireplace. But, gathered with my students at one table, I told stories and tried to be a good host.

C. DALE YOUNG

ON DONALD JUSTICE

I would be neither a poet nor a physician had it not been for a teacher's statement. In my last year of the MFA program at the University of Florida, a poet who offered me kindness despite the fact I never thought I deserved it, sat listening to me have a mini-nervous breakdown in his office. I had deferred starting medical school for two years, and that time was coming to an end. I was in a kind of panic. I was worried that medicine would silence all poetry in me, that it would drain me of any creative impulse whatsoever. I was contemplating studying for a Ph.D. in literature, certain this would keep the poetry flame alive. But my teacher looked perplexed. He already understood something that I wouldn't understand for years to come. It was then the poet, my teacher, stated, somewhat matter-of-factly: "We always find time to do the things we want to do."

The poet who listened to me and reassured me was Donald Justice. I am, even to this day, deeply indebted to that man. Some would think it was his knowledge of poetry that impressed me. He did, after all, appear to know virtually every poem you could cite, many times by heart. Others would think it was his brilliance as a teacher that drew me to him. In fact, despite learning more from him than from any teacher I have ever had in my life, this is not the case. I was drawn to Don Justice because he possessed a kind of wisdom, an ability to listen, to make you feel as if he cared about you and your work. Mark you, he was a demanding teacher, but you always believed he was just trying to make you a better poet, a better person.

"We always find time to do the things we want to do." Is there a truer statement? We always find the time. I carried that statement with me all throughout medical school, internship, residency, all the way into my current practice of medicine. There have been times when I have felt overwhelmed by the study or practice of medicine, but I rarely worried about poetry. I knew I would always find my way back to it, that I would always find the time to write, no matter how small or scattered that time was. I learned slowly what Don Justice already knew: I cannot not write poems. Medicine taught me discipline as a writer, but what made me survive as a poet was Don's simple statement. He somehow knew I belonged in medicine. I think he knew also, while I sat in his office so many years ago, that I might have given up that dream and that responsibility in order to write poems, when really I didn't need to give up either. In a strange way the man, and his statement, gave me permission to do what I needed to do, what I have continued to do.

It is funny. I teach occasionally at conferences, and now I teach in the low-residency MFA program at Warren Wilson. I find, at times, in the way we hear our parents' words rise from our own mouths, Don's words and cagey questions escaping my own lips. It is unlikely I will ever be as a good a teacher as Don was, but from him I have learned to listen, to ask questions, to lead people to the answers as opposed to simply telling them. It is a trait I use not only in the classroom but also in the clinic. It is strange: I know full well that Don passed away, but it is hard for me to believe it. I always expect to receive a postcard from him, or a note about something that he recently read. Sometimes, on a foggy evening in San Francisco, when the slightest of winds slips through the portico leading to my front gate, I can almost hear the cadence of his voice. No, I am not psychotic: I do not hear his voice. I hear the *pattern* of it, something like a sigh, something exasperated but hopeful at the same time.

MAYA LANG
ON RON DEMAIO

When I was a girl, I got in trouble for reading too much. My parents, Indian immigrant scientists, had little patience for the books I carted home from the library. I tried to select paperbacks that were not obviously for teens ("smut!") or suspenseful ("nonsense mysteries!"), but even the classics were met with frowns. My parents didn't own books other than *The Physician's Desk Reference* and *Principles of Structural Engineering*. We didn't even have cable. They regarded me wearily, wondering why I wasn't like my industrious cousins studying for the SAT.

We achieved a truce of sorts: so long as I did well in school, I could read what I wished. I studied science during the day and read novels at night. I learned about writers who were doctors, from Keats to Chekhov. I told myself there were a lot of us doing one thing during the day, another late at night—a lot of us whose outward faces differed from our interior lives. Surely, one could not simply be out in the world as a writer! Better to keep such embarrassing activities private, to go about the good work of satisfying one's parents and being impressive.

This fairly bleak worldview—that I could not be who I really was—seemed noble at the time. Self-sacrifice has its own allure. I'm quite sure I would have given into its pull and become a miserable but competent doctor were it not for a mentor who entered my life when I was fourteen.

Ron DeMaio founded an arts program at my public high school that managed to be both rigorous and cool—a rare combination. Everyone wanted to be in the Student Television Arts Club. STAC met for half the day, from 12:30–3:30, and one could audition in any of six disciplines (art, dance, drama, music, voice, writing). In a school of 1,500 students, it accepted about thirty.

STAC was Julliard. It was *Fame*. It was the only way to escape the horrors of high school while still in its halls. STAC put on improv shows, made short films that won awards, and ventured from Long Island into Manhattan for field trips. Crucial for my purposes, it also sent students to the very best colleges. I explained this to my parents, who sighed before allowing me to apply.

On the very first day of STAC, Ron had us write letters to our future selves. I remember sitting there, stunned, before meekly asking if the letters would be graded.

When we saw plays and Broadway musicals, Ron arranged for the casts to talk with us. Gregory Hines spoke to us after his performance in *Jelly's Last Jam*. I understood, for the first time, what it might be like to be a successful artist.

Once a month, we had workshops in our respective disciplines. Writers studied with authors like Helen Schulman. We wrote stories and critiqued one another's work, a kind of mini-MFA. I stared at the workshop leaders as if they were unicorns. Here were writers pursuing their craft full time, able to eke out a living. Maybe it wasn't easy. Maybe they had to teach workshops to make it happen. But it was possible.

Ron devised Willy Wonka–like experiments for us. He might drop us off at a surprise location with a bag of video equipment, or tell us to compose a performance piece based on a color. "Think about that letter you wrote to yourself," he would say. "Would you write it differently now? Are you meeting your standards?"

The single most important lesson I learned from Ron that influences my writing still has nothing to do with craft; it has to do with our relationship to risk.

While I generally loved STAC, there was one aspect of it I dreaded: improv. Once a week, we had a class that consisted of theater games, mental and physical activities designed to hone our improvisational skills. It was sort of like gym with the added pressure of being funny.

At fourteen, I was bookish, anxious, and cripplingly self-conscious. I envied the actors, so at ease in their bodies, able to speak in made-up tongues and mime animals. I knew how to be funny and commanding from behind a keyboard. I just didn't know how to be that way in person.

With improv, there is no delete key. You can't go back and rewrite a scene.

You can't hit the pause button and go for a walk to contemplate a character's possibilities. You can only leap, trusting in your instincts. You learn to make a choice in the moment and commit to it. You learn that sometimes your choices work and sometimes they don't but that the important thing is to stick with them.

As a novelist now, I wish I could offer up a turning point: one afternoon, perhaps a crisp day in autumn, when I took a risk and made everyone roar, thereby finding my confidence. "From that point forward," I would recount, "I felt more assured." If anything like that occurred, I don't recall it. What I remember is the shock of surviving. I faced down my biggest fears (of failing, looking like an idiot, appearing uncool) and I *did not die.* This was news.

The hardest part of writing might be the first draft. How do you start? What if you make the wrong choices? How do you carry on knowing that what you have is flawed? A first draft is a journey into the dark with questions and doubts for company.

Improv—as much as I dreaded it—taught me how to ignore the voice of doubt in the creative moment. Criticism can be invited in later, as I am revising, but heeded early, it derails the process. To make something out of nothing: that is the goal of improv actors and writers alike.

It is easy for writers to get in our own way, to chastise and berate ourselves. We want to dazzle, to be lauded for our talent, to have editors and agents and readers sit up in astonishment. We want our fingers on the keyboard to spin magic. Set up this way, writing becomes a dreaded exercise where your task is to elicit thunderous applause. Set up this way, writing feels like improvisational comedy in front of your whole school when you are an awkward fourteen-year-old.

What Ron DeMaio taught me was to not be ruled by the desire to impress. He taught me to listen to my own voice over the demands (real or imagined) of others. He taught me to not mind failing, which in turn taught me how to take risks.

Being a writer involves a constant dance with disappointment. Failure lurks at every corner: in the scene that doesn't quite work, the rejection letters from agents and journals. Even "successful" writers feel it when they are bypassed for awards, when their published works don't sell enough copies, when their newest book fails to live up to the hype. Writers are always starting from scratch, trying to prove ourselves once more. We are in an improv skit that never ends.

But when you love the process, you don't mind. Focus on the audience and you are doomed. Focus on how they perceive you and you become self-aware. The reward cannot be the applause; the reward is losing yourself to the moment and forgetting that the audience exists. Creativity blooms in the absence of judgment.

Tell yourself to write something dazzling and things probably won't go well. You'll be too hung up on sounding clever. But tell yourself to write something terrible and you will feel your body relax. Tell yourself to write something that will probably be awful, that no one will ever see. Tell yourself that you needn't write one word, that it doesn't matter much anyway. Tell yourself this not to trick yourself into performing well. Tell yourself this because it's true.

Permit yourself to fail not so that you can ignore the failings but because you will be better for them. When an idea enters your head and a voice peeps up to say that the idea will surely flop, cheerfully agree. See the idea through. Either you will flounder or you will fly, but either way, you will learn.

When I finished the first draft of my novel, I sent a copy to Ron. I wanted him to tell me if it was any good—if I should chuck it in the trash or stick with it. Really, though, that manila envelope was a missive to my fourteen year-old self. I wanted to know if I had done right by her, if I had written something that would make her proud.

All these years later, I remember what I wrote that first day of STAC in my letter. I sat there for a long time, contemplating the blank sheet of paper, before finally scribbling a line: *Whatever you're doing, I hope you're still writing.*

The best mentors do not spout wisdom or anecdotes, attempting to fill you with their own stories. The best, like Ron DeMaio, challenge you to write your own.

MECCA JAMILAH SULLIVAN

ON AMY

I committed to writing when it landed me in the principal's office in the fifth grade, placing me in league with the rule breakers, for once. I had just discovered both Toni Morrison's *The Bluest Eye* and Ntozake Shange's *Sassafrass, Cypress, and Indigo,* and though I was not nearly certain what either was about, each left me with an irresistible sense of possibility. I knew I loved books by then, but it hadn't quite occurred to me that there were people who spent their lives writing them, or that I could be such a person one day. Dizzied and ignited by these writers, I had written a story about a girl who was being abused by her alcoholic father. I was not being abused, and never have been, but as the daughter of an activist and a social worker, I was hyper-attuned to injustice. Child abuse, like racism, AIDS, apartheid, police brutality, and wildlife endangerment, shaped—however abstractly—my gathering worldview. Writing that story gave me a place and a purpose for feelings I could not explain. So I submitted it to my teacher, bright with confidence and anticipation—both newish feelings welcome in my fat black ten-year-old girl life. When the story came back to me with no gold stars or purple-penned adulations, I was shocked. Instead there was just a note: "Mecca, please see me." It devastated me then. And I couldn't be more grateful.

I was shocked, in part, because of the connection I felt with my fifth-grade English teacher, Amy. Amy was tall and white and thin and blonde, qualities I had by then learned were egregiously overvalued in my elite, smart-kid school and beyond and qualities against which I therefore raged. But Amy was also a lesbian, which meant something important to me, though I couldn't name it. She was twenty-five—an age that seemed young to us only on her—and a recent graduate from Teachers College, not too far from my house in Harlem. Ours was the first full-year class she had taught on her own, and so a sheen of newness rested on everything she did.

And she did a lot of new things. On top of the essays and reading responses we were accustomed to, Amy (who encouraged us to call her by her first name—a triumph of coolness) had each of us purchase a marble notebook, which would serve as our journal. We were to write in the journals regularly, not for a grade but simply for the experience of writing. Every twenty pages, she collected the journals and gave us comments on Post-it notes, usually in green or purple pen. We could write anything we wanted, and she would read and comment in detail. If we wanted a page to remain private, we could fold it over and she wouldn't touch it.

I don't know whether it was blooming creativity or my ravenous drive to be the favorite, but I was all about these journals. I filled three marble note-books by the time the year was over, recording reflections and inventing sto-ries on everything from homelessness in New York to the Rodney King verdict to my parents' arguments to the ceaselessness of time.

While the writing itself was important for me, her feedback was what changed things. She told me I was a writer, that my writing was powerful. She called me an "exceptional observer" of the world around me. But she also pushed me to revisit ideas that were underdeveloped. When I handed in work that was careless and uncommitted, she told me so, and her disappointment stung.

In one entry, I mused on the name of the "art company" I planned to develop. What purpose I had in mind for the company I'm not sure, but I was confident that the title should be an acrostic of my first name. I had come up with _____, Educationally, Culturally, Correct Art, but was stumped on the "M" adverb that would begin the title. I submitted the question to Amy in the journal, partly, of course, to see if she was really reading and would care enough to respond. "Morally?" I asked. "Check yes or no." Brilliantly and graciously, Amy drew a third box, labeled "not sure," and checked that one. Then she offered a list of better adverbs for me to consider, some of which I had never encountered before. She pushed me to revise, to pursue standards I could not quite see.

This was what it meant to me to become a writer—laboring toward a world past my horizon. Amy called me her sweet and gentle poet, a title better than chocolate. And I felt I could earn it—not just by being who I was, but by valuing my voice enough to work toward it.

Acrostic, excerpted from Mecca Jamilah Sullivan's journal, 1992

In that sense, Amy showed me more than what it meant to write: she showed me what it meant to teach. In one of my many gushing missives in the journal, I mused: "Amy, why is it that I like you so much? One thing is that when we have discussions, you don't get your opinion into it, and so even if somebody is totally OFF in their disgussion [*sic*], you find something positive about it." Prepubescent swooning notwithstanding (that entry continues: "I know that the last day of school will be terrible. I will cry so much that my eyes will probably go dry I bet."), it's striking to see how much that approach shapes my pedagogy today. In the classroom, I listen athletically, searching students' voices for the important ideas they have yet to discover there. When I mentor young writers whose work I admire, I encourage them to notice their voice everywhere and to look for drafts in everything. I tell them to listen to their texts, their emails, and, yes, their journals for traces of voice that can be culled into what they really have to say. When they're sweet and gentle, I try to treat them that way, and I give them my time as honestly and full-heartedly as I can.

These are things I learned from Amy, my first writing mentor: to pursue my voice in unfamiliar places, to take responsibility for it, and to believe that, if I did, my work could mean something, and someone would want to listen.

It's that meaning, that mattering, that I understood when my writing got me sent to the principal. Concerned, as any young teacher might be, Amy had mentioned my story to the principal, who called my parents into the office to see if things were all right at home. I don't know the details of those exchanges or how they affected my poor parents, who gently explained what had had happened on the bus ride back to Harlem. I do know that I was terrified and mystified by this new world I had stepped into—one in which my writing could do real things in the world.

So as much as my writer self took shape through Morrison and Shange, it also took shape through Amy. She taught me to take care with my voice and showed me the breathtaking possibilities of its reach. What Morrison and Shange whispered into my ear, my fifth-grade teacher wrote in bold purple handwriting just beside my own: writing matters, so treat it that way I had no idea then, of course, how few people believe this in adulthood. I couldn't be more grateful that I learned that lesson young.

Notes from Amy, excerpted from Mecca Jamilah Sullivan's journal, 1992 eventually protesting, roommates. I had been writing in my little notebooks for six or seven years; now, for the first time, I "saw" what I wanted to do.

I wanted to write poems that were smart, funny, complicated, and formal all at the same time, like John Donne's. I had a lot to learn.

I don't insist that this was the right direction, or even good advice. What happened was it got me to write and read at a higher and more committed level than I had thought possible. Bobo Rudd's suggestion and John Donne's poetry could only take me so far. But they gave me a friendly push forward, and this is all we can expect from our mentors.

Looking for a mentor is a normal impulse. Even the agoraphobic Emily Dickinson asked advice of strangers such as the critic and editor Thomas Wentworth Higginson, which, of course, she never followed. From the coffee houses of London to the cafés of Paris to the MFA programs of American universities, writers young and old have searched for guidance and friendship from talented and like-minded contemporaries. There are many ways to get and use advice. Your job, as a writer, is to find the right way for yourself.

STEFAN KIESBYE

ON IRVING FELDMAN

He gave me rides home, the generosity of heated seats in Buffalo, New York. After class, which ended at 10 p.m. with only one more shuttle bus going back to town, we left Clemens Hall, wind rattling us every time, scraping our faces. Buffalo has two seasons, winter and July, and July never comes.

His car was a Saab. I took his class fiction in the fall, poetry in the spring— five times. Someone once joked that I was graduating in his class. It was always the same classroom, 308, with fluorescent lights and beige linoleum and windows that wouldn't keep the cold out.

Irving wasn't the cuddly type; his wit was a serrated knife. I wanted to relax in his presence. I tried. There were rumors of students running out of his class, crying. I was awkward, with a thick German accent and a dictionary. In his class, I swapped my language for this new one, testing each word—would it withstand his scrutiny?

I can conjure up his voice, raspy and sure of itself whenever he launched into a joke. His laughter could wake the dead. He said, "Being understood is better than being praised." He was unforgiving, his affection for students separated completely from his judgment of a particular piece of writing. After he made us read our poems, he read them aloud himself. We listened, rapt. He gave our writing a different life; he said, "See? Do you see? Do you hear it?" We never received written comments but instead scribbled down what he said as fast we could; we collected his words like scars and medals. When I was stuck, first class, John Barth also offered to give all of his students a reader's comment or "blurb" that each could use as each made his or her way in the world. Martone's "blurb" reads as follows: "Among our wealth of excellent new American short-story writers, Michael Martone is one particularly worth reading."

Martone has used the quotation, with deep appreciation, on each of his books—except the nonfiction ones where it would not quite fit—and on all the accompanying promotional material. Perhaps because of the abiding affection and regard he holds for his teacher's gesture, Martone loves the genre of the "blurb" and is very happy to write one for anyone who asks.

Martone enjoys the discipline the form imposes to capture the essence of the work and something, too, of its author's style or voice. There is a lyrical compression to rendering a good blurb. Martone has, several times, considered writing a book made up entirely of "blurbs" and has often made up "blurbs" for his own books, creating authors who are impressed mightily by his, Martone's, writing ability, his originality, his sensitivity, his utter readability, etc. John Barth, during the time Martone studied with him, concentrated on instilling in his students a thorough understanding of the formal construction of a story, employing the insights of narrative theorists to describe technically the workings of plot. Freytag's triangle, the famous upside-down checkmark, was utilized as a kind of can opener or crow bar to crack open a story.

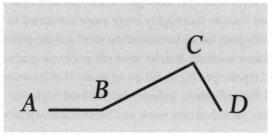

Freytag's triangle

Martone took these lessons to heart, and, years later in his own classes, routinely draws his students' attention to various parts of the story under consideration—its ground situation, vehicle, rising action, climax, and denouement. John Barth, in conference, years ago, told Martone that what he, Martone, was writing were not technically stories. Martone said that he suspected that. What his teacher said exactly was: this is not a story, technically.

He was referring to something called "Fort Wayne Is Seventh on Hitler's List," a collage of thematic incidents that concerned scrapbooks, his grandfather, and airplanes. Martone understood how this wasn't a story. He had always had (and still does have) a problem with the vehicle part of the formula, the story's "one day" pivot that animated the potential energy found in the story's ground situation. Martone has always been most interested in the ground situation. Martone's teacher went on to say that this was a descriptive distinction, that his writing was up to something else. It was (and is) technically anecdotal, a series of interesting events, a rich tapestry of details. And, in the end, they settled on calling these things "fictions," a designation that has always seemed much more accurate.

One day, a week before spring break, John Barth asked Martone if he would, during the coming spring break, be interested in doing a little yard work. Martone, being a long way from home and in need of some extra money for the typing of his thesis, took the job. In addition to pruning the shrubbery, picking up the felled deadwood branches from the winter, and raking the decaying leaves left over from the fall, Martone had to cut, trim, and apply fertilizer to the lawn. At the end of the week—its individual days memorable for the amazing sandwiches his teacher built for him each noon and for the forty minutes of conversation exchanged as the sandwiches were consumed—Martone worried about the consequences of his yard work, especially the application of the fertilizer. John Barth had been working, when not preparing lunch, on reconciling the editorial queries attached to the galleys of his current massive novel so did not oversee Martone's labor with the caustic chemical. A week later Martone walked up North Charles Street to inspect his work. His fears were realized. His mentor's lawn was striped brown and browner, the grass burned in a pattern that traced last week's progress back and forth, back and forth over it, a singed graph inscribed on the property. Martone stared at his handiwork. There was nothing to be done. Perhaps, Martone hoped, he won't notice. In any case, nothing, thankfully, was ever said about it. Of all the things that hadn't happened to Martone during his life to that point (both factual and fictional) in which, he believed, nothing much happens or is supposed to happen, this event was as much of such nothing he ever experienced.

OUTLIERS

briefly, asked what Ira thought about me and my new job. I was confused. Thought? About me? I was pretty sure he didn't think about me at all. I was pretty sure he didn't even know where I worked now. Once, long ago, he had been my mentor, and briefly I had been his mentee. But for much longer and more recently, I'd been his *employee*. He had others, even a new one to replace me. We worked well together sometimes and not so well other times. I can say of my twenty-five-to-thirty-one-year-old self that I was hard working and smart, but I remembered how nice it felt to be an intern, and sometimes I resented the loss of that feeling, and sometimes that showed up at work. I was young and idealistic and I wanted this to be something more than a job. It was a great job, a meaningful job, but, really, it was just a job.

And I wanted Ira to be something more than the boss I complained about. I wanted him to be my mentor still. But it got complicated.

Here's what I can say with many years between me and that time: maybe a mentor doesn't give you the key to succeeding. Maybe a mentor is someone who makes you feel like you're capable of something, while also putting in front of you an impossible task. Maybe the best mentors give you the crutch to lean on and the situation that forces you to lean on it.

What I know now about my job that I didn't then is that I was never going to be perfect at it. I was never going to be an expert the way I once defined expertise.

This idea that someday I'll know exactly what I'm doing is something that any mentor knows is probably false. I'll eventually know better; I'll be more confident, and I'll succeed more often perhaps, but if I'm doing good work, there will always be struggle. One of the best lessons I learned from Ira and other "experts" in my field is that even they couldn't do the hard work of radio in their sleep. They didn't always know the right answer; they weren't always certain. They trialed and they errored. They fucked up. It didn't always look like it from the outside, but now I see it. I went to my colleagues for help a lot, but they also came to me. They came into my office, closed the door behind them, and sank to the floor in frustration, and we talked through whatever the problem was. In round upon round of edits we reshaped whole stories into better versions. Even Ira's stories. Nothing ever worked perfectly the first time. It never does. And that's not failure.

During late-night recording sessions with Ira, he would second-guess some decision and he would ask me for advice and I would have to tell him what I thought. Or he'd get yell-y when recording voice tracks. "Am I yelling?" And I'd say, "Yes, you're yelling." It's as if he were yelling, "Diane! Help me!" I didn't have to be infallible. I just had to know enough to do my job. And a big part of my job, I'm realizing, was just to be able to help. I lost track of this often in my years there. I don't know why.

Maybe mentoring is more about joining the people you admire in the work you all love. Your colleagues, mentors all, give a little to you and then you give back. You make their job a little harder some days, but you know some days you'll make it easier. They believe in you, even when it gets complicated. That Ira believed in me at some point was what mattered most, even if in the present moment he was squinting like there was no tomorrow.

We are still friends, Ira and me. At least, I think we are. He loves my husband. Everyone loooooves my husband. He was Ira's intern too, a couple of years before me. It was one of the many connections that brought my husband and me together. I doubt my husband ever cried in front of Ira, and I imagine that helped keep their relationship simple, easily navigable over the years. But my husband never worked for Ira. He was Ira's intern and Ira was his mentor and they never muddied the waters with all the stuff that comes after. But here is what I can say after all this hand wringing. Ira taught me everything I know about how to tell a story, about emotion versus sentimentality, about what is interesting and compelling, about narrative and pacing, and about simple, conversational, effective sentences. And if he didn't teach it to me, he helped me uncover my own singular instincts for it. I would not be the writer I am today if I hadn't worked for him. And I mean *worked* for him, not interned. I got to learn from him for six years, not six months. He was my boss. I was his employee. In the end, that was the prevailing relationship. But I guess that doesn't have to mean he stopped being my mentor.

The Post-it from Ira Glass that Diane Cook
found on her desk

MARY GAITSKILL
ON THE OLD GUY

The only mentor I've had in terms of writing was an old guy named David Kozubei, whom I knew in Ann Arbor, where I went to school. I say "old guy," because at the time I was twenty-four and, to me, a guy in his late forties was old. I also say it because there *was* something old about David that had nothing to do with years and everything to do with his seeming to exist out of time and place.

In 1979, I glanced into a store window and saw an old guy with enormous glasses strapped to his big, bald, egg-shaped head sitting behind a large desk surrounded by leafy plants and book cases arranged in a sort of diorama. I went in and met David: it turned out that his encampment of desk, plants, and dioramic book cases were all that was left of his legendary used bookstore, David's Books. It turned out that he sat in this "store" and read all day, that he had read nearly everything ever written in the English language and had something to say about all of it.

During the course of our friendship, he was able to buy and maintain another used bookstore, a huge place where he also sat and read all day. I was an undergraduate at the university but I was getting very little out of the classes in terms of writing. Because I was a high-school dropout with a lot of years spent away from home and school, and because I had transferred to the university from a community college, I also had some trouble finding a place socially. David's store was one of the only places I felt peace or at least relief from despair, and a sense of possibility. I don't know why this was, and I didn't know then either; I just liked to be near him. David seemed to me like a particularly gentle angel whose sense of humor had caused him to take a mildly comic form.

However, when I began to show him my writing, I discovered that he was not always gentle, and could in fact be a devastating critic. But his criticism fascinated me; it was almost always more precise, original, and intelligent than what I was hearing from the few professors I was able to get any feedback from at all. Even now, when speaking to a class about literary style, I paraphrase David. "Style," he said, "is a by-product."

I said, "That means incidental."

"Not true," he replied. "It means an inevitable discharge that occurs as the writer follows what for him is the correct—that is, the only—path available in creating his world. It's a discharge in the sense that the appearance of a plant is the inevitable result of its inner structure, and, in writing, has a similar relation to the inner nature of the work." It's a definition I've never forgotten. It represents an ardent, individual way of thinking and being that I remain grateful for and, I'm sure, in some secret way influenced by.

KEVIN CANTY

ON HARRY CREWS

The first time I laid eyes on Harry Crews was in the English department corridor of Turlington Hall, a modern and fairly swanky building on the palmy grounds of the University of Florida in Gainesville. I was a newly arrived graduate student, wondering what I was doing there. I'd been out of college for fifteen years or so, and the smell of the place, the look and feel of school, was completely foreign to me, something I'd outgrown a long time before.

Down that hallway came a man who did not belong there. He wore a sleeveless white t-shirt, sweatpants that had once been black, and a pair of ancient rotten athletic shoes. He had a tattoo or two. There was something wrong with his legs; he walked with a hitch in his step, and he seemed to be listing a few degrees to starboard. Slowly he moved down the hall and past me, scowling, not bothering to notice me, which was fine. Something seemed to be pissing him off and I didn't want it to be me.

This is the thing you noticed about him, the larger-than-life, outrageous Harry Crews-ness of the operation. He was dented, battered, bruised, upright, and angry, and he was not going to take any bullshit from anybody. This was the public Harry Crews, reinforced by the writing and the legend, and it attracted acolytes and myrmidons from far and wide. There was the big guy in tiny shorts, then a girl who looked exactly like a boy, and always the cast of extras who wanted to say that they'd shaken hands with Harry Crews, had a drink with Harry Crews, studied karate with Harry Crews, started a rock band named Harry Crews, taken Harry Crews to the fights. He was a one-man rock-and-roll show, right there in the English department.

This was the first thing you saw of him, and for a lot of people the only thing they saw, and both Harry and his audience seemed largely content with this. "Show us the tattoo you don't remember getting, Harry! Tell the joke about the country boy fucking the cow!" Over the course of a couple of years in Gainesville, though, another side of him swam slowly into focus.

First off there was the writing, which was sharp, quick, surprising. The voice was always Harry's voice, gruff and accented, but he knew how to make music out of it: "The afternoon had come up Cadillacs." Also there was this knack for taking an idea that seemed to be a gimmick at first—guy eats a car—and making something bigger and more interesting out of it. And always the classic O'Connor move of taking a thing and blowing it up to enormous and grotesque size to make it visible. The quote from Flannery herself could be taken for a key to the scriptures: "When you can assume that your audience holds the same beliefs as you do, you can relax a little and use more normal means of talking to it; when you have to assume that it does not, then you have to make your vision apparent by shock, to the hard of hearing you shout, and for the almost-blind, you draw large and startling figures."

Then there was the workshop, which at first seemed to be another act in the Harry Crews Show. Nobody who was in attendance that first semester is ever likely to forget the words, "You mean to tell me that she's *fucking* the *dog?*" (She was.) After a while, though, I started to see the outline of his way of working, a set of tools I could maybe use myself. He liked a clear storyline, a brisk pace. He liked a story to stick to its business. I don't think I'll ever rewrite a story of mine without hearing Harry's voice in my ear, asking, "Son, what's this story *about?*" It's a terrorizing question but it seems like one you ought to be able to answer. In the course of two years of working with Harry, I picked up dozens of ideas about story that I still use in my workshops today, ideas that tend to seem obvious at first glance but seem, actually, kind of profound when applied to a story. "Nothing will happen to a reader unless it happens to a character first," for instance. Seems simple enough, right? And yet how many stories go wrong by forgetting this?

Finally—and this did take a while—there was the example of the man himself. Beneath the public Harry (or maybe just alongside it, coexisting) was a dead-serious worker who got up at four every day to get his writing done. He had somehow survived his dirt-poor upbringing in Bacon County, Georgia, to make a writer out of himself. He was teaching in the same graduate program that had rejected him when he applied out of college. He had refused to take no for an answer and persevered to write original and successful novels. And this is maybe where I learned the most from Harry, not from tips or tricks or from the writing, but from the fact of the man himself. Beneath the bluff and bluster and braggadocio was a man who got his pages written, who respected his craft and did the work.

And this, I think, was where the scowl came from. He looked at us and saw soft white middle-class kids who were not getting their work done, who were asking for respect without bothering to earn that respect. Of course he was pissed. He had made a place for himself at the table and now we came along, expecting a place already set for us. So that's the one great thing I learned from Crews: none of us belonged there. None of us had a right. If I wanted a place at the table, I'd have to make one for myself, alone in a room with my computer and my printer and my imaginary friends. Which in the end is what I did. And maybe I might have done it without Harry's example and Harry's help, but I'll never know, because I was lucky enough to have these things.

RODRIGO REY ROSA
ON PAUL BOWLES

It's been twenty-six years since I first set foot in Tangier. "It looks like Sicily, with a touch of Greece and the south of Spain, without the camels," I thought, half-asleep, pressing my head against the window of an old school bus that was taking me, together with fifty or so North American students, from the Boukhalef Airport to the American School of Tangier, on the rue Christophe Colomb, which now goes by a name out of *The Arabian Nights*, Harun er Rashid. Willows, poplars, and Roman cypresses lined either side of the road that was leading us through the hills and fields; poppies rose above the ripening wheat, oleander betrayed the wetness beneath the dried-up streams, and the palm trees shone in the sun, the Atlantic's dark-blue horizon in the distance. I don't know why, but all of this filled me with a sense of well-being, as though I were under the effect of some drug; during that sleepy trek in a decrepit school bus, and after the flight from New York, already Tangier held the promise of adventure. Most of the students were fledgling painters or photographers from New York City, but some of us were aspiring writers who wanted to show our work to an author whose impressive body of work I had only begun reading three or four weeks before setting out on this trip, a man whose name the students uttered with an almost fearful reverence: Paul Bowles.

In *Advertisements for Myself* from 1959, Norman Mailer, the cranky old know-it-all, proclaimed: "Paul Bowles opened the world of Hip. He let in the murder, the drugs, the incest, the death of the Square." And the caustic Gore Vidal, so fastidious in his taste, wrote the following in his introduction to Bowles's *Collected Stories* in 1979: "The short stories of Paul Bowles are among the best ever written by an American. . . . As Webster saw the skull beneath the skin, so Bowles has glimpsed what lies back of our sheltering sky, . . . an endless flux of stars so like those atoms which make us up that in our apprehension of this terrible infinity, we experience not only horror but likeness."

That afternoon, after a light snack in the school's dining hall and an inaugural speech delivered by some professor or other, the students were assigned their rooms, and I'm almost sure everyone fell asleep. The dream that accompanied my first Tangier siesta seemed like a good omen, although it wasn't particularly pleasant. It was a vivid dream, and now, more than a quarter of a century later, I remember it clearly. It belonged to a category of dream I'd call "of an invisible presence," a type of dream I often have. The dream is static. The dreamer finds himself in a room identical to the one in which he is sleeping. The dream reproduces the circumstances, the *reality*, of the sleeper exactly. But suddenly he senses something wrong: the dreamer knows he's not alone, even though he hears and sees nothing. There's someone there, beyond his field of vision, in total silence. The dreamer feels observed. He wants to turn over, face that presence, which may be hostile. He lacks the strength to turn over (he is facing the wall), he tries to open his eyes, but he can't lift his eyelids either. It is then that he realizes he is dreaming. He wants to yell, but no sound comes out of his mouth—in the distance, he can hear the crickets, the call of a muezzin, the whistling wind. Finally he awakens, opens his eyes, turns around. The room, as expected, is identical to the one in the dream. No one is there. And yet . . .

One afternoon, two or three days after our arrival, we saw Paul Bowles for the first time. He was accompanied by a tall Moroccan man who held his round, balding head erect. They were crossing the sports field that separated the American School from the student dorms, where the writing workshop was supposed to take place. Bowles at age seventy was a thin man, with perfectly white hair; an unruly tuft of it glimmered beneath the three o'clock sun. They both walked quickly, but in a dignified manner. I don't remember how the Moroccan, who was Bowles's driver and trusted friend, was dressed. The American writer wore various tones of beige and white, and sunglasses with tortoiseshell frames and opaque lenses, which lent him a distant, modern flair; there was a mineral, almost metallic, dryness about him, it seems to me now. Disheartened, I sensed that my initial forays into narrative fiction, their outmoded style—a style that undoubtedly revealed (that I undoubtedly wanted to reveal) the influence of Jorge Luis Borges—couldn't possibly interest this "hardline existentialist," which is how my older colleagues had referred to Bowles.

I think it was during that first session, though it could have been a week later, when Bowles declared that he did not consider himself a teacher, that he didn't believe you could teach anyone how to write fiction. If he had accepted the offer to lead this workshop despite his skepticism, it was because the school director had succeeded in convincing him that there were people willing to pay money so that he would read their manuscripts and give his opinion about them, and that was all he was prepared to do. And then he added that he wouldn't have done it had it not been because he needed the money, because he wasn't what you could call a rich man. Someone may have asked him if he hadn't made a lot of money with his books. In any case, Bowles said that the literary success of a book (the only kind of success that should concern a serious writer) was no guarantee of profit, and while books sometimes provided just enough to get by, they only rarely enriched those who had written them. "If some of you are under the impression that I can teach you to write best sellers that will make you lots of money, you're in the wrong place," he said with a smile.

For our introductions, he asked us to mention, in addition to our birthplace and how long we had been writing seriously, our favorite books or authors. I can't remember the authors I mentioned other than Borges, but I do remember that this reference caught his attention. Moreover, the fact that I was from Guatemala led him to approach me after class and tell me, in Spanish, that he had traveled throughout Guatemala and Mexico, and that if English wasn't my native language, I could write in Spanish, which he had no difficulty reading. Borges was also an author he admired and he had read his work in Spanish, he added, and, as I was to learn later, he had been the first to translate a Borges story into English ("The Circular Ruins," published in *View* in January 1946).

At the next session, Bowles suggested that we meet in his apartment, which was close to the school, instead of the student dorms. He told us he could offer us a cup of tea while we discussed our work, and I don't believe anyone was opposed to the idea. Abdelouahaid, his driver, could pick up the older members at the school (the majority of my colleagues were over fifty) and take them to the Itesa Building; the younger ones could walk.

The Itesa Building—where Bowles had lived since the 1950s and where he remained until two weeks before his death in 1999 at age eighty-eight—was on the slope of a hill surrounded by barren fields that brought to mind the

countryside, with goats and sheep grazing here and there, but a countryside
under threat from the homes and buildings that were sprouting in every direction like a plague of mushrooms. It was an Italian-style apartment building
with smooth, wide marble stairways built in the fifties. Bowles's apartment,
on whose door I knocked for the first time one afternoon at the start of the
sacred and fearsome month of Ramadan, was on the fourth and last floor.
Nowadays other buildings block the view, but in the early 1980s you could
still see, toward the north, a blue patch of the Strait of Gibraltar (an inverted
triangle that rose up between Marshan Hill—covered with small Moroccan
homes that looked like Legos in all the possible shades of white—
and Monteviejo—a hillside made green by the gardens of the European
residences), which the people of Tangier affectionately call *la coupe de
champagne.*

"There are places in the world that contain more magic than others."
Bowles once wrote something along those lines. Be that as it may, for me that
small apartment, its thick curtains almost always drawn, its Berber rugs, its
walls covered floor to ceiling with books, its handful of striking pieces of
African art, the collection of Moroccan drums and *qasbas* (always available in
case a *jilali* came to visit and felt like playing some music), the smell of sandal-
wood incense combined with burning kief or the scent of tea—this place contained more magic than any other I had known until then.

At first, Paul and I talked mostly about Borges's fiction, about Bioy (who I
hadn't yet read), and also about traveling through Central America. I don't
recall our speaking about my writing (fortunately), and though Bowles had
ceased being just an author whose work I admired and a "hardline existentialist," I still didn't believe that, beyond those pleasant conversations aided by
kief and tea, he would take an interest in my attempts at narrative. When I
expressed my desire to visit the Moroccan interior—especially the Rif—
Bowles encouraged me. He told me I could miss a few workshop sessions, that
he didn't think I would be interested in hearing what everyone had to say
about each other's work, especially considering that they wrote in English and
about life in the United States, and he even loaned me maps of northern
Morocco for the trip. So I counted myself dismissed and concluded, with the
simplemindedness of a twenty-one-year-old, I should admit, that it was all for
the best. I told myself that next time I would skip the workshop sessions in
English and—I assume I consoled myself in this manner—at least I would get
to know a bit of Morocco. I visited the Rif, I walked among the unending fields
of cannabis in the unstable Ketama region, and I returned to Tangier satisfied

with my little adventure, believing I had accomplished everything I had set out to do in that place. A few days before returning to New York, Bowles asked me, in that formal tone of his, if I would let him translate the stories, or rather, the prose poems that I had shown him during the workshop. A publishing house in New York that specialized in *extravaganzas* had requested a contribution from him for its catalogue, but he didn't have anything to send them at the moment. It seemed to him, he told me, that if he translated what I had written, they just might be interested in publishing them. Of course I gave him my permission, and we agreed that he would send his translation to my address in New York so I could review it and, if it was to my liking, we could submit the work to Red Ozier Press, the small publishing house for rare books. That is how our long collaboration began, a necessarily asymmetrical collaboration, given the fact that a reluctant master translating the work of an apprentice is never the equivalent of the latter translating the work of the master, no matter how valiant the effort.

The last year I spent a significant amount of time in Tangier was 1998. King Hassan II was about to die, and his son would bring about many changes, most of them purely cosmetic. But the outside world had changed as well, and those changes were evident in the life of the city. There were female police officers in the street, new settlements of migrants from the countryside appeared with increasing frequency, and ghettos had sprung up, inhabited by immigrants from other parts of Africa, for whom Tangier was the last stop before setting out to breach Europe's fortress. Truly, the city would be transformed to such a degree that, of the Tangier of the 1980s, one could repeat what Bowles had written when comparing the city he had discovered in the 1930s to the one he saw anew in the 1950s: "only the wind remains."

I stayed, as I had so many times during the fifteen years that I persisted in visiting the city, in the Atlas Hotel, built in the art deco style at about the same time as the Itesa Building and where I had begun writing the only novel of mine that takes place in Tangier, *The African Shore*. It was winter and the heating at the Atlas was still deficient, so when I was invited to stay for the remainder of my visit in a nineteenth-century European mansion surrounded by gardens in the Monteviejo—and with views of the cliffs overlooking the Pillars of Hercules and the town of Tarifa embedded in the Spanish coast—I considered myself the most fortunate Guatemalan on the whole of the African continent.

By then Paul had become an emaciated old man in chronic convalescence, confined to his bedroom and unable to read due to cataracts, although always full of wit. His aesthetic activity was limited almost exclusively to listening to music—which sometimes entered his room in the form of the calls of the muezzin from the three or four mosques nearby, whose voices recalled the modulation of flamenco singers, or from the drums and *rhaita* solos during the nights of Ramadan.

Here is a list of memories—written haphazardly—of the things we talked about during all those years at the Itesa with Paul: The discipline of traveling. Conrad and the sea. The sounds of the jungle and the desert. Graham Greene, Norman Lewis, R. B. Cunninghame Grahame. Westermarck. Raymond Chandler, Patricia Highsmith. Moroccan fatalism. Jane Bowles. Kafka, Ivy Compton-Burnett, Gertrude Stein, Flannery O'Connor, François Augiéras. The feeling that the body is an obstacle. The idea of death as a final liberation. The effects of kif. The inventive talent of Mohammed Mrabet. The disadvantages of alcohol. Fiction writing as a controlled dream. Style as instrument. The physical act of writing—placing pen to paper—as a propitiatory ritual or the source of so-called inspiration.

I've since lost the notebook where I jotted down the traces of a dream I had, but if I hadn't written them perhaps I would have lost the memory of the dream as well, one of the last dreams I had in Tangier, one that I'll attempt to describe now.

I was staying again in that magnificent home in the Monteviejo neighborhood in Tangier, with its gardens and view of the strait. The owner, Claude-Nathalie Thomas, who translated Paul's work into French, had loaned it to me in her absence, and I was alone. It was winter, and in my second-story bedroom in that house on the road to Sidi Masmoudi, a fire of olive and eucalyptus wood burned merrily in the small fireplace. Downstairs, in the entrance hall and small courtyard with its glass ceiling, the full moon of November in the year 2000 coldly lit ninety-eight cardboard boxes stacked upon the black-and-white checkerboard floor of ceramic or marble. The boxes, numbered and labeled by my own hand, contained the books, notebooks, and papers belonging to the personal library of Paul Bowles, who had died one year earlier, having bequeathed to me this incredible inheritance. A day or two later I would have to transport these boxes from Tangier to Spanish territory, and it would be necessary to sneak past the vigilant customs agents on both sides of the strait. Under no circumstances were they to become aware that those papers and books were anything more than a bunch of dusty old volumes and scribblings, and not the personal library and literary legacy of a celebrated author. In other words, an inheritance. And the general opinion was that an inheritance left in Muslim lands by a North American *nazrani* to a Guatemalan one would not easily leave Moroccan territory.

I dreamt that I awoke in that house, in the room with the fireplace, and a fire was burning in the dream as well. I walked out into the hall and looked downstairs at the center of the courtyard. Suddenly I was down there, without having taken any stairs, among the boxes of books and papers, only in the dream they were now open. On the circular black tile that marked the center of the courtyard, there was a life-sized metallic bust upon another metallic pedestal, a bust of Paul, an elderly but upright Paul, with the tuft of hair over his forehead and with a slightly haughty expression. But now the boxes have caught fire, and I realize that it is a cremation ceremony. I think: "Of course, Paul asked to be cremated." Now Abdelouahaid, in whose company I had first seen Paul twenty years earlier, is at my side. We both watch the flames incredulously, filled with sadness. We hear a scream, a horrible scream of pain. It is coming, unbelievably, from the bust. Abdelouahaid and I look at each other, and it is he who says, although I was already thinking the same thing: "It's Paul, he's inside. We have to get him out!" We pass through the burning boxes to reach the bust, which is smoking and looks as though it is about to melt. Abdelouahaid sees (and I see that he sees) some metal buttons along the nape and back of the bust. We rush to unfasten them. Inside the bust, suddenly liberated, stands an old and very weak Paul, staggering and unsteady in his camel hair robe, the Paul to whom I had said my last farewell on the eve of his death in the Italian hospital a year earlier. Abdelouahaid and I place his arms on our shoulders and lead him through the flames; we exit through the hallway, where we can already see the starry night of Tangier, the silhouettes of the Roman cypresses beyond the Moorish arch of the magnificent house at Monteviejo with its grand doorway, which is wide open.

Translated from the Spanish by James J. López

KEN BABSTOCK

ON THREE BUILDERS

Somewhere in Dublin in the very early nineties, working for two build-
ers, Hugo and Tony, on a long job in Temple Bar, I felt glimmers of an
unspoken support for my odd off-site passion—poetry. I couldn't have known
then, but essentially we were serving in the sub-basement of the vanguard of
the bubble that would later ruin the country fiscally. At the time it was simply
welcome pay packets, theater on weekends (Brian Friel, Samuel Beckett,
something in Russian, *Juno and the Paycock*), and union breaks, when we sometimes talked books. I'm sure I seemed to them as young and clueless as I was,
but they never sneered. There was no dissonance or distance, to them, between a volume of Mahon's verse and a mallet and chisel; Michael Longley
and a length of rebar; *The Hawk in the Rain* and a hawk and trowel; a spirit level
and *The Spirit Level*. Once, in a pub (it may have been the Temple Bar, before
it became what it did when the dragon began truly spitting fire), they introduced me to a woman named Clodagh, first by their nickname for me,
"Canada," then—and I should face it, they *might* have been mocking—as "a
young poet." It didn't hurt.

Then five or six years later, in Vancouver—strange parallels—another
builder, this time English, who'd lived as a young man on the same London
street as either Alan Bennett or Harold Pinter. He was the exact shape and
build as Martin Amis, though quite a bit older, and once, over tea again
(unions!), asked me point blank: "So what is it with Martin Amis, then?" Has
anyone ever answered that satisfactorily? And again, he knew of my extracur-

ricular vocation, and he quietly, without noise or bizarre interrogations, approved. He simply approved. I'd begun publishing poems in journals by then, but was still a couple of years away from my first book. Phil just took it on trust I was serious. No advice. No long inquiries. No "I could have been . . ." (though I suspect that was a part of his past somewhere). He just gave me work, the loan of a tool belt, leniency when I showed up to a job paralyzed by hangover, and a lift home most nights. That, and long, empty hours that bloomed within a rhythm of repetitive labor. We worked quietly. Only spoke when we had to, so those soggy days and weeks in West Van, Kitsilano, or Shaughnessy eventually felt like a "writing space." I shaped lines in my head, many of which vanished when written, but some stayed. All of "Deck. It's a Deck," from my first book, *Mean*, perhaps too obviously. I still remember meditating for days on why "sump pump" contained everything I needed when uttered at work, but when written down, became an example of mortgaging Hopkins.

I'd like to thank those three men—equal parts brother, uncle, gaffer, example, and reader—for the work, the quiet, the way they blended the world in ways most of us forget are possible.

ALEKSANDR SKIDAN

ON BORIS OSTANIN

1

I met Boris Ostanin in 1989 upon my arrival at the Free University, where he was the chair of the poetry department. Having already read Barthes, we probed Ostanin with the question "What is writing?" In response, he told us stories about Gaston Bachelard falling off his bicycle and how the fall manifested itself in the psychoanalysis of water and fire. (It is necessary to note that Ostanin had developed a peculiar relationship with a bicycle himself: his other favorite story was the tormented, exhaustive, spinning pedals of Molloy; from the bicycle, he transitioned to a scene in which Molloy coaxes money from his mother by means of inflicting codified knocks to her forehead; quite possibly, the unfortunate Molloy was metonymically associated with Krivulin, whom Ostanin would piggy-back into conversations quite frequently.) He talked about Elena Shvarts and Sasha Sokolov. It was through Ostanin that I first heard of Alexander Vvedensky and Leon Bogdanov. In class, he dragged in new and old issues of the *Hours*. Unfortunately, after a time, the Free University had to move its "lectures" on Liteynyi Avenue to the Writers' House.[1] Whether the reasonably well known neighbors were affecting the atmosphere of our gatherings, or writers had made this place absolutely useless, or the style of "teachers" who didn't really teach anyone anything had somehow dimmed our enthusiasm; or we were half-wits; or whether all of these together had combined with "ambition" to publish some "official" journal: whatever it may have been, our meetings found us moving from one apartment to another. . . . In Vasya Kondratiev's book *Strolls,* there is a story dedicated to Boris, but I won't quote it; I merely want to bring to mind the bit about farewell, a farewell letter, which is written to all of us, this city and its ruins, to all that, on top of which is erected this strange non-thing, which is poetry. (Even the names themselves, which have surfaced here, whether out of place or in place, rustle on a tongue that is forgotten, as if it doesn't exist . . . did it ever exist at all?)

2

Once, Ostanin gave me a good scare when he informed me that he had decided to change the year, day, and month of his birth, and along with that, his first and last names. I couldn't imagine how it would've been so simple to cheat one's fate. As though she doesn't know all of our tricks. If she were to be deceived, perhaps it would have to be another way. . . . Ostanin changed his telephone number, his apartment. . . . Now he publishes and edits books. But to tell the truth, the best article on Nabokov was written by him. In it, there are more than forty plausible explanations offered (and then rejected) as to why the credited author of *The Gift* elected the pseudonym "Sirin"; it also offers exegesis, pulling into its orbit all of Nabokov's creative work, both in Russian and English. One of them, psycho-biographical and at the same time strictly anagrammatic, concerning Zina (and Zina Mertz) is particularly effective. For me, Ostanin remains the first to have cracked open the horizon of reading beyond the gloomy fortification-serfdom of meaning, and emphasized the multi-channel, multi-wheeled nature of critical ascent into the unknown. (A masterpiece of such criticism remains the script on the subject of a famous glove, on the occasion worn by Anna Andreevna Akhmatova on the wrong hand, the dialogue played out by Boris Ostanin and Arkadii Dragomoshchenko during a session at the Free University.)

3

At one of a series of critical seminars in Jyväskylä, Finland, in 1994, when yet another presenter yet another time attempted to exhaustively get to the bottom of . . . what appears to be "genuine realism," Ostanin remarked that the word "exhaustive" had exhausted itself and that the time had come to find a different rhetorical flourish. What he meant was that there is always something rather than nothing, some residual, elusive remnant, seeping through the sieve of any and all hermeneutics.[2] The tracks of the name in the text are melting away, as well as the tracks of what was held there ("the truth"). (The author may be the first critic of his own text, and moreover, he truly may forget about it forever; and so I am certain that Ostanin does not remember this episode.) Also melting away are the traces that a name was there, and so on and so forth. But why not what was held in the occupied space, even though deprived of any currency of meaning, as soon as the talk turns to realism, the what-is-held in the sense of an estate? After all, a real writer must have an estate, if not a fate. As such, let's take into account a specific kind of era that was melting away before our eyes. A very specific one. That was the great era of meaning, which demanded of us, and which was none other than, that demanded itself, as if it, the meaning, could not have gotten by without us. We were forced to exhaust it.

Translated from the Russian by Violetta Marmor

NOTES

1. Liteynyi Avenue is notable for a number of significant historic and cultural sites, such as Bolshoy Dom ("the Big House"), home of the former KGB and its successor organization, the FSB; the nineteenth-century Varvara Dolgoruky mansion; Muruzi House with Joseph Brodsky's apartment; the Nekrasov Museum; the Zinaida Yusupova mansion; and Mariinsky Hospital.
2. The Russian word *ostatok* (remnant) and Ostanin's name share a common root. The author is engaging in wordplay here.

TONY D'SOUZA
ON THE EXQUISITE LADY

My becoming a writer is entirely due to a woman I'll call the Exquisite Lady. In 1992, I came back to Chicago after a few months spent riding a bicycle and working odd jobs in Alaska. I was beginning college at a small liberal arts school in Wisconsin called Carthage. Though the setting on Lake Michigan was beautiful, I had conflicted feelings about being there. I'd been accepted to West Point but hadn't been able to pass the medical exam because I'm color blind. Carthage had recruited me to play tennis; it was the only other school I had applied to, and even though they'd offered me a scholarship, I felt it poor consolation for the end of my military dreams.

My experiences in Alaska had changed me. The idea of going up there after high school had begun as a pipe dream concocted with a friend; when he'd backed out at the last minute, I went alone, using my savings from two years working nights and weekends at McDonald's. I rode more than 1,200 miles that summer, nearly all the way up to Fairbanks, slept rough almost every night, fell in love with a pretty Alaskan girl at Denali, and had many quiet moments to begin to know myself. Coming to Carthage and sharing a small dorm room with a sheltered, religious boy from rural Minnesota was confining; I had trouble expressing the changes I'd gone through, missed the girl, and felt isolated and alone.

Not long after school began, Carthage announced a writing contest with a cash prize. I wrote the first story of my life, about a man I'd met who lived in a tent on the Nenana River, a survivalist with a love for poetry. My story placed third; there was a note from the Exquisite Lady—our school's writer-in-residence—scrawled on the copy returned to me. Under five hand-drawn stars, she'd written: "You can be a real writer if you want to be . . ."

The next day, I was in her office. The Exquisite Lady was like no one else at that school. She had svelte pageboy hair; she dressed all in black, was cool, urbane, and sexy; even in that first meeting, she talked about New York publishing, her stories in the *New Yorker,* the book contract with Farrar, Straus, and Giroux that her agent was trying to close. But mostly she talked about me, about my story, told me it was different and spoke of something exciting and real. She said that I had to improve my vocabulary and use of language, but she could tell from just those two single-spaced pages that I had it in me to be a real writer. She said she wanted to work independently with me, that though it would have to wait until the following semester, she'd make a reading list in the meantime. She sent me off to the library with an order to read Hemingway's *In Our Time.* I left that meeting giddy from having so much attention lavished on me by someone like her, and spent the afternoon sitting between the stacks, reading "Soldier's Home" in *In Our Time* over and over again.

The Exquisite Lady and I conducted three independent studies together—I was the only student she did that with. These classes all had different titles, like "Study in Fiction," "Study in the Novel," but those were just covers for what we were really doing. Once a week for three hours, the Exquisite Lady and I would meet in the faculty lounge, where we would smoke cigarettes and go over the stories she had assigned me to read. She'd given me a black three-ring binder filled with college-rule paper, and we discussed characterization, setting, language, and eye for detail in Eudora Welty, Mary Gaitskill, Alice Munro, Tim O'Brien. She led me to the works of short fiction that guided me, including "Powerhouse," "Royal Beatings," "The Girl on the Plane," and "The Sweetheart of the Song Tra Bong." The binder became filled with pages on Aristotle's poetic theories, diagrams of the story arc, and terms like *bildungsroman, deus ex machina,* and *in medias res.* She introduced me to *The Decameron, Tristram Shandy,* taught me the roots of the canon. She went over my own fiction with equal measures of ruthlessness and praise. At the end of each of those meetings, our ashtray would be filled with Parliament butts. I loved being her pet, being seen walking around the campus with her beside me.

At that time, the Exquisite Lady was in her late thirties, divorced, the mother of a nine-year-old son. I had no idea about the difficulties of making a living as a writer, hoping for a book, a full-time position, tenure. She talked of the writers she was teaching like they were friends. Some of the people she'd studied with at the Iowa Writers' Workshop were putting their first books out, and she'd always hang on her door a poster announcing their publications. Everything she told me to do, I did: I wanted to please her, fantasized about meeting her at a hotel in the city, taking off our clothes, making love. Once, I invited her to one of my fraternity's keg parties. When she actually stopped by and I heard her voice in the hall, I was stricken with panic and hid in the closet in my room until she left. During our last appointment before I graduated, she told me how apply to graduate school. A few years later, I did.

More than anything else that I learned from the Exquisite Lady, I learned discipline. Her deadlines were hard and fast, and I never missed one. My writing came out of a desire to express my sense of the world to someone else, but it also came out of passionate love. She was the most accomplished, attractive woman I had ever known. Every one of the words I wrote when I was first learning the hard task of making myself sit in the chair, I wrote them for her.

BYRON CASE
ON L.

I was a precocious, bookish boy of seven. A friend of my parents, L. was a suave classicist, in his early thirties, lean, with neat dark hair and a spruce mustache—handsome, in an unobtrusive way. The house he rented was small and tidy, and my mother and I often went there on weekdays, as part of our regular outings. My meticulous mind was unburdened by its neatness: perfectly ordered bookshelves in every room, plain bone-white walls, not a trace of bachelor clutter to be found. Busts of Homer and Socrates flanked L.'s big blue typewriter.

After a glass of German beer with my mother, L. led me up to his shrine of words, the desk on which that imposing typewriter sat. At the keyboard, he propped me up on his knee and asked me to tell him a story. He was a speedy typist and clacked at the keys fast enough to keep up with my dictation. My tales generally ran to just a few pages, after which L. would present them to me with ceremony, the way one might with a gift. Sometimes he put them into colorful binders with labels on the front, bearing the titles. These I treasured.

L. was forever encouraging me to write. It was to this end, and because I was home-schooled and socially awkward, that he arranged a pen pal for me. Every couple of weeks I received a letter from Ugsbay Unnybay, an honest-to-goodness extraterrestrial living on earth. I was sworn by him and L. to absolute secrecy about his existence. "Absolute secrecy" did not, in this case, extend to my parents, who of course knew all about my alien friend, including his resemblance to a toilet plunger. For reasons I didn't understand, they were consistently amused by my excited reaction to letters from Ugsbay. (I would be eleven years old before I learned that Mister Unnybay's name was Bugs Bunny in pig Latin.) Our correspondence spanned a couple of years, during which time Ugsbay, confined to his hideaway, pressed regularly for descriptive anecdotes about my life on earth. In return, he provided similar ones about his home world. A benevolent manipulation; of course, Ugsbay was really L.

Would I have known if L. and my mother were having an affair? My father certainly had suspicions. He shared them with me long after he and Mum divorced, once I was a teenager. Given this disconcerting element, true or not, L.'s presence in our lives gave me one of my earliest glimpses of the complexity of human relationships. Questions arose about how I was supposed to regard my beloved childhood mentor, assuming he had a part in my parents' split and all of the tumult that followed. In a terribly unwriterly fashion, I elected to remain in uncontemplated ignorance, never broaching the subject with my mother.

I turned to writing full time at about age twenty-eight, after six years in prison, where I am still (the facts behind which are unsuitable and too convoluted for a forum such as this). The act of putting words to paper in this gray nine-by-twelve cell is my gentle escape from hard surroundings, while publishing grants me a voice this exile would otherwise silence. Where most of the prisoners around me languish in institutionalized stupors, mine is the vibrantly intact inner life of a man only bodily displaced. Part of me always remains *out there*.

If writing thus far has saved my mind from the deadening effects of imprisonment, it was L. who gave my writing its earliest boost. I cannot say that without his influence I wouldn't write today, since I was writing before I could ride a bicycle. Perpetual encouragement, stylistic exercises masquerading as alien correspondence, and those prettified manuscripts that made me further appreciate words' presentation—it is undeniable that without these indulgences from him I might never have drawn on the full benefits being a writer affords.

I don't know where he is now, but I like to think that he'll someday see my name in print and experience a frisson of pride for having, however tangentially, helped put it there.

was in order. I was the last one to speak. I did my best imitation of Cubby's driving style, which involved drifting dangerously into other lanes while cursing at the other drivers about being too close to his car. To my great relief, everyone broke up laughing. His ex-wife said to me later, "You channeled him!"

Perhaps the lesson that Hubert Selby taught me that has had the most profound and lasting effect came after he had read some writing of mine. He fairly scolded me, I would like to think, because he thought enough of me and my work to take the time to do so. He told me that my ego was getting in the way of the writing. At the time, I was standing there with another writer and mutual friend. Selby ripped both of us for doing this.

He told us in a few different ways that it was the story that was important, not the writer. He said that the writer must do all he or she can to get out of the way so the characters in the stories will find their reality and receive their due respect but mostly so that that their truth can be told.

There was no misunderstanding. There were no questions to be asked. The lesson was as clear as it could possibly be and it rang loudly in my head. From that moment to now, I strive to get out of the way of the writing, to prevent my ego from separating me from what the real task is—to tell the truth.

When a writer can achieve this smallness of self, his or her writing can pick up astonishing amounts of clarity and power. You may sometimes actually surprise yourself when you read back what you have just put down when you allow what it is to be all it really is.

My way is to treat everything, everyone, every action and situation as "normal" without distancing and thus insulating myself by judgment. Whether it's a dead body or a beautiful wide-open space, I try to let it all happen to me and hit me as hard as it is supposed to.

This can be an incredibly painful way to go through life.

I am also of the opinion that writing, music, or any other "artistic" pursuit should inform and do considerable damage to the "artist." As it passes through the writer, real damage will be sustained, like loss of health, shortened lifespan, alienation—a lifestyle that others see as insane, undesirable, and practically impossible.

Or, you can dummy up, block all the punches, and go the distance, defending yourself against life instead of letting it do its thing to you.

Here's a blanket statement I can live with: all great writers are, on some level, great fighters. Even the most meek and retiring take on life, they strike and are struck. From that comes the strength, the beauty, and the truth.

Hubert Selby, Jr., who was one of the most gentle and generous people I have ever met, was also one of the angriest people I have ever known. He argued with his god, he spoke out loud to his dead father, and he never held back. He and life raged constantly, relentlessly. The better examples of his work are a testament to that bravery and that enormous love he had for all of it.

Guts, basically.

SHEILA HETI

ON SUSAN ROXBOROUGH

I didn't know a single grown-up woman. I was seventeen, living in a house on industrial, bleak, Bathurst Street in Toronto. It was the mid-nineties. My boyfriend lived in one room and a girl lived in the other room and there were always high school kids dropping by, because no one's parents were around. I would wake up early while everyone was still asleep and take the subway to Random House, down near the bottom of the city. I was too young to need breakfast. I roamed the office in my coat because I didn't have appropriate clothes and I was always cold. The only reason I had a job was because of a woman named Susan Roxborough.

Susan was Naomi Wolf's publicist in Canada. Naomi Wolf had published *The Beauty Myth* a few years before and was the feminist from whom I first learned about feminism, so when I heard that she was lecturing in Toronto, I bought tickets and went to hear her speak, then stood up during the Q&A and explained that she had changed my life. I went down to the podium and gave her the zines she'd inspired—or rather, I gave them to an attractive brunette nearby—feminist zines I had put up on the walls of my high school the year before. Only later did I come to understand that I had given the zines to her publicist, after she wrote me a letter saying she liked them. Did I want to meet with her—Susan Roxborough—about the possibility of creating a book of writing by teenage girls for Random House? Naomi would write the introduction. It took me three months to receive her letter (by which time there were three letters), which had been sent to the P.O. box mentioned in the zine—

three letters, each more urgent and bewildered than the last, because I never checked the P.O. box, because the only letters that had been sent there were hers.

During my first meeting with Sue, she realized I needed a job and arranged for me to be hired as publicity assistant. At the time, the Ontario government paid for young people to work in mentorship environments. I was now the only person in the house on Bathurst not on "student welfare." I would photocopy press clippings that came in huge envelopes, which had been scissored out neatly by clipping services, with the name of the author underlined with a ruler and a pen, topped with a white tag bearing the clipping agency's name and date. I'd put the clippings in the author's file in the long gray row of metal filing cabinets in the hall. Then, when authors had new books coming out, I would go into their files and photocopy the best clippings, and those pages would be sent out with the books. I didn't have a desk; I just roamed the halls and waited for a publicist to call me in with a task. That's what I did, apart from stealing books from the book room   contemporary hardcovers by the Dalai Lama or cookbooks by Bonnie Stern or the latest novel by Carol Shields—to sell at used bookstores so I could buy myself lunch, or buy other used books for myself that I wanted even more than lunch.

I had one other friend at the offices; she was about twenty-four and seemed more sophisticated than I'd ever be (which turned out to be true), a woman with the exotic name of Jasmine Zohar, whom I once invited to our house on Bathurst for a dinner party. Her whole being radiated disdain and distress, which made our foolish company stand out in unflattering relief (we served her "peanut butter soup") and I knew I would never invite her again, and that I should not ever invite Susan. Perhaps I would have known this anyway: Susan was too special, too much mine, and too oddly hovering between parent and guardian angel for me to imagine her ever inside my dreary life with my friends.

Susan was in her early thirties at the time—brilliant, soft-spoken, tough, loving, and unsentimental. I couldn't imagine she had real fears or insecurities, but in retrospect, she seems like any woman whose life is not quite settled, for whom the dramas of men are something significantly more painful than whatever glamour a teenage girl might attach to them—genuinely painful, not exotic. I would hear the publicists talking about their love lives. They always seemed grave.

I sometimes went to Sue for advice, but more important was the fact that I was around her every day. If I saw her in the halls, or through her office window, it meant nothing could collapse too completely. My parents were divorcing, my boyfriend was sleeping with other girls—only Susan radiated safety. If I picture that time without Susan Roxborough, I feel scared. I would have been living out in the cold, out in the wilds, without a responsible eye. But everything would be basically okay because there was Susan. She had given me a job. She was working with me on my first book. She convinced me to go to university. She closed the door whenever I came to talk to her in her office, and listened to me with her wide blue eyes. I knew she didn't gossip about me with the other lady publicists, whom I liked but did not love. I could always close the door on the wilds of that first year of living away from home, and sit in a chair by Sue.

A person needs only one figure of understanding in order to not feel they are a random, spinning particle in the universe, without destiny or care. In those years, which my grandmother once called my "lost years," that person was Susan Roxborough.

Just last month, recently divorced, she visited Toronto with her eleven-year-old daughter, and came and sat in my apartment, where we talked about our lives. We gossiped about the people we still knew in common—and Sue was gracious, careful not to say anything mean. And about a matter that had been bugging me for years, she was the only person able to respond in a way that calmed me.

Susan now lives in Seattle, and she spoke of a desire to move back to Toronto, "home." I hadn't realized she felt her home was here, and I felt too shy to tell her that, when I was a teen, "home" was a hallway near her.

MIKHAIL IOSSEL
ON GILBERT SORRENTINO

Unbeknownst to himself, Gilbert Sorrentino has been the only true bridge spanning the two ontological halves of my literary being (such as it may be): the Russian and the American ones. Indeed, he was the first and only American writer I had encountered, in English, back in the old U.S.S.R., of whom I truthfully could say to myself: now, this guy, despite his being an American, is a better writer than almost anyone I know!

The last sentence of one of his better-known short stories, "The Moon in Its Flight," reads, "Art cannot save anyone from anything." I discovered that story in Joe David Bellamy's slim paperback anthology, *Superfiction or the American Story Transformed,* which was among the small pile of predominantly avant-garde (read: unreadable, to us) books given to the semi-underground Leningrad literary Club-81 that I belonged to in the early eighties by the met-aphorically Birkenstocked trio of visiting American experimental poets from the San Francisco Bay Area.

As I was leafing through *Superfiction'*s onionskin pages, deceptively fragile to the touch, that last sentence fairly jumped out at me. Not even my woefully limited command of English at the time was able to diminish the immediate poignancy of its simple truth. Right then and there, I was hooked on Sorrentino's writing for good. It was, as the hackneyed phrase has it, love at first sight. Never before or after have I experienced such an instantaneous connection with a piece of fiction, especially one written in English.

"The Moon in Its Flight" became the first full-scale American short story that I translated into Russian.

Then, less than a decade thereafter, during my Stegner Fellowship stint at Stanford, unbelievably enough, I was participating in his postgraduate fiction workshop. Quite the heady journey for an ordinary boy from the Leningrad suburbs! From the other, past-tethered shore of my life, the likelihood of this eventuality would have ranked on a par, say, with my having a boozy night with Ernest Hemingway at his Key West abode.

What can I say about Sorrentino as a live person? In class, he was benign and relaxed, as inordinately quick as one fully would expect him to be, keenly perceptive and, much to many of the workshop participants' pleasant surprise, highly entertaining: full of caustically funny little anecdotes dating back to the golden, post–World War II period of American publishing, and in particular the early years of his editorship at the legendary Grove Press and Evergreen Review.

What else can I recall? He, too, had a low threshold for boredom when presented with the archetypal MFA student stories, if you know what I mean—especially the ones rendered in the "quietly understated" minimalist vein.

Fortuitously, I got to spend some time with him outside the classroom as well. His office was small and windowless, cluttered from floor to ceiling with all manner of printed matter. He smoked cigarettes in his office: that's how long ago this was. One day I showed him the old issue of a Leningrad *samizdat* magazine with my translation of "The Moon in Its Flight." "This is my story?" he asked, somewhat incredulously, regarding warily the faded typed sheets of crinkly onionskin paper: the couple dozen or so pages' worth of barely legible Cyrillic lettering. Indeed, it was, I confirmed. "So then, can you read out the last sentence for me?" he asked. I complied: "Iskusstvo nikovo i ni ot chevo ne mozhet spasti." He shook his head, with an ironic little smile of phonetic wonderment, and said quietly, in his soft voice, "I'll be darned."

What else was there to say?

"I will be the darned ones!" That's how Google has dealt just now with the task of translating "I'll be darned!" into Russian. *The darned ones!* I just thought I'd share. There's not any hidden, symbolic meaning to this pointless little bit of information.

How about tasking Google with restoring to its original English my Russian translation of the last sentence of "The Moon in Its Flight": "Iskusstvo nikovo i ni ot chevo ne mozhet spasti"?

Here you go: "Art and no one from anything he cannot save." Art—and no one.

EDIE MEIDAV

ON PETER MATTHIESSEN

For the rest of us, the memories of past existences are but glints of light,
twinges of longing, passing shadows, disturbingly familiar.

    —Peter Matthiessen, The Snow Leopard

M eet anyone, questions start. Do you take a person's posture as a first premise, if not a complete moral code? And if a particular man is married to a beautiful illusion of the literary life, and if there comes your way over such ramrod posture a twinkle, what then?

In our first sight of the legend, some joke already winked. Was his about how to manage passion behind all fronts? How unforgettable Peter was, tall at a creaky antique table, gleaming out at twelve fidgety undergraduates under the roof of a college that considered itself fancy.

A few of those huddled around that table bore numbers after names already overfamiliar from being engraved onto the frontispiece of campus buildings, children of generous ancestors whose buildings' cornices offered excellent refuge for college finches to nest, nurture, fight, excrete, reproduce, and graduate from the nest before dying.

Whatever our names or cornices, we who stared at the legend lacked. Ancient in the way of adolescents, we could hardly understand ignorance the way he did. Scions, bastards, aspirants, freaks, whoever we were, we had come to Peter's nest to be nurtured and perhaps reproduce, but first we needed to ogle. There sat literature, his spine tugged as if a rope from Melville's first whaler were pulling it upright. Behind such presence stretched years of adventure and Zen practice, a man arriving too late for our understanding. Too late for his time, creating work that played with time, clearly he needed nothing from us. Obelisk and icon yet with such genial humor, a tease familiar to me from having grown up with a brother. In a spirit of upright sportsmanlike jest, Peter started that first class, all brotherly understanding and avuncular tease, Peter's joke our constant thrum: as if to say "don't tell me you take any of this literature hoo-ha seriously?" But also "you must take this sentence to the death." Because this sentence mattered and then the next also. And every now and then the eye of grace would open and our teacher would become grave in saying even X needs to cut this word from this sentence. Even X, and how blessed X would feel!

Even X knew something—but could you grasp that shimmery thing? I felt lucky to be there, having applied later than the others with a handwritten note deposited at an English office, a first missive hiding all ambition. He would have thought it too long but accepted me anyway, tall man with a lengthy biography who favored short, hardworking, enigmatic sentences. As in "the finches don't live here anymore." Or "Peter died."

The question in relation to any mentor becomes how best to honor the very person who teaches you honor. He would suggest entering such a question by the front door, but because he died last year and my vision still clouds, the back door to the columbarium seems the best one to open.

Consider that usually you expect to find literature in the literary mentor, someone expounding on tomes of books. Someone like the first true writer I had met, a man hoisting literature as suavely as any Manhattan salon host, the debonair Walter Abish, who sported his own courage along with an unexplained black eye patch, Abish offering up a plate of pralines before declaiming that writers should write what they did not know: he himself favored the habit of writing about countries onto whose landmass he made a point of never setting foot, as the page itself could contain all valor. The following week, he saluted me at a café before leaning over my shoulder to cross out words. "Carve," Abish said. "Make your sentences sinuous," causing me to think of Italian sculpture, how one could carve from your work alone a life you loved. Sinuous! Carve! How would anyone not be charmed? If Abish offered a key, perhaps I misused it, since after that point, what I mostly wrote that year were uncarved stories from the view of older men in love with sinuous younger boys, especially one older Asian monk and an older art model. All a way of inducting myself into whatever stories had mattered to me, never so old as I was in that class, a first-year proto-Buddhist college student from out west surrounded by polemic-wielding east-coast sophisticates.

"Oh, sure," said Abish, "when I want to get a story into the *New Yorker*, I write a *New Yorker* story, but the real places to write for are the *Paris Review*,

Conjunctions, and *TriQuarterly*," in this way offering up distant goalposts, impressively shadowy binaries: in a world of tall mirror-sided buildings and Manhattanite verticalities, cultural grace depended on exclusions.

Only later I stumbled into Peter's world, Peter who embraced the globe so much he found it deficient, a writer made of a world hunger so counterphobic it had the paradoxical strength of ether. Did his aura come from having sought out death so often? His cologne was of someone born into privilege who then slummed by seeking out dirt, risk, injustice. His posture arose from one distinct imperative: stride lightly through halls of privilege and ditches of its absolute dearth.

After years of correspondence, plans, phone calls, and occasional sightings, I finally made a pilgrimage with a friend to visit his home out on Long Island. First off, he delighted in showing us the hobbyist galleon ship which his buddy Vonnegut had given him: a ship encased in glass, a way to contain adventure. Next Peter wanted to describe the walls' framed 1960s photos of semi-naked aboriginal Papua New Guinea swordsmen at war. "There I was," he said, "right here, crouched among those tribesmen!"

As we'd guessed years earlier, for Peter, coming up against death meant life more fully lived, a struggle like literature's own: you could not survive without paying attention. He talked of that aboriginal battle with palpable longing. Poisoned spears thrown by men naked but for their pointy loin-gourds might have been one of the best ways to die: die from a spear and you surely count as someone upon whom nothing was lost.

It happened that while describing the thrill of aboriginal death, Peter had just begun to undergo severe treatment for leukemia. Out in the Gobi Desert two months earlier, he'd fallen to his knees, reduced to crawling. He had returned, gotten diagnosed, almost recovered. Before the photos, he had picked us up near the train station and then, as soon as he could, outside his house, showed us a giant whalebone he had truck-dragged from the beach. "Come see how the natives live," he said, luring us into the house of literature, just as he had done so many years earlier. He was excited that some wildlife people, wishing to honor his environmentalist legacy, had invited him out to Cape Cod to sight the one giant mammal he had never seen. "The great blue whale!" And how could Peter not love such an Ahab prospect? The contortions to arrange such a trip almost impressed us more, as coordinating our own visit had been harder than glimpsing a mythical whale: no cell phone, computer, or answering machine could sully Peter's universe. Meeting him meant that complications abounded, complexities not involving his treatment but rather his wife and the delicacy of lunch plans.

We sat on that visit, girls again, perched gingerly on a couch while he murmured in the kitchen. After a long consultation, he extracted two glasses of water which he brought us, talismans of the endless scotch and whiskey that had once flowed. Near that couch on that gray day hung photos of him shirtless and hale-fellow-well-met with authors: Mailer, Vonnegut, Salter, and always some obscure unnamed dark-haired woman gadding about in a beach scene on Long Island or on a boat, the men sticking out their skinny ribcages in the manner of fifties photos, back when ads for strongmen still boasted of kicking sand back at bullies. These were hearty livers. Vonnegut died falling down the stairs, Mailer died when his kidneys gave out, and so far Salter and Matthiessen had kicked enough sand back at death to outlive their photographed fellows. Once Long Island had been uncool and these lions had chosen it, their isthmus of cunning, exile, and loud drunken hijinks away from the monolithic isle of Manhattoes. Matthiessen was of the Upper East Side and Hotchkiss but willed himself to be one with the people, with Long Island potato farmers or anyone soon to be dispossessed, a lover of Conrad and Dostoyevsky both, a humble servitor in strange dinghies across the world, or so his living room proclaimed. The water he offered us in a glass was as clear as the man who offered it yet also a domestic token of how hard it must be to be attached to a person dancing lightly through so many realms and tribes.

What about his work? He was trying to finish a novel. "It might kill me," he said wryly. "It's me or it!" He had won a National Book Award for his last novel, a retelling of his Florida stories. Not giving up the literary struggle, not yet; for his kind there would be no ballyhooed retiring from the practice.

Outside he showed us the bare gray zendo where he served as priest: he had already chosen a successor, and he relished telling us how he beat with a stick the backs of those whose postures sagged. "Some had a tainted practice," he confided, going into a story about one particular woman: we knew already that some women were good at getting their thorns into him.

When we had been students, rumors had swirled, most of them true. As a young man, Peter had quarreled with his parents and then renounced them, taking on the ideal of the hobo or the beatnik without naming it as such, not jumping rails with Kerouac but working with fishermen on Long Island. With George Plimpton, he'd founded the *Paris Review*. In that impossibly optimistic time, when being a spy lived on the same congenial plane as being a writer, he had worked as a cultural emissary for the CIA in Paris and then wrote *The Snow Leopard* on the Tibetan plateau. Teaching at Yale, for which he took the jitney to the city and the long train up to New Haven, came about because he had paid attention in the wrong way. *In the Spirit of Crazy Horse,* his risky book, had backed the Indian activist Leonard Peltier, and the FBI had sued him for libel. While legal fees had flattened his wallet and made him teach for a spell, the truth telling deposited something into a more personal bank account, one that mattered more: from behind bars, Leonard called him regularly, promising that one day, on some native plains beyond, the two men would run free as thoroughbreds.

Peter's lessons to me over the years could perhaps boil down to one: *Don't make the mistake I did; only use your writing for fiction.* What did he say to others who might call him a mentor? Claire Messud, Amor Towles, Michael Ravitch, Sharon Guskin: each has some Matthiessen mentorship in their literary code, though a legion unknown to me must cover some great Gobi-like tract.

Once I sighted him in a courtyard at school writing in a tiny book. "I write every day; then I transcribe the notes." Later that week he called me for a meeting that would end up helping me through every waitress job I would be fired from and every soul-killing moment with an alcoholic boss or under fluorescent lights: he asked if I could represent the school in some national contest, and also, did I have any writing I could send his editor?

If I needed to sit immediately after with a friend on a curb outside, floored by the message, slapped or kissed by an emissary of future grace, does it matter? If I misinterpreted his words to mean I should type in beatnik frenzy on onionskin paper for two weeks and mail such randomness to his editor, does any of that matter now?

The week he died, I was making plans to trek out the following weekend to meet him. Because the last time I saw him, at the Sag Harbor train station, he had said, quite clearly, "I want to see you again, Edie. I want to meet your family"—offering a flinch to which I paid no attention until, literally, the hour of his death, when I was helping my kids toward sleep but felt the pressing need to call.

"Too late at night," my mate said. "Try in the morning."

And in the morning, as I was trying, figuring out how to get to Long Island, my mate delivered the news: I was too late. As the ninth century claimed, the devil is in charge of timing, though Peter surely would have made a joke about clinging.

What probably matters most: the gift of belief he offered, one that sprouted. When I can, I try to replicate his act with others, with students or friends. On that last visit, in his living room, I admit I became teary. "You really gave so much," I told him. "You believed, it meant everything, I'm hoping your gift continues."

His twinkle also turned a little teary but, tellingly, the posture stayed a yardstick. "I've lived a good life," he said, "loved what I've done, have been very fortunate. I hope to keep on living but won't suffer if I don't."

That he had that gift of belief in others mattered to him as well, he said, especially since it helped limit the regrets he then mentioned—how he had lived, as well as his doubts about the worth of his writing out in the world, but as far as I was concerned, his candid humanity only added to the legacy.

As if obeying James's injunction to be someone upon whom nothing was lost, Matthiessen's presence alone invited you into the party. You didn't have to go globetrotting to pay attention. You could just find the humor and gravitas of each moment. Did the joke come from years of hitting people's spines with his favorite cane during Zen practice, from sitting still on a cushion, from crouching down like a young Peter O'Toole among murderous tribesmen in Papua New Guinea? Or did it have nothing to do with boldface bravery and the notations made about extreme geographies? The joke may have been that for all we need to care about the details, whether they are about justice or love, texture or loss, our last legacy is attention. If usually the mentor offers literature, instead Peter offered the twinkle. And could you not call that the gift of life itself?

MEGAN MAYHEW BERGMAN

ON TAMMY WHITE

I take the winding dirt driveway to Tammy's farmhouse, pausing to let a neighbor's guinea hen scurry by. A small herd of angora goats is grazing in the first pasture. A black potbellied pig nibbles grass peacefully in their midst, not even looking up at my station wagon. Before I get to the house there are two coffee-colored alpacas, recently sheared, each nesting in a sunny spot, legs tucked, fuzzy lips pursed. I roll down my windows. Sometimes you can hear them hum. Alpacas, Tammy has explained, just want everything to stay the same. They worry easily, and then they hum.

I park my car and approach Tammy's front porch, where a rogue dairy goat with a silvery-blue coat is standing, looking at me with ambivalence. A white peahen rustles nearby. The turkeys cackle in the distance, a surprisingly musical sound for such ugly birds.

The dogs push through the front door with their noses, two elderly springer spaniels and a border collie puppy named Nessie, who runs circles around all of us until the space closes and I am at the door.

I let myself in, because Tammy keeps that kind of house. It's one of the few places I feel comfortable making myself a coffee, but today I don't have to, because Tammy is kicking off her muck boots, having come in the back door, and is filling a mug for me. Her hair is in braided pigtails, and she's wearing a short dress with leggings, and little rooster earrings. Tammy always beams. I figure she even beams when she's alone with her sheep, but it makes you feel good, as if you're responsible for all that glow.

When I moved to Vermont from North Carolina a few years ago, I was desperate for warmth. Tammy had warmth in spades, a sort of dogged positivity paired with emotional honesty that I found refreshing. Plus, she's the first to plop a steaming hot strawberry-rhubarb pie on your counter when you need one. I learned that's not necessarily a southern gesture, just nice.

I often ask myself: what is it I like so much about Tammy's place? Is it the smell of pies baking? Is it the handspun yarn in progress in the corner, a gorgeous strand coming from what looks like an indigo-colored cloud of cotton candy? Is it the serious-looking Maine coon cat that climbs into my lap, or the dog hair on the couch that makes me feel at home? The humble paintings her children made years ago, the jar of peacock feathers, the basketful of fresh eggs? Is it the uber-nurturing way Tammy guides you through a conversation? Allowing tangents, but always circling back to the heart of the exchange, and pressing just the right book into your hand as you leave. Or if not a book, a few hot biscotti wrapped in a napkin, or a dozen eggs, slipped onto the passenger's seat of the car as you depart. She has a remarkably graceful and giving nature, but not haplessly so—intelligently and mindfully so.

I think what I love most is the way Tammy places a premium on creativity and meaning. She annotates her cookbooks, jotting down when she made a particular dish, and for whom. She throws beautiful, inclusive parties, coining the term *festive farmwear* for the marriage of her white peacocks, which I, as a justice of the peace, conducted dressed in a full red skirt and plumed hat. She inscribes books, remembers birthdays, sends care packages, and curates her life, right down to the car she drives—a cream-colored vintage VW convertible, usually stuffed to the brim with dogs, daughters, and pies.

No, maybe what I love most is her sense of fun and exploration. "I leap and don't look," she says whenever someone remarks on her undertaking another demanding project, like beekeeping, or chainsaw lessons. She's the first to teach someone else one of these skills, too. She's my chicken dealer, my go-to canning resource, the first to answer a text about barn-stall maintenance strategies, and she once taught me how to embroider so that I could make customized handkerchiefs for my husband. I embroidered away, badly but with great happiness. Tammy has a contagious energy, and her "leap don't look" philosophy is contagious. Learn how to keep bees if you want to keep bees. Rescue a sheep and put it in the back of your pickup truck if your heart tells you so. Write the Great American Novel if you want to write the Great American Novel. Anything is possible. Anything. Make yourself vulnerable and have at it.

I sort of fell into my adult life here in Vermont, the one where suddenly I was a mother, farmer, and writer with little training. I met Tammy when I needed to be emboldened. I needed to feel as though I could take artistic risks, as though I could write my first novel after two story collections, as though I could manage the apple trees and raspberry patch and enormous gardens and goats I had inherited. I needed someone who understood households with cats on the table and children underfoot and the urge to still bake a good cake even when it's ten o'clock at night.

For most of my life, I have battled the urge to be a hermit, to tuck myself inside my safety zone and stay there, enjoying my own company, dreaming my dreams, thinking my thoughts. But the years I lived that way were far emptier than the days I live now, dogs and kids underfoot, jam boiling on the stove, novel-in-progress eating up a quarter of my brain at all times. I finally feel as though I want to share myself with the world, be it through pie or through words, but I need coaching, constant reminders that it feels good to give. It feels good to leap.

There is a sense of magic about not just her farm, but Tammy herself. She watches my daughters some days, and more than once I've picked them up only to hear the familiar response: "I don't want to leave."

And I get it. I never do either. Thanks to people like Tammy who make us bleeding-heart eccentrics feel loved, and at home, not just inside their walls, but in ourselves.

POLINA BARSKOVA

ON THE TEACHER

1. THE RAILWAY STATION

Every Thursday after the meeting, our train ride would exhaust itself at the famous rail station—the mammoth old rail station melancholically stuck amidst the city obsessed with constant self-renewal. (It would change names like an elderly beauty changes her face.) We would run down the whirling staircase slippery with the vomit from the night before, with the remains of the art nouveau lascivious floral debris. "Do you remember what happened here?" my teacher would ask me sometimes. "Yes," I would mumble and nod—indeed I do.

That now-rusty, dilapidated staircase once served as the setting for one of the most pathetic tragedies of Russian poetry—poet Annensky, a dignified gymnasium teacher with a proud mustache, who didn't dare to publish his sonorous poems until his forties and even then did so blushing like a rascally schoolboy, died there. I mean he died right on these steps (I always would wonder which step it was exactly) of a heart attack.

With the overreaching generosity of guilt, the poet Annensky was posthumously proclaimed by his students, Gumilev and Akhmatova, to be one of the forefathers of Petersburg avant-garde poetry. His porous, gentle heart had suffered many blows during his lifetime, but this final, decisive one came, as is not uncommon, from a publisher.

Right when the poet had braced himself to enter the tight little world of Petersburg literary exaltation, the coveted chair was snatched away by another debutante. This *another* was mysterious, exotic, young, and sexy: she would send her poems on expensive lilac paper smelling of patchouli and hint at the gothic and convoluted mysteries of her international origins and destinations. The publisher, taken in by these charms, chose to publish her rhymes instead of his poems. Eventually and inevitably, she proved to be a fake, a practical joke, a mystification. But by then Annensky was already dead of his silly broken impatient heart.

So every time my teacher and I walked down this staircase and he asked me, "Do you remember what happened here?" I would think of this heart coming locomotive-like to its stop and about the beautiful, beautified mask, the mask of beautiful words worn by the younger, more promising (promising what and to whom?) talent under which was the smirking face of a prankster.

2. THE STREET

Every Thursday of every season for almost a decade I would rush to our meetings via one of the most solemn and peculiar streets of what was then Leningrad. Each side of the street consisted of one very long, very classical building colored yellow and with many columns rising up rhythmically. The building rising on the left housed the Ministry of Engineering, Construction, and Regulation; on the right was the oldest and most celebrated ballet academy in Russia and thus in the whole wide world. I would pass tiny perfect ballerinas on the way to their lessons—all aglimmer like a school of fish. Every girl in the city dreamt at least for a moment of becoming one of them. Even I enjoyed my chance to try on a pink *pointe* shoe made of silk covered in chalk, only to raise my head and see weariness on the examiner's face. "Thank you, next!" she said. I would peek at the ballerina world through the huge dusty windows: study how their perfect iron bodies, united by the magical count, "une, deux, trois," moved together—a perfect docile caterpillar.

I met that ballet teacher years later at a literary party and reminded her of my failure. She smiled awkwardly. In order to create a dancer, you need to shape a strong body, an impeccable sense of discipline. "But what is needed to create a poet?" she asked. I smiled awkwardly.

3. THE ROOM

The room where our meetings took place was situated in a bleak huge building by the bleak wide river. All the Leningrad newspapers were published there. Our room housed the newspaper for the young pioneers—*The Sparks of Lenin*. The sparks of Lenin in the city of Lenin were not burning with much cheer then: the empire was at its last stinky sigh.

Every Thursday we, the aforementioned sparks, the Soviet schoolchildren between the ages of seven and fifteen, would gather there to be turned into poets. I was first attacked by the muse at eight, waiting outside of the liquor store while my mother, a nervous beauty, was booze shopping. I proudly recited my rhymes to Mama. She later shared her astonishment with a friend, who directed her to my future teacher—the bald, well-wrinkled man with the alcoholic nose and the lively eyes of a raccoon. He said, "Of course, she can come. We meet every Thursday, from 4 to 6 p.m."

We adored him. Our teacher, with the funny last name of Leikin (sounds like "watering can" in Russian). Indeed, he was watering us—thirsty, blind seeds in need of better words.

He would read us strange poetry and then make us read strange poetry out loud. Once, when I was thirteen, he handed me a volume of Annensky and instructed, "Please, choose a dozen and read to us next Thursday." Obviously, I did not understand a thing about the poet's world—bleak, hopeless, elegant, filled with irony. Yet its sound consumed me. Like a huge building with the windows too large to be seen through (a railway station? a ballet school?), each poem was filled with cold air, and I became drunk on its oxygen. Alliteration after alliteration, I gobbled up the book: I wanted more. The empire was rotting while its confused teenagers recited Baudelaire and Celan, Brodsky and Gumilev, Tsvetaeva and Parnok.

After a weekly portion of incomprehensible, addictive poetry, we played games. Every Thursday he'd invent for us a new one. Not your boring charades and awkward bouts of sonnet lacing but real games He would bring us a page of contents of an imaginary book. ("Imagine," he'd say, smirking, "I've lost the book, and only this remains—let's write poems with these beginnings.") He would make us write poetic monologues: "I am Hamlet," "I am a parrot," "I am a white night," "I am C—." He would read to us seven translations of a famous poem made by his translator friends (I met Le Charogne and Todesfuge for the first time through him), and we would have to compare the translations. And more, more.

But the most important part was when we would read our own poetry. He would never assess, nor praise, nor criticize. His comments were specific, funny, caressing. And yet—from the expression of his smile, from the length of his pause after a poem—we knew what he *really* thought. And we also knew that the one whom he asked to read last was the king of the room.

When my time came to read at the end of our meetings, I understood that sweetness-bitterness of being proclaimed—a poet, the poet. I wanted nothing more than his approval; I feared nothing more than his disappointment. During our train rides after the meeting we'd be silent (enough said already) and I would furtively study his ugly dear face trying to read in it the guarantee that my little voice could last somehow.

"What will you do if you stop writing?" he'd ask. "What will be interesting about you? Is there anything interesting at all?" he'd tease. I shuddered with fear. And then at the railway station in the winter brown twilight we'd smoke our last cigarettes. (I started when I was twelve.) He'd ask, "So, who died here?" And I'd say, "Annensky." "And who killed him?" And I'd say, "Cherubina." He'd accept my passwords, kiss my forehead, and disappear into the crowd. And I would rush home to write more in order to please him, to make him happy.

I knew he was a poet: but his poetry, gloomy, baroque, and inspired by self-loathing, did not impress me. His real gift was to find the gift in others, like geologists do with their minerals—hidden in the deep dark soil. He would nourish and praise that gift, would observe with acute curiosity the bearer of the gift, a vessel, so to say. Then these children would inevitably stop writing. Another of us would be appointed the last reader. The ex-favorite would stop coming on Thursdays, fade into the past.

For some reason I persevered: out of stubbornness or fear of silence—who knows?—I continued writing. This is another story to be told at another time.

One evening when I walked away from the station, I understood, to my own dismay and nauseating embarrassment, that this was my last ride with him. I knew I never could not come back—I absolutely did not know why. And indeed: I never saw my teacher again (no matter how often my peers and his friends would repeat that I "literally broke his heart"). Almost daily I imagine our meeting, at one of *our* places, and how I say, "Sorry"—to this day having no idea what for.

ROSEMARY SULLIVAN
ON LEONORA CARRINGTON AND P. K. PAGE

When I was a young woman trying to convince myself I could be a writer, I met the remarkable Canadian poet P. K. Page. She had just published an article called "Traveller, Conjuror, Journeyman," in which she described art as magicianship. "The point of art," she said, "is to alter our way of seeing." Her voice, so candid and playful, made me want to seek her out. I still remember that first visit in 1975. Her suburban home in Victoria, British Columbia, looked ordinary on the outside, but entering it was like walking into an exotic mind: on the shelves of her living room were Mexican candied skulls and gaudily painted trees of life, Mexican paper flowers and Australian bull roarers, and her walls were filled with her own paintings—one depicted strange strings of dancing vegetation reaching towards the sun through scarlet air; another was of stippled silver moons. We became friends on that visit. P. K. published two of my poems in a book of short poems she edited called *To Say the Least.* I had thought at the time she was just being kind, but I realized later that my poems wouldn't have made it into her anthology had they not struck a chord in her.

What is a mentor? Someone who travels ahead, throwing back wise hints; who instills confidence, offering a rationale for making art. P. K. could be playful and witty and we had fun, but she was also serious about what I would call her *metaphysical appetite,* a hunger I shared. We used to tell each other our dreams. I became her dream keeper, remembering dreams long after she had forgotten them. In one of her dreams, she saw two dogs standing in a field.

Each had two blue eyes and, above these, a third eye, which was human. The thought of the dream was "If their third eye is human, what is our third eye?" She called this an *informational* dream. Like D. H. Lawrence, one of her favorite writers, she believed that "we are a mystery to which the mind can gain little access." We both loved the fact that dreams are antic and serious at the same time. In one dream, she walked into a field at the center of which was a gigantic egg. A voice said: "You can't be beaten unless you're broken. Unless you're broken you can't be whole." She laughed when she described it: "It's the cosmic omelet." The insight of the dream, she told me, was that we have to be raw, open to suffering, if we are to learn anything.

We talked endlessly about romantic obsession, with all its pricy pain. We had both fallen in love that way. She is one of the voices behind my book, *Labyrinth of Desire: Women, Passion, and Romantic Obsession.* It begins with a fictional love story set in Mexico, which I then take apart to wonder over the myths we repeat in that "ghost story" we call romantic love. Is such love really autoerotic, a projection of all that we long to claim in ourselves? When the obsession is over, we wonder who is the stranger standing before us.

It's curious that, in the long years of our friendship, it's her aphoristic statements I remember. She once told me: "If the planet is a plant, perhaps you are a nodule of growth." I tried to make that my mantra.

It was P. K. who sent me to Leonora Carrington, another mentor. Leonora was famous as the lover of Max Ernst, but it was her own work as a painter and writer that turned her into one of Mexico's most important artists. She lived in the same imaginative space as P. K. did.

I still remember my first encounter with Leonora in 1995. I was dumbfounded by the Spartan rigor of her house in the Colonia Roma district of Mexico City: a dark entrance, cement floor, interior patio with scraggly trees and plants. It seemed cold and austere until I saw her sculptures. They filled every corner. They were under the stairs, beside the cat litter, behind the door, on the sideboard. Like bronze dreams: a sphinx figure with a human head held tenderly in its palms; a strange desolate god with a door that opened in his body; a Mary Magdalene riding backwards on something resembling a pig. I would later learn that this sparseness of furniture and decoration was calculated. Leonora would tell me that, apart from her books and artworks, everything in her house was dispensable. "I can pick up and leave at a moment's notice," she said.

All the warmth of the house was collected in the modest kitchen. As we sat at the table, with its checkered tablecloth, tea canister, ketchup, and bottle of tequila, Leonora immediately put me at ease by discussing the new "corset" she had just bought at Price Choppers in Florida to support her sore back—it was the kind train porters use for a weak back. She was thrilled with it. And then she told me I was sitting in the seat where Aldous Huxley had sat. She had always admired him, but she liked him especially after he came to Mexico. I was not surprised that Aldous Huxley would have sought out Leonora because, like P. K.'s, all her work is about perception.

Sometimes you meet someone with whom you connect immediately at the deepest level. That's what happened as I sat at Leonora's kitchen table.

She began to reminisce about those days in the early 1960s when she and P. K. had begun their friendship in Mexico. "P. K. had a wonderful eye, a very textured verbal sense. Once I remember her sitting down to a particularly unappetizing dish of rice and calling it 'congealed blood.' Nothing more needed to be said."

But our talk soon took a higher note as we began to speak of our mutual interest in Jung and I discovered what a quiet afternoon with Leonora would always be.

"Jung was absolutely right about one thing," Leonora told me. "We are occupied by gods. The mistake is to identify with the god occupying you." Leonora told me she was possessed by Demeter, the mother, so obsessed was she with her two sons. "They are adult, have nothing to do with me, and yet I am still tied umbilically." "Who occupies you?" she asked. I felt nailed to the spot. "I have no idea," I replied. "My guess would be Diana, the huntress."

Our talk turned to books, influences. "These days I'm interested in Fritz Capra, the meeting of physics and consciousness," she said. "It's not who we are, but what we are that's important. We have taken a wrong turn, refused magic, and swapped the power of instinct for intelligence. The mysteries which were ourselves have been violated. Wisdom has been covered up. There is a lot of dogmaturd to clean away. Our machine mentation is the problem—I am, I am, I am."

But then she corrected herself. "The problem is not ego. It's the mannequins. I have one for my gallery, one for each of my sons, one for Tchiki [her husband], one for my cats." I took her to mean the masks we put on so casually. She told me she'd spent a week in Canada living with Tibetans when she was on one of her investigations. "I liked the Tibetans because they were so reasonable," she said. "But I got bored."

She said she preferred the shamans to the psychoanalysts and the priests. When she worked with the shamans in Zinacantán she learned from them that the soul has thirteen parts and an animal spirit companion. It is possible for a part of the soul to get lost because of fright and to leave. "That seems to me eminently believable," she said. "It has happened to me."

I asked her what she meant. "Entities do enter our lives," she explained. "One I experienced was malevolent. It has happened six or eight times since I was very young. It was a thing without shape or boundaries, amorphous. It comes as a sound. It was voracious, sucking, a sucking force, and inside this entity were millions of other entities, equally voracious, crying desperately, one of which was me. As in hell."

"Was this evil?" I asked.

"Yes, evil is an entity, a force with its own momentum. Like Hitler."

"What moves it?"

"An absence of attention. That is the only thing I can think of," she replied. "The only thing we can do about evil is pay attention."

I told her that I had recently had the strangest dream. I had visited the Egyptian collection at the Metropolitan Museum in New York and had been dazzled by the hieroglyphic image of the human eye on birdlike stick legs. In my dream there were four eyes on legs staring from their corners into the center at something that I could not see. In the dream I knew that if I could just see what they saw I would understand all the mysteries.

She didn't dismiss the dream. She simply said: "There are phases or layers to reality that we don't have the equipment to experience. But there are moments you see, and then you lose it."

"The human apparatus is limited by body and time," she added, "but it can open up more. The world is marvelous. It looks at you. You look at it."

Every time I went to Mexico over the years, at least a dozen times, I made sure to visit Leonora. In those early years, we also talked about romantic obsession. At the age of nineteen, she had attended the Amédée Ozenfant art school in London and, through a school friend, met Max Ernst. The meeting, she said, was a "shock amoureuse." She was still young and got caught up in the "love madness."

In the spring of 1938, Leonora and Max Ernst moved to Saint Martin d'Ardèche, where they covered their home with sculptures and shocked the neighbors, who peered through the hedges, by painting outdoors—naked. That summer Ernst painted his marvelous *Leonora in the Morning Light* in which Leonora stares out at the viewer from a landscape of minotaurs, unicorns, and skeletons, herself an exotic dream creature suspended from a phallic vine. When I look at that painting now, knowing it's of Leonora, I always feel overwhelmed.

Leonora talked about how in early September of 1939, just days after France and England had declared war on Germany, the French police ordered the arrest of all "enemy aliens." They knocked at the door in Saint Martin d'Ardèche, put Max into handcuffs, and took him away to a hastily improvised internment camp set up in an abandoned brick factory in the town of Les Milles just outside Aix-en-Provence. Ernst had lived in France since 1922. It never occurred to them that he might be included in the roundup. It took Leonora three months of cajoling bureaucracies before Ernst was released from Les Milles through the intercession of the poet Paul Éluard. In May he was denounced by a neighbor as a spy, arrested again, and returned to Les Milles. The injustice of it still made Leonora shake.

In June 1940, as the German army advanced on Paris, two friends pressured Leonora into joining them as they fled by car across the Pyrenees to Spain. There was no point in waiting for Max, they said. Who knew where he might be? But the terror of not knowing what had happened to Max was leading to disaster. In Spain, under the pressure of anxiety, Leonora began to spiral out of control. She was institutionalized in a hospital in Santander. Her multiple experiences of being shackled and given the drug Cardiazol to induce seizures were so horrendous that she came to call them "death practice."

"At least when you go mad, you find out what you are made of," she could now say laconically.

"Why didn't you try to get out of France?" I asked her.

"We should have left after Max was released from the concentration camp the first time," she said, "but Max couldn't imagine a life outside Paris. Paris was freedom." Paris was the City of Light.

At the exhibition *Entartete Kunst* organized in Munich by Joseph Goebbels in 1937, Max Ernst had been labeled a degenerate artist. There is a picture of Hitler standing in front of Ernst's painting *The Beautiful Gardener*. Over the painting is a banner that reads "A Slur on German Womanhood."

I asked Leonora why totalitarian minds are afraid of art. "Because it gets inside," she said. "It can terrify you or give you joy."

She told me: "The Nazis opened up a forbidden door in the soul. I suppose if you have to stake this little bit of ground that says you are a superior race and then defend it, something horrible always happens. When you claim certainty, when you say that you know."

Leonora planted the seeds for my book: *Villa Air-Bel: World War II, Escape, and a House in Marseille.* From her I learned about the villa where people fleeing the Nazis in 1940 found shelter and of the marvelous man, Varian Fry, who founded the Centre American de Secours, setting up secret escape routes across the Pyrenees, forging passports, and trading money on the black market. He saved at least 2,000 people who would certainly have ended up in German concentration camps. Researching and writing that book was one of the most extraordinary experiences of my life.

Leonora died in 2011 at the age of ninety-four, one year after P. K. died. When I look back, it is always Leonora's humor and outrageousness that I remember and even try to emulate. She was brilliantly adept at one-liners. Over the years I collected them.

Once she said: "Tchiki's doctor said we come back as energy. 'What?' I asked him. 'You mean as traffic lights?'"

She said she went to a Freudian analyst once, who told her she was not adjusted. "To what?" she inquired.

And she ended a conversation with a Jesuit who asked her if she believed in God by asking: "Which one?"

Once when I asked what she was reading, she said. "A book on criminal profiling. That's the kind of book I enjoy these days." We laughed. "I love detective stories," she added. "Why?" I asked. "It appeals to the inner criminal, the killer in us all."

It intrigues me to think that my mentors have always been women. It's deeper than simple gender affinity. It's more about what Leonora would call the search. She once told me: "We still must meet the female. Buried under so much pain. There is the biological fact. The two genders. But never have I heard an adequate explanation of what the meeting of the two sexes would mean. The kind of explanation where you say: Ah! Yes!"

Leonora was sometimes called a feminist and claimed Margaret Atwood as one of her favorite writers. But no label sat easily on her. I will always remember her comment that "women's spirituality is grounded in everyday reality, which makes it sane. Men kick free to abstraction, metaphysics." This is dangerous. "The compartmentalization of the mind/body is convenient for institutions to control us."

A while back I found an article on Leonora, I don't remember where, but it quoted a letter she wrote to André Breton, which I copied down. Breton had asked her to participate in an exhibition of eroticism in Mexico City in 1959. She wrote, describing her intended contribution: "A Holy Ghost (albino pigeon) three meters high, real feathers (white chickens', for example), with: nine penises erect (luminous), thirty-nine testicles to the sound of little Christmas bells, pink paws. . . . Let me know, Dear André, and I will send you an exact drawing." Breton, it seems, did not write back. Leonora had come to dislike the surrealist myth of male artistic genius, the grandiose gesture, the erotic raiding of the female muse. She had some simple advice about painting. "Painting is like making strawberry jam—really carefully and well."

I learned from both these women why you make art. Writing is hard. It is also a humble act. When you are in the throes of a writing project, you will find yourself asking: Why do I do this to myself? The answer is simple: it's the search that gives meaning to my life. It is my ongoing conversation with the world.

LINEAGE II

PADGETT POWELL

ON DONALD BARTHELME

Don Barthelme once said to me, "The trouble with teaching is you spend all your time working on someone else's rotten manuscript when you should be working on your own rotten manuscript." This is signature Barthelme. It contains the making of a joke by repeating two syllables or two words or two phrases, at which he was very good: "And I sat there getting drunker and drunker and more in love and more in love." Sometimes the two words are so good you do not need repeat them for the joke to obtain. One night Don's wife, Marion, reported, not without a tinge of worry, that the neighbor's dog had nipped their child. Don said, "Does she warrant it's not *rabid?*" "Warrant" and "rabid" had not been heard in a while; their archaic novelty was funny and gently suggested we not worry overmuch in our modern bourgeois fatted travail. "Does it have rabies?" would not have managed this humoring balm. Another time Marion reported that a strange young man had come to the door, vaguely menacing somehow. "Did he have a linoleum knife in his pocket?" Don said, nearly laughing himself.

"Rotten manuscript" also contains his careful self-deprecation. The repetition surprises twice: we do not anticipate a prudent teacher calling a student's manuscript rotten, and we certainly do not anticipate Don Barthelme's calling his own manuscript rotten. He was always prudent to not promote himself in just this way. If he praised himself, he detracted, and the praise was seen to have been but a set-up: One night he said, "I am going to read a story called 'Overnight to Many Distant Cities,' a lovely title I took from the side of a postal truck." This capacity, this tendency toward what he called "common decency," lifted him from the mortal street where he was a pioneer writer— arguably, I think, one who began with "bad Hemingway" (cf. *Paris Review* interview) and refracted that through Kafka and Beckett and Perlman and Thurber and changed the aesthetic of short fiction in America for the second half of the twentieth century in equal measure to the way Hemingway changed it in the first, and Twain before that—well, from this high mortal street to, in my eyes at least, a kind of high mortal deity. Don was God at the University of Houston, loved by some of us and not by others, like all gods, and if he was not always godly he was always goodly to us. He was a biggie and he was goodly. He was a strange New York biggie who was, even more strangely, from here, and he was back with some benevolent plan. It had a powerful effect. We were lowly sun-addled Aztecs to his Quetzalcoatl, and it felt like we'd been waiting for him a long time without knowing it.

In my own case we entered into a special affair when I discovered by accident that if you demanded good fathering of him, he who spent a third of his time writing about bad fathering, a phrase he considered redundant, he would oblige you. The day we met him, he came up on Glenn Blake and me to shake hands and trapped us in tiny school desks we couldn't get out of quickly. We struggled to get up and stand as boys with proper manners would—here came Andy Warhol, in an urban-cowboy suit, on a slight vodka tilt, bearing down on us, and we'd better stand up. He saw us trying to be good boys. (He did not see that we were caught so flat-footed because our previous teacher here would not have deigned shake hands with us.) Within a few weeks I was saying to him in a manuscript conference, "Don't you *ever* withhold a comment from me. I am not here to be coddled. I came here to meet women. And I am not going to write a thesis. If I have to do this I am going to write *a book*." "By all means," Don Barthelme said, chuckling, closing the manuscript, both of us chuckling. A boy demanding more rigor, not less, of a father! A man who theretofore felt all fathering tantamount to botching and bullying! We gave it a try. I say this now because I did not say any of it at the funeral. I avoid funerals and weddings.

On a night when he had asked if the neighbor's dog was warranted to be not rabid, or if the boy at the door carried a knife, Don Barthelme handed me a story in manuscript and said, "Here. My latest." He was showing me how it actually worked, or *that* it actually worked. When we saw one of his stories in the *New Yorker* we thought it had sprung full-blown from on high. I was to see that it started on unspoiled paper, and you spoiled the paper by typing very neatly with good margins and no mess and sent it to Roger Angel and *then* it looked the way it looked in the *New Yorker*. The paper was spoiled on that typewriter over there by the door where the boy with the linoleum knife and the boy who had disappointed us by not having a linoleum knife so we had to supply him one had tried to gain entry. There were watermarks from the stem of a glass on the wood by the typewriter.

MIKE SPRY

ON PADGETT POWELL

Padgett Powell may be surprised to learn that I would call him a mentor. I was never a student at his highly respected creative writing program at the University of Florida. In fact, we've only been in the same city three times in the years we've known each other, and for no longer than two weeks at a time. And for the first six days he knew me, he thought my surname was Spray, made no apologies for having that information incorrect, and made no attempt to rectify it once informed of the error. He still occasionally calls me Spray, but now I take it as a sign of friendship and respect, which it most certainly, knowing Powell, is not.

The mentor/mentee relationship is a precarious one in the world of writing, because more often than not the parties are writers, fighting for the same piece of a very small publishing pie. I've been very fortunate in my short time in the industry to work with writers who have been very good to me. For the most part, the advice I've gotten has been more than helpful. In the early days of what I will humbly refer to as a career, though my parents may disagree, I took the advice of more experienced writers as law. As I got older, I took that advice as suggestions meant to help form my own decisions. The problem, especially in Canada, where the writing community is tiny, is that unfortunately some people are only out for themselves, so their advice can be malicious self-serving vitriol dressed up as counsel.

And perhaps that's why I do list Powell as my mentor. Because he and I don't play in the same sandbox. We aren't part of the same community, so there's a distance in our relationship that is of great benefit to me. I doubt it is of much benefit to him. Powell is one of the most interesting and dynamic American writers of his generation. And he has no tolerance for bullshit, which I put high on my list of qualities I look for in people. We met in Saint Petersburg, Russia, in 2006 at a summer writing program. He dug into our work quickly, and honestly. There was no placating. No niceties or pandering for the sake of tenure review or good student evaluations. He was keenly interested in taking what we had written and making it as good as it could possibly be but more importantly making us better as writers. In six three-hour classes over twelve days.

The sage wisdom and learned advice I received in that workshop I keep in mind every time I write. Partly because of the genius of the advice and partly because of the manner in which Powell delivers it, with his southern drawl, dry wit, and straight face that gives nothing away. Among the many quotable moments in that class that I still reference as often as I possibly can are:

- On my inability to write believable dialogue: "Master Spray, you write excellent dialogue, sir. You just don't allow anyone else to talk."
- On my sense of humor: "Watch your Coy Quotient. It's creeping up there."
- On a student's writing that I thought bordered on parody: "You see what you've done here? Master Spray believes it to be parody, but you haven't given him permission to laugh."
- On my arriving late to one of the sessions: "Someone needs to help this man. He quite obviously has problems."
- On a student's writing that was obviously autobiography, a no-no in Powell's class: "This could have been called 'My Name is (Student's Name) and This Once Happened to Me.'"
- On writing from experience: "If it happened to you, don't write it. It'll never be as interesting to the reader as it is to you."
- On Donald Barthelme's thoughts on the purpose of humor in fiction: "Break their hearts."

It's within Powell's anecdotes about Barthelme that his understanding for the mentor/mentee relationship is found, and their relationship is part of the reason that Powell is so good to those that he has worked with. His affection for Barthelme is both endearing and evidence of his respect for the benefit of mentors in the writing world. Barthelme was Powell's mentor, and Padgett has passed his wisdom down the line to the next generation of American writers. One day, if it hasn't happened already, essays, theses, tomes will be written on this writers' tree.

My favorite Powell stories are private. They exist in our correspondence, and I must say that his emails are evidence of his genius as a writer. In fact, his emails are better than everything I've ever written. Sometimes, when I'm stricken by writer's block or writer's laziness, I go back through our exchanges and I am quickly entertained and inspired. My favorite story I can share is from August of 2006. Padgett and another writer, whose name escapes me but who very much resembled Mark Hamill pre-motorcycle accident, came to visit me in Montreal. I took them on a tour of the city, up the mountain, down the mountain, The Main, Schwartz's. Powell was Powell, filling moments of silence in conversation with questions about my life and Montreal. "Where do you buy knives here?" "You tried this Viagra shit? She'll like it." "Where do your blacks come from?" Powell being Powell.

I lent the two writers my apartment for their stay, and Powell my laptop (his had been stolen a few days earlier in New York), and I crashed at a friend's. When I returned the next morning, I found that Powell had surfed some very strange websites, written an op-ed piece for the *New York Times,* and completely rearranged my home. Tables and chairs had been moved, couches resituated, paintings rehung, rugs thrown out. "Mr. Spry," he said, noticing my stunned surprise, "you were missing a cockpit. A man's gotta have a cockpit. The laptop is over here on the table, no longer attached to the Internet. It'll improve your writing tenfold. I was going to throw out your printer, and I would have been doing you a favor. I fenged your place." And he was right. With the apartment in that configuration I went through one of the most prolific writing periods of my life, finishing my first book and a good chunk of what would be my second. I had only been missing a cockpit. Who knew? Well, Powell, of course.

After that visit I briefly considered applying to Florida for my master's degree to work with Powell. But I stayed in Montreal and did my MA at Concordia because I was in love with a girl. That turned out to be a poor decision on both counts. The next time I saw Powell, in the summer of 2010, he asked about the girl, whom he had met on his previous visit and had taken quite a liking to. When I told him she was long since gone, he noted: "Ya, she was already gone then. I could see it in her eyes."

"Thanks for telling me," I joked.

"You would never have seen it."

About once a year, Powell and I have an email exchange that lasts for a few weeks. Inevitably it's a highlight of my year. One of the difficulties I've found in writing, or more specifically the writing community, is trust. Other than Powell, there are only a handful of writer friends whom I trust implicitly. Having that in Padgett, and for him to have been so kind with his time and advice, has made me a better writer. And no matter where I've lived, I'm sure to feng my place properly, sure to ensure that I have myself a good cockpit.

make up some good shit

Directive issued by Padgett Powell on the manuscript of Kevin Moffett

SAM LIPSYTE

ON GORDON LISH

Gordon Lish taught me to write. The class I took met every Wednesday night in the apartment of a gracious and talented woman named Eleanor. We began at six in the evening and ran well after midnight. Gordon Lish taught me to write and how to sit still and pay attention. This is mostly what writing is about. Maybe you don't have to sit. You could stand, or walk. But you have to pay attention. You can always tell by the first page whether a writer has paid attention, has listened to what he or she has said. It's shocking how many people don't listen to what they say. Maybe that's why other people sometimes shout, "Are you listening to what you are saying?"

Gordon's method of instruction was a mixture of demonstration and critique. He would speak for a long while, for four or five or six hours, in grammatically complex and perfect sentences, weaving the elements of his lecture—a certain philosophical tract, the condition of his shoelaces, a terrible misunderstanding with a stranger, a childhood memory possibly misremembered—into some playful and profound totality. These improvisations contained the lesson and were the lesson. They were also some of the grandest examples of art I've witnessed.

Toward the end of the evening, Gordon would invite you to read some of your sentences. He had the best ear and the best heart, and he was always honest. Honesty can resemble cruelty, but you can always tell the difference. You can always feel the difference. Or I could. Some people got to read for a long time but he usually stopped me in the middle of the first sentence and said something like "Bullshit!" And he would be right. Because in those days I still thought there was an easy way to make writing easier. But it turns out that all the ways to make writing easier are very hard.

Some of the people who were lucky enough to be edited by or taught by Lish wrote some of the best fiction of our time. Who are these people? The list is out there. You can look it up. I looked it up. That's why I sought him out. Gordon taught me countless things about writing and about being an artist. I won't tell you what they are because he still teaches. You can still seek him out. Okay, I'll tell you one thing he said. Though it could be two things—I'm not certain. Gordon said, "There is no getting to the good part." Then he said, "It all has to be the good part."

NOY HOLLAND

ON GORDON LISH

first knew about Gordon Lish from an article Amy Hempel wrote for *Vanity Fair,* I think, a piece called "Captain Fiction." I was fresh out of college and working an entry-level job at *Esquire,* busing tables downtown at night. I had written a story or two, didn't know much but knew enough to feel invited by the lavish, heated, exalted way Gordon spoke about fiction—really about being alive. I went straightaway to Columbia and stood in the receiving line, dumbly unsure of myself, waiting my turn for the interview.

I don't know if Gordon was wearing his jumpsuit back then, with the tail of his belt hanging loose, and brogans, and his many-feathered hat—I think this rig came later. Mark Richard came later, who sat on the heating vent, and Diane Williams, and Will Eno—years later. This gets to be a long time and a lot of people ago—late eighties, early nineties—Sam Michel, Dawn Raffel, Michael Kimball, Yannick Murphy; Amy Hempel, Jason Schwartz, Lily Tuck, Ann Pyne; Ben Marcus and Peter Christopher and Victoria Redel and Richard Blanchard—to say nothing of so many others, stellar at the time, who turned to photography, welding, I don't know, wrote for a time and quit.

For me, Gordon and my first idea of myself as a writer began at Columbia, amid student protests against investments in South Africa—shouting outside the window, leaves coming down, a hallway bright as a hospital. When I got to the head of the receiving line, Gordon asked me one question: "Why are you here?"

It was "just awful—dreadful," the story I'd sent him. There wasn't a sentence in it he could stand to read but one. (He read the sentence aloud. I've forgotten it, a shame: I owe that sentence my seat at the table.)

I come from a quiet family. I'd been to a college where teachers wore tweed. Called young women *Miss*. Spoke softly. But very soon here was Gordon with the dial turned up, talking nooky and Bloom, the nuthouse, Artaud, the implicative load, the hours he could go without pissing. He was irreverent, even lewd. He spoke admiringly of Paglia (who had shredded his book and sent it back to him—"for use in the men's room") and told biting, hilarious, Schmolovitz jokes.

"Why are you here?" The question persisted. To what end, what effect, what possibility?

At Columbia I began the first fiction I would publish, a story called "Absolution." When I finished the story, Gordon wrote to my mother—she was in Tuscaloosa, dying—an extravagant letter of extravagant claims, and he encouraged her to help me. (She always wanted to and did.) My life was taking opposing turns—heady, painful, a bewildering loss I had begun to believe I could make something beautiful from. With sufficient desire. Desire is everything—this was at the heart of Gordon's teaching.

Gordon didn't last at Columbia. Before long he was conducting private classes in New York City apartments. We sat on the floor at Christine Schutt's place—six hours, nine—late into the night, the traffic thinning. And a kid—Will Schutt, lovely poet—cracked the door, an eye in the dark, giddy, and looking on.

Fidgeting, pissing, food, thirst—we were briefly beyond all of it—any daily numbing concern—jobs to go to, rent to pay. I know how this sounds. The feeling wasn't so for everyone, but I wasn't alone in feeling it, and for me it was absolute. The class was church. An intoxicating faith. A drug to last the week until we could get ourselves up from the Village or across the country or over the river to sit back down. People came at great cost repeatedly and some—reading aloud, he always had us read aloud—some never made it past the first sentence. He'd say, "What have you got, Kimball? Let's hear it. Come on, Raffel. Let's see if you can beat Richard. The scourge of Richard."

"You lost it," Gordon would say. Or "You had it but you got tired. Don't get tired. Exhaust the object. Why are you here? What is wrong with you?"

These were not rhetorical questions. There was no discussion. There was reading and listening to others read and listening to Gordon speak. Perform. His teaching was a demonstration of what he wanted us to practice—shapely, obsessive, unafraid; a lot like juggling fire. I watched in awe, thinking, How in the world can he bring this around—bring this thing back to that other, when each is so distant and different?

Gordon seemed often in peril of losing his way. He improvised, invented. He vivified the plain and the daily. Talked shit, told jokes, made use of it, of everything, the snippet overheard. He repeated sentences, phrases we had written—"things best left kept secret"; "my brother and my's room"; "I saw a man hook a walking stick around a woman's neck once"—and followed with his wild praise.

We were writing into history. We were the gods of the page.

There was no "outside," no public: the comparison was each to each. It wasn't school. It was your life, and you stood on a precipice and you had to commit or fail. Fail better.

Gordon was preacher, father, guide. Rogue. Raunchy, divine. We wrote to have something to hold against death—a rebuke. To beat death. What an achy, invincible feeling I could have, sitting cross-legged on that floor. What panic at the years passing.

I met Sam Michel in that class and we married, and we've been married for twenty years. Sam and I see Gordon some, and we talk on the phone, and once, in New York, when our boy was still small, we went to a playground together, uptown, Central Park. Cracked jokes, pushed our boy on the swings, forgot the time, talking. Dusk came and we turned to go home but by then we couldn't: we'd been locked in. It was a tall spiked iron fence—no way we were getting over it. We whistled and yelled and waved our arms and, as we did, a fat raccoon sorted quietly through food in the trash. At last help came, surly, scolding. But you can't scold Gordon Lish.

I never saw him soften. I never saw the man shrink from saying plainly what was painful to hear. People hated him for this and still do. Well, let them. For my part, I will go to my grave saying thank you thank you thank you. For belief in what is possible, thank you. Stamina. Nerve. Not publication, not popularity in the moment, but something that has a chance to endure. Gordon's teaching continues to make it, for me, easier to bear—even to hunger for—the isolation, the rebuke, the feeling of needing to stumble through my own peculiar darkness.

The sentence the sentence the sentence. Accretion. Torque. Swerve. Implicative load. Loosening of associations. You want your sentence "to lean and hearken to" the sentences which precede it. Music, you want. The gaze. You want, when you finish reading, not applause but a stunned regard. The spell cast and lasting. Some kindred soul whispering *more*.

CHRISTINE SCHUTT

ON ELIZABETH HARDWICK

Before I met Elizabeth Hardwick, I had imagined the woman who described Virginia Woolf's fiction as "all chorus and no plot" as mannish, shapeless, Gertrude Stein–like, dressed in black and unadorned; instead, she looked like a pert sidekick actress from the forties: mobile face, red mouth, hair middle-parted in a ruffled curl, amusingly approachable, really, but I lacked courage. "Miss Hardwick?" I asked—hardly bold. Just to cross the street from Columbia to Barnard had unsettled me, but she said yes to my request to join her writing seminar, and once at the table, I felt more at ease, especially when it turned out we were the only two in the room to have read and been impressed by Renata Adler's and Harold Brodkey's recent fiction in the *New Yorker.* Our shared enthusiasms for other writers—Nadine Gordimer among them—boded well, and after our first creative assignment to write about ourselves by way of introduction, I was the obvious star and emboldened by her favor. What did it matter if my Robbe-Grillet imitation ultimately failed? All the other work I turned in she liked, liked a lot. And in her office at the end of the term, she said, "If you should . . . ," and here memory fails me mightily because I'm not exactly sure what she said except to describe what followed as supportive mumbling. I want to plug in "need anything" when it couldn't have been those words. Would Elizabeth Hardwick really ever say, "If you should need anything"? But that was how I left her, feeling fully funded. A year later, I sent her my first novel, asking if she thought it was finished. Hardwick responded quickly, inviting me to talk about the manuscript at her apartment on

West Sixty-Seventh Street, the same apartment she had once shared with Robert Lowell.

Not for the first time, I thought my life was about to begin.

Why is it then I remember only what I was wearing and the sofa we sat on? The floor-to-ceiling bookshelves, book ladder, reading lamps, long table, Persian rug—I know the interior from photographs of Hardwick at home. I didn't notice them then. I saw only Hardwick's serious and curious expression as she looked at me. We sat close on the sofa and she asked, "Do you love your husband?" Was the husband in my novel so transparently my own and was he unloved? Did I love my husband? I did not answer convincingly.

At some point in our meeting, she said, "It takes character to be a writer." The word *character* stunned me: I had never heard it before.

And as to my first book? "Ah, well," she said, "we all have a first novel in the drawer."

Hardwick told me there might be a job at the *New York Review of Books* if I was interested, but I left her thinking I should have a baby. Nevertheless, I met Roger Strauss about the vague job, and the word *flailing* comes to mind when I recall how I paraded so-so skills and talked about my fiction. End of summer, late seventies, high stink on Union Square, I stood for a time looking up at the offices of Farrar, Straus, and Giroux, sorry again not to have noticed more and thinking I should have a baby. I did. I had two.

Some fifteen years later, I sent Elizabeth Hardwick my first book, a collection of stories, *Nightwork,* in hopes she might consider writing advance praise. She called a few days later to say she could not—and not because the writing wasn't good. The writing was very, very good, but my subjects: "What you do to children," she said. "What is your story anyway, Christine?" I laughed a little by way of answer.

But how did our conversation end?

"The writing is very good."

"I'm sorry you can't say as much."

I said good-bye and thank you and hung up unharmed. In the years between, I had read and written and stored away such things as would sustain me as a writer: mentors often turn away from the apprentice's realized work. Think of Emerson's cool response to Thoreau's voice once he had found it and Moore's criticism of Bishop when the poet began to sound like herself. Now I had found my voice and my subjects and although my mentor could acknowledge the gravity and grace of the prose, she could not—would not—endorse my subjects.

June 5, 1978

Dear Christine: I like your story very much. All of your family
stories have seemed excellent to me-- very convincing, interesting.
Perhaps the writing of the last few sentences could be a little
stronger. Just the very, very end. I think it might end on
a sentence that starts with "he" rather than a reference back
to yourself. Or perhaps end on a rhetorical question-- how can one
honor such modesty?-- or something like that. Just a few words to
make more of an impact at the end, a verbal winding up I mean.
I am very happy about your baby boy, Nicolas, with an "h" I see,
as I look back at your letter. Your life will never be the same--
an old saying, and very true. You didn't say how you were going
to manage the teaching and the baby-- very difficult, especially
since children up to the age of 6 or 7 are always sick with something
or other that terrifies you. But I assume you have a good plan. It
is important to work and I imagine that you must like everyone else
for the money. Writing will be hard for a few years, but it will
come back and continue . I wish you luck along with the great
pleasure of the child. I must say I still love Harriet more than
anything in the world-- and what is so extraordinary, love her more
than myself. That I suppose is the real experience hidden in
all this.

   Have a good summer. I am always here to help you in any way I
can and so don/t be shy about calling or writing.

                                        Affectionately,

                                        Elizabeth H,

My own memory sours things. What I have is a letter from Elizabeth, written a year after I showed her the
novel that belonged in a drawer, and it is as generous a letter as it can be, starting, "I like your story very
much [I'd sent her a new story]. All of your family stories have seemed excellent to me—very convincing,
interesting." She ends the letter, "Have a good summer. I am always here to help you in any way I can and so
don't be shy about calling or writing. Affectionately, . . ."

Such things happen, I thought, and was sorry and not a little sad, but also happy to feel dispassionately undaunted. It takes character finally to withstand the knockabout, shaming pursuit of writing literary fiction, and I had character—enough to answer elliptically, to say to Elizabeth Hardwick, "My story . . . ," and laugh. Pleased to have said just that, pleased not to have bumbled through an answer to whatever was my story but to have gone on writing stories as every writer must, alone.

This is splendid. I particularly like
the pace and tone of it, the way you
have the style in your own control.
Of course in a sort of "survey" like this
a dozen things couldbe substituted for
the ones you have chosen. But I like
all of your choices, except perhaps for
a slight reserve about death. Very good
indeed.

*that was written without
J. 3. Perhaps it is too much
to take her all the way
into the marriage. the banker
bothers me - he seems unreal.
the last line is good.*

Typed and handwritten comments from Elizabeth Hardwick to Christine Schutt on fiction written for her class

TOUGH LOVE

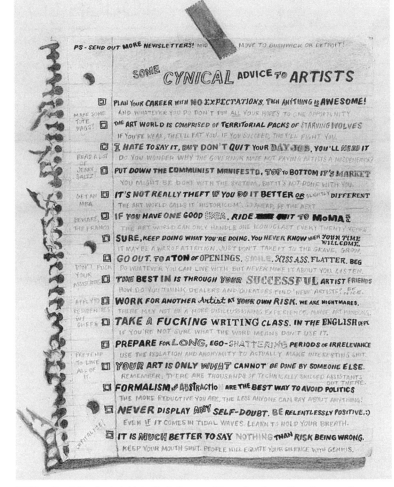

William Powhida, *Cynical Advice for Artists,* graphite, colored pencil, and watercolor on paper, 2012. Reprinted courtesy of the artist.

DEB OLIN UNFERTH

ON JOHN PROBES

My early mentors were hardly mentors, more like alcoholics—their fallen conditions somehow signaling to me deep insight, evidence, no doubt, of my own fallen condition—but I loved them. My favorite was John Probes, a photographer on extended hiatus.

Probes's advice tended to be cryptic. "The problem with drawing a line in the sand is that it's sand," he'd say. It does make sense: obviously a line in the sand can be rubbed out with a shoe or covered over in a wind. If you want it to stay, you have to be prepared to draw that line again and again. You may spend your life at it.

Other guidance was less clear. "Never do anything on Tuesdays" was one he repeated for years. He said it with fervor and a stern severity. If I tried to get him to meet me out on a Tuesday, he would not. I never understood what he meant but I also felt committed to the meaning not mattering, or mattering in an unorthodox manner. Maybe the form, not the content, was the point: sometimes one must have the courage and audacity to say the word "never" at the beginning of an imperative sentence. Or maybe it was a lesson about randomness? The randomness of rules? Or about the tremor of "never," a word to pair only with absurdities?

I do think he did mean something by the content, too. I think he meant I should never do anything on Tuesdays, but I never knew why not. What's wrong with Tuesday? That gap—his not being able to explain it and my not being able to figure it out—the universality of that gap, was part of the lesson.

One night (at my request) he and I spent several hours compiling a list of rules to live by. I wrote the rules down, but then I lost them and couldn't remember them. Losing those rules has been one of the great tragedies of my life. In my most unhappy, miserable moments, I think, If only I could remember the rules.

All I have of them is a postcard he sent me some days after we made the list: "All but the first three rules may potentially be redundant; possibly confusing."

But what were the first three?

Once (and I think it happened only once) he got angry and wrote me a letter saying he didn't want to mentor me anymore (though he didn't use that word): "Though I sincerely regret it, and it does upset me deeply, I do not feel it is necessary for my participation in your aspirations."

I don't recall why he was angry, but it must have had to do with his drunkenness and my not understanding it, or my not understanding what dark places a true deep-level drunk will go and must be allowed to go. (I never understood. The last time I saw him, ten days before his death, he told me he thought he was dying. "Let's just get out of here," he said. "Put a sign on the door that says, 'Gone dancing.' I mean, who'd really miss us?" and I'd been annoyed and didn't understand.)

At the bottom of the angry letter, Probes added, after the signature, so that it looks almost like an afterthought: "Anything you need from me you've got. The End." So it seems his anger lasted only as long as it took for him to get to the bottom of the page.

When he died (found by a neighbor after six days, his body soaked into his bed and ripped off the mattress by paramedics), I felt the deepest, most prolonged despair I'd ever experienced. I went to his apartment and sifted through his belongings like wading through murky water and turning up muddy stones. The darkroom chemicals, the rotted food, the empty vodka bottles, the old photography books. I was looking for more hints, more words, any piece of Probesian wisdom—I needed it. (Still do, badly.) I took home his kitchen table.

This was 1999, spring. He missed the millennium by months. He would have loved it. The nothingness of it, the banality of one day passing into another, a thousand years done. He would have made something of it and then I would have laughed and been confused. I would have thought about what he'd said, always.

I've carried that kitchen table up innumerable flights of stairs, back and forth across the country, I pulled it out of a dumpster when some movers mistook it for garbage. I've used it as my writing table all these years.

The kitchen table that Deb Olin Unferth took home from John Probes's apartment after his death and has used as her writing table ever since

ERICA DAWSON

ON MARY JO SALTER

In the summer of 2013, Mary Jo Salter, a friend of hers, and I were having dinner at an Italian place in Saint Pete: drinking bottles of malbec; me complaining about how people never tell grad students, who hope to be professors, about the daily administrivia; her telling me about teaching at Hopkins, my alma mater.

Poetry stuff. Professional stuff.

Then, when her friend got up to use the bathroom, she looked me in the face and asked, "How are you doing?" with such emphasis on the "doing" that I felt as if everything I'd been talking about was just inertia. So I told her how I was for real, what I obsessed about when I couldn't sleep. She caught a glimpse of her friend returning to the table. She looked back at me and held the stare for a split second too long—the same emphasis as on the "doing." She didn't say anything else.

About a year earlier, at a different table, this one at the Sewanee Writers' Conference, Mary Jo, who was on faculty, sat with me in the staff-only kitchen of the French House—the spot where those late-night conference moments happen. Earlier that morning I had concluded my part of a staff reading with "Ideation X," a relatively new poem about the summer before at Sewanee, when I was in the middle of what had turned out to be a breakdown. There, in the kitchen, Mary Jo let me finish whatever inconsequential nonsense I was saying. Then she asked about the poem and I said, "I'm much better now," and she gave me an expression that let me know I didn't have to be better.

Years before that, in 2006, I was sitting in my Cincinnati apartment, eating Special K, and the phone rang. It was Mary Jo Salter. (Back in the day I called her by her full name, with that awestruck formality reserved for people you admire.) She told me she'd picked my manuscript as the winner of Anthony Hecht Poetry Prize. I couldn't speak. She asked, "Erica?"

In the seven years between that phone call and the second bottle of malbec in Saint Pete, I started calling her Mary Jo and thinking of her as my fairy godmother and, eventually, my poetry big sister. We'd both grown up in Maryland. She was the professor I wanted to be. We could geek out over a headless foot.

What I love most about Mary Jo is how there's no bullshit. When I first saw what she'd written for the foreword of my manuscript-turned-book, I was thrilled that she was so direct: none of that lofty theorizing, none of that "look how smart I am while thinking about this book" nonsense. I was all about what she was saying when I read, "For all her straight talk, her sensuality is also tinged with wit—most amusingly in this parenthesis '(conquered, I came).'" Mary Jo was referring to a line from "White Dwarf," a self-portrait in which I describe myself as a sexpot wearing fishnets. I was less happy about the sentence that followed—"She likes sex"—because I knew my dad and brother were going to have enough trouble with the poems themselves. I asked if she'd mind if we cut the "she likes sex" part.

We did and I wish we hadn't. Mary Jo understood the book, the speakers of the poems, me, and all the connections in between. She was being forthright about my being forthright on the page. At that point in my life, I pretty much kept the candor to the poems. I didn't let it out of my mouth. Now I like it when, with a simple question or a look that's all sincerity, she calls me out on keeping my mouth shut, or talking too much about nonsense. If I got to see her more often than the occasional summer, I know she'd keep me in check all the time.

The other day I was reading Dickinson, one of Mary Jo's favorites. I came across "The Gentian weaves her fringes," and the line, "Summer—Sister—Seraph!" I'm going to make that the subject line next time I email Mary Jo. When she writes back, she won't address it, but she'll sign the note "MJ." I don't know if I'll ever be able to call her that.

NICK FLYNN
ON PHILIP LEVINE

I think about Phil Levine nearly every day, whenever I sit down to write. He said something to me once—I assume he wouldn't remember, and if he did he wouldn't know the long-lasting effects his words had on me—but these few words set me—my life, my writing—off in another direction from the one I was headed. I'd handed in a poem for our one workshop together at New York University—I don't recall which poem, or if it ever even became a poem— and after he read it he turned to me and said, "You have more light inside you than this."

By the time I made it to NYU, I'd been out of school for a long time (ten years or so), working at various jobs ("lousy jobs," as Levine would say about his own jobs in his twenties, though I suspect neither of us found them completely, or merely, lousy). I'd been an electrician, an okay carpenter, a ship's captain (with a bona-fide marine merchant's license), a caseworker with homeless adults. I liked the jobs, and if I didn't I made it clear and was fired— every restaurant I ever worked in fired me. My mother had worked in restaurants my entire life, after working at her truly lousy bank job all day. She worked nights at bars or restaurants for the tips, and we lived off her tips—she drilled it into my brother and me that if we didn't have enough to tip well, we didn't have enough to go out (which meant I almost never went out, except to bars, until I was thirty). During my ill-fated attempts at restaurant work, if a customer was surly or rude to me, I'd go into a silent rage, or if they tipped poorly I'd chase them into the parking lot and throw the money at them—clearly sublimated and misdirected defenses of my mother and what she must have endured.

That I can write about this now is thanks to Phil Levine—his poems gave all of us permission to write about the actual, day-in-day-out circumstances of our lives. That I can actually look someone in the eye and call myself a poet is thanks to Phil Levine. He made what seemed an unlikely path seem noble. His definition of a poet, I once heard him say (on the radio? in an essay? from a stage? to my face?), was someone who can look you in the eye—I took this to mean something about integrity, something about doing the best you could do. It was not simply a calling, which might suggest a lack of agency—it was something you had to become, to rise to, to embody. It would require everything. He once said (in an interview? in our workshop?) that being a poet is the one job in the world where you wake up every morning and nothing you know will help you to approach the task at hand, which is to write a poem—if you had remained an electrician, you would know how to get the lights to come on. But you are now a poet, and each day you must invent the world. Not the world, but your place in it. In this Levine is similar to another poet whom I also think about nearly every day, each time I find myself in another poem. Stanley Kunitz said that if you read a poem you like, you must become the person who can write that poem. It is a life's work. How one lives one's life is important. These are things Phil Levine has said to me, over the years, or that he has written in essays, or that I culled out of his poems. It all blurs together now.

In 1992, twenty years ago now, I met Phil Levine in that workshop. It was my second year at NYU. When I first got there I was hungry to sit around a table and listen to real poets talk about poems. I saw it as another apprenticeship, not much different from the one I'd gone through to become an electrician. I was writing like a fiend, in a glorious fever—grateful that I'd escaped the burning house of my twenties (or so I believed). I'd already studied with great poets at NYU (Olds, Kinnell, Matthews), but I knew Levine was coming, and he was the reason I was there, though I didn't know it at that point, not fully. You see, I was, and likely still am, a blunt tool, a dull instrument. I need poems drilled into me, I needed to be strapped to a chair. At NYU Sharon had welcomed me into the community of poets and instilled the sense of poetry as a gift. (I believe she even quoted Lewis Hyde's The Gift.) Galway recited Yeats, we'd all go on retreats, the entire class, into the woods, to write. At NYU I got to study with Ginsberg, who cried when he talked about Kerouac, and who hit on me—he hit on everyone (male). But my last semester Levine was coming, we all knew he was coming (like Grendel), and we knew he would kick some ass. Levine made me want to show up each week and make him pay attention, if only because he didn't let a lazy word or phrase slip past. Anything that was false, or untransformed, or tired, he simply skipped over—he wouldn't waste his, or anyone else's, time. He was exactly what I needed.

I already knew him from his poems, everyone did. *What Work Is* had just come out. (I think of it as his *Some Girls*—a masterpiece coming years after his early fury, especially *They Feed They Lion*.) His poems did what I hoped mine would one day do, not only in their seeming effortlessness, but in the their unlikely vistas, opening. At some point I read his essay on Berryman. I identified with him sneaking into Berryman's Iowa workshop, unregistered, with his pride at getting over. I identified with his hunger to learn, after those years of lousy jobs. I identified with the fact that he stuck it out. He found a poet who was his (Keats), just as Kinnell had Yeats, and Olds had Lucille Clifton, and Ginsberg had Blake, and Kunitz had Celan. One line from his Berryman essay stayed with me (this is from memory)—"A poet doesn't play fast and loose with the facts of this world." Levine attributes this to Berryman, but what could it mean? Berryman, after all, had poems with talking sheep in them ("I hope the barker comes").

I cannot claim Phil Levine as my teacher alone—he belongs to many, most notably, and poignantly, Larry Levis, who would die young a few years after I met Phil. Levine's love of Levis was manifest, and generous, and profound. His reputation as a hard-ass followed him, and was deserved, yet it made his generosity that much more genuine. In workshop, I happened to find myself on his good side, or at least that's how I remember it. If he humiliated me, or my poems, I don't remember. He was committed to the poem, we were being offered the chance to be part of a long tradition, stretching back centuries, we were being invited to gaze into that river with him, to be a part of it.

I was writing poems then that were dark, brooding, gloomy. (Some might say I still am.) Levine turned to me one day, during our weekly workshop, and said that he didn't believe the poem I'd handed in. "You've got more light in you than this," he told me, looking me straight in the eye. His words pierced me—it was as if someone had really seen me, had acknowledged who I was, had pulled aside my mask of gloom. He did not use the word *luminous*—this is not a word I would associate with Levine—it's not demotic enough, not of this earth. I knew I had light inside me, and that somehow I would have to find a way to let some of it into my poems. It would take me years, but Phil's voice stayed with me, his faith that there was more than darkness inside me, inside any of us. He had seen it (at least he said he did), years before I could.

A poet's job is not to play fast and loose with the facts of this world. What this would come to mean to me is that there is a world, one that demands—requires, rewards—our attention to it, the kind of attention Simone Weil describes as a type of prayer. The world is made up of hidden patterns, as-yet discovered physical properties, and it is our job to both honor these patterns and to invent new ones. To imagine. Berryman's sheep say what sheep would say, as far as we can imagine, if we are able to listen . . .

ROY KESEY

ON ROBERT DAY

In high school I had three excellent English teachers—more than my quota, surely—and in my early college years I had three more. These were my mentors for reading fiction and for thinking about it out loud. Later there were a few creative writing professors who gave me good notes. One of them, the poet Robert Day, was my advisor for the portfolio I put together to fulfill the thesis requirement for my BA at Washington College twenty-something years ago. We didn't meet in person all that often, but I remember our first conversation well.

> *Robert Day:* [Flips quickly through the first thirty or forty poems in the folder.]
>
> *Me:* [Clears throat.]
>
> *Robert Day:* [Stops flipping. Reads silently through the poem he's stopped at.]
>
> *Me:* [Straightens in chair. The poem he's reading is one that I wrote a year ago while studying philosophy at Oxford, and I'm particularly proud of it.]
>
> *Robert Day:* So.
>
> *Me:* Yes?
>
> *Robert Day:* If I'm not mistaken, what we've got here is your classic beaver shot.
>
> *Me:* Um.

Robert Day: Right?

Me: Well. It's, um. It's a lyric poem? With a—

Robert Day: Okay, lyric, right. Classic metaphorical beaver shot.

Me: I guess I'd characterize it more as—

Robert Day: You write a lot of these, don't you?

Me: Beaver shots?

Robert Day: Lyric poems.

Me: Yes.

Robert Day: You know what you maybe ought to do? Write some narrative poems instead. Just for the hell of it, you know. Just to see how it goes.

That right there is some kick-ass mentoring, folks. It only took me another few years to move from narrative poems on to narrative prose, where I've mostly hung out ever since. Hats off to you, Robert Day. I owe you one.

SABINA MURRAY

ON VALERIE MARTIN

SOME GUIDELINES FOR MENTORS

Be Harsh

The first thing Valerie Martin told me was that what I had written was boring. This was in 1985, in response to a one-page assignment in an introductory fiction class at Mount Holyoke College. What the particular charge had been is lost, but I remember that I had chosen to excise all of my alien Australian and gothic Filipino upbringing from the piece; I had crafted a true fiction by creating a fake identity in order to write some false prose. I can't remember what I wrote because it *was* boring, and why clutter my mind with that? I was mildly astonished—embarrassed really—not to have landed my first college fiction writing assignment with a shock-and-awe caliber performance. *That* I recall with stunning clarity. "Boring" was usually not my problem.

Be Open to Changing One's Opinion

I'd had an unconventional upbringing. I spent my childhood in western Australia and relocated to the Philippines when I was twelve. My Manila high school experience, which bordered on the macabre when it wasn't fully entrenched there, was profoundly difficult for the average American girl to relate to. My anecdotes were about the tying of chickens to the trees in the backyard so that they wouldn't be blown away in the typhoon, or about the neighbors sacrificing a cow that I had grown fond of to stave off the mother's cancer, or about boldly knocking on the door of the cute guy across the street (who happened to be Imelda Marcos's nephew) and inviting him to usher at my friend's family concert—a fundraiser to send a miraculous statue on a tour of California. The next piece I wrote for Valerie's class dealt with a manipulative babysitter who convinces her charges, who idolize her, that she has a deformity—a tiny hand that is growing between her breasts. As a sign of friendship, she will let the little girl touch this hand. The story ends with the girl reaching towards the sitter and we know that all she'll find is that people lie and, when bored, they torture the innocent. Valerie found this story rather good.

Hold Protégés to High Standards

I wanted to write an honors thesis for my senior year, which, incidentally, coincided with a semester that Valerie was on sabbatical. "I'll do it," she said, "but you have to write a novel." At the time, I was twenty years old. Had I been older, I would have found this daunting and might have declined, although I didn't decline much in those days. I probably had some delusional response like "No problem." But that is lost in what followed: the wash of writing—sometimes all night before one of our deadlines—and in the final weeks before my thesis was due, the onset of an awe-inspiring case of chickenpox. All the women who hadn't grown up in the United States were coming down with it, and when the English girl in my dorm landed in the infirmary, I knew my days were numbered. A pre-med genius friend from Hampshire College was so impressed by the circumference of one of my lymph nodes that he photographed it and made it the subject of a paper. And my thesis, *Slow Burn*, did get finished, the last pages penciled on a yellow pad as I soaked in a tub full of Aveno.

I did think that getting published was easy in those days—part of the necessary glamour of youth, which helps one get out of bed after the novelty of reaching the drinking age is tapped. And Valerie did make it look easy. She put in me in touch with her agent, said nice things, ushered me through a couple of drafts, and was as pleased as I was to see the book come out.

Stay Interested

I thought my struggles were over. It's understandable. My future was, in its usual way, undecided, and my past offered nothing but childhood, so this first step into publishing felt permanent: I'd made it! But (and I'm sure you see this coming) I was wrong! I not only have the distinction of having sold my first book at twenty but also that of having been washed up at twenty-five. Valerie did not give up on me through these years. We stayed in touch, even though

I'd moved to Texas for grad school and was still living there. A lot of things happened. I got married, had a kid, and, thank God, another book, and some jobs, another kid, and a couple of other books. I might have been catching up with Valerie, who also had a family, but she always stayed a step ahead. I won the Pen/Faulkner, and she won the Orange Prize. I may have had two kids to her one, but she had two grandkids to my . . . dog.

Stay Interesting

And now, and significantly in the present tense, Valerie is still writing some of the most thought-provoking books out there. Of course she does not write for me, but it would be easy to see how I could be so deluded. *The Ghost of the Mary Celeste* is a creepy, gothic book with a wildly inventive structure. *Salvation* examines the life of Saint Francis—who, obviously, is a saint along with being a cipher—and wonders at his experience of life as a man. *Property* has a nasty narrator who gains sympathy as she pursues her tale of victimizer and victim. And all of Valerie's books—such as *Trespass,* in which a main character dies early on, and *The Confessions of Edward Day,* where an unplanned incident alters the characters—derive from a quintessential curiosity about the possibilities of writing. But we don't spend all our time talking about books.

Be a Friend

Although the bookcase of the mind is always present, and we both have a conversation style that approximates taking books off shelves, perusing, commenting, reshelving, and moving on, Valerie has stayed interested and present in my life, and I can say the same about hers. Ultimately, we have reliable respect for each other as practitioners of the form, one that keeps us in a society—like Masons—with its own equivalent of secret handshakes, whispered codes, and odd rituals. Valerie will always be my mentor, even though I am now on my sixth book, because it was she who ushered me into this world of writing, who—with a combination of criticism and kindness—opened the door.

RUI ZINK
ON ALBERTO PIMENTA

I first met Alberto Pimenta (born in Porto in 1937) in about March 1984. I was a young student with a penchant for malice trying to organize a provocative five-day stunt known as Pornex '84 and had boldly approached the formidable poet Melo e Castro at Cais do Sodre station, inviting him to be the keynote speaker. Although no fee could be offered (Portuguese tradition), Melo e Castro accepted but noted: "The one you should talk with is Pimenta." Both of them were legends, pioneers of the experimental poetry movement, outsiders with panache. Pimenta, for those (like me) who knew of him, was not only an incredible and virulent poet but also the man who in 1977, three years after the Carnation Revolution, dared to inhabit a cage in the zoo under a sign reading HOMO SAPIENS. When I called him, I mumbled my rehearsed speech: "Sir, we are students. We want to organize this artistic and intellectual debate on porn, since ours is a thinking university and, although we can't pay a fee, it would be an honor, sir, if you'd be so kind . . ."

He cut me short. He gave me his address and told me to drop by in an hour. I had seen pictures of him, but I didn't know that by then he had completely shaven his head. I shivered when this large, scary, Greek-satyr, smiling man greeted me while opening the door and ushering me in. Yep: Martin Sheen meet Colonel Kurtz. I do love Alberto, but he was never a pretty sight. Once a colleague of mine said, involuntarily quoting Dennis Hopper, "But the voice, ah, the voice! When we listen to the voice we forget everything else!" And she was right. He is—always has been—one of Portugal's most charismatic presences at a reading, a debate, a presentation. A force of nature. Oddly, at age seventy-four, still an outsider. On the other hand, not odd at all. Not at all, Alberto.

He listened to my sales pitch and immediately he was game and, as was his habit, he had a better idea. Then, in the ensuing rehearsal, he had a dozen more better ideas. Working with him could be exhausting. One worked hard on something and, next day, change of plans. Ah, but always a plan, always a plan. Hard work too. Damn.

For nearly twenty years we had weekly lunches, sometimes more than once a week, where we enjoyed a friendship among equals that I also could never stop seeing as my very own private master class. He taught me that in art the only room for chaos is in the reader's mind. That discipline is the keynote to apparent anarchy. That genius requires work. That, while in many ways the opposite of a bureaucrat, the artist shares with that creature the need for deceit: bureaucrats pretend they work a lot, artists pretend it comes easy to them. And both depend on the audience to buy that. Both are, in a way, creatures of darkness, except that artists don't fear ruining their nails as they dig out for light and air.

Partners in crime across the years, as well as in (sigh!) teaching . . . I don't know what else to say about this never-ending friendship. Oh, maybe this story from 1985: Alberto was launching a book at the Lisbon book fair, and he lured me into going around the pavilions asking people to sign a petition to censor his book. In those days I looked like a Boy Scout, and dozens of people signed it, proving that even at a book fair the longing for inquisition is hard to suppress. When I finally arrived at his stand, he was quite upset: "How dare you try to censor my book?" Pre-planned answer: "Sir, I am a righteous Portuguese citizen. I have the right to censor whatever I want." Alberto leaped into a frenzy and we did some wrestling moves, Andre the Giant versus Hulk Hogan, or Godzilla. A few minutes later, after beating me up, he asked: "So, do you still think my book should be censored?" My jaw broken, an eye half out, I nodded: "Yes, I still think that your book should be censored." In a blink he transformed his mood and heartily opened his arms: "Me too!" Then off he went to a osculograph session. [*Author's note:* an osculograph is the same as an autograph, only you do it by putting the instrument's baton to your lips and kissing the signed copy.]

Way to go, Alberto.

ANYA GRONER

ON BETH ANN FENNELLY

In Oxford, Mississippi, what matters is story. Just outside the visitor's center, a statue of William Faulkner sits on a bench, holding a pipe, his bronze body turned toward the empty seat beside him as if listening to an invisible conversant. Brochures encourage tourists to walk a few blocks to Rowan Oak, the columned house where the Nobel prizewinner outlined *A Fable* on his plaster office walls. Other literary sites include the city fire department, just up the boulevard, where the author of *Big Bad Love*, Larry Brown, was stationed until he quit fighting flames to write full time. Down the road at the University of Mississippi, Willie Morris, who wrote *My Dog Skip*, taught fiction. John Grisham audited his class. Later, Barry Hannah moved to town. Then came Tom Franklin, Jack Pendarvis, Chris Offutt, and Richard Ford.

Reciting these names is a kind of conjure work. At bars, aficionados trade stories. When drinking, Faulkner would don a stolen air force uniform and tell friends about aerial stunts he performed during a war he never fought in. Barry Hannah was sitting on a nearby sidewalk eating salad with his hands when a woman approached and asked if she could store her boat in his empty garage. "Not unless we're hitched," he answered, and so they got married. Another time, late to class, Hannah emerged whiskey-wild from the grocery to discover he'd left the top down on his convertible during a rainstorm. He drew his pistol, shot four holes in the car's floor, draining the waters, and drove to class.

When I entered Ole Miss's MFA program in fiction, this legacy of gritty

American letters intimidated more than inspired me. I had no degree in English and was sure my admittance letter had more to do with a bureaucratic mixup than actual skill. To address my fears, I volunteered first for workshop.

"American fiction is over," my professor announced the next week. Inspired by my prose, he lectured on bad writing.

"Is this supposed to be ironic?" he asked me later. "It's not."

While Oxford's male population boasts top-notch writers, the women about town are world-famous beauties. Hair salons, dress boutiques, and shoe depots fill the brick buildings on Oxford's square. Lady shoppers flutter in pink and turquoise and yellow, teetering on heels, no outfit alike.

"Ole Miss has the prettiest women," a fellow MFA bragged to me the very same week I attended my terrible workshop. "They come for their MRS degrees."

I glanced from my beaming classmate to my ripped shorts and paint-splattered sneakers. I was thinking about what he didn't say, that Oxford's literary family tree was filled entirely with men, that for decades this town had failed to nurture women writers. I didn't want to get married. I wanted to write.

During my years at Ole Miss, the fiction faculty consisted only of guys, but the poets included women in their ranks. Not until my third year did I cross genres and take a class with Tom Franklin's wife, Beth Ann Fennelly. By then, I'd gained more confidence in my prose and in myself. Poetry, however, was new territory.

"She's a diva and she's fierce," my friends warned. "She doesn't mince words."

"Good," I said. "I want to be fierce, too." I'd recently witnessed Beth Ann read from her newest book, *Unmentionables*. She wore a green silk dress, which offset her long red hair, and entertained a packed house with taboos—her crushes on shirtless college boys, the sensual surprise of kissing her baby's mouth, cow tipping in Illinois, the danger of the brag. In one poem, words shortened to broken syllables until language dissolved altogether and she started to howl.

Back in my apartment, I read from Beth Ann's first book, *Open House*. In her long poem "From *L'Hôtel Terminus Notebooks*," I was surprised to discover my own doubts mirrored—only rather than turning away from her anxieties, as I'd done, she had transformed her toxic thoughts into a character, the troublesome Mr. Daylater, a man whose sole purpose was to interrupt and discredit her.

—Mr. Daylater: Don't you use no fancy words, girl.

—Why can Bob Dylan record a song ten different ways, expanding and cutting it, changing the tempo and tone, poking fun at himself even, but a published poem is locked, historical? I think—

—Mr. Daylater: Using qualifiers like "I think" is a mark of female speech. You lack assertiveness, or want people to think you do.

—Well—

—Fillers are feminine too.

Though Mr. Daylater silences the narrative voice in this passage, the poem eventually gives way to Beth Ann's voice alone. Naysaying Mr. Daylater is shushed.

In class, Beth Ann was ruthless. "What is this?" she said. "I can't connect here. You've got a clause problem. A verb problem. No lyricism. No heart." When she critiqued me, I listened. So did everyone. She pointed out our best lines. Our writing had to be that strong, always. During office hours she asked if I wanted to hear the good news first or the bad.

The best compliment a teacher can give is her highest standard. One afternoon, I was at Beth Ann's house discussing a story with her husband Tommy. We were sitting in the back yard, beneath the shade of an orange umbrella, when she opened the sliding glass door to check in with him about picking up the kids.

"Why are you smiling?" she asked when she saw me. She'd recently called me out for lazy punctuation, errors so appalling she threatened not to let me graduate unless I got a perfect score on a grammar quiz she'd administer herself.

"I'm smiling because I'm scared," I told her.

"Good," she said. "You should be."

After Beth Ann left, Tommy assured me that her quiz was a compliment. "Trust me," he said. "She's toughest on the people she cares about most."

Beth Ann's ambition encompasses not just her writing and her teaching, but also her relationships, and she rejects the old trope that successful women must choose between family and career. With three kids and two careers, Tommy and Beth Ann have one of the busiest, and happiest, marriages I've encountered, and she wouldn't have it any other way. In her essay "Everything But: Creating Tension in Love Poetry," Beth Ann argues that, in life, love works best "when it's light on conflict." Love poetry requires the opposite scenario. "For half my life I've been luckily and stupidly in love," she laments.

DAWN RAFFEL

ON HER GRANDMOTHER

My grandmother was a conservative woman but her advice for apply-ing for any academic program or job was rather unorthodox: when they ask whether you know how to do something, no matter what it is, say yes. "You'll figure out how to do it," she said. "You'll have to."

My grandmother handled the finances for the family business for decades, and she did it meticulously. As far as I know, she never applied for a job.

But I'll admit to heeding her advice more than once, beginning with a summer journalism program for which the prerequisite was the ability to type. (This was back in the Dark Ages.) On the first day of the program, we students sat at long tables for a long day in front of our machines, and for hours I vacillated between misery and panic. At around four o'clock in the afternoon, the guy sitting next to me looked over and remarked, amazed, "This morning you didn't know how to type. Now you do."

Okay, this is a terrible strategy if you are applying to be, say, a heart sur-geon. But I've talked my way into gigs where I had to pick up a fistful of skills on the quick before my boss could figure out I didn't know what the hell I was doing. (The only job from which I was ever fired, knock wood, involved serv-ing overpriced steaks while wearing a plastic miniskirt and a holster, and I was sacked more for having a reprehensible attitude than for incompetence, although I was also guilty of that.)

While one can argue workplace ethics, it occurs to me that my grandmother's advice is second to none if the job you want is to be a writer. You *don't* know what you're doing, no matter how many books you've written before. You don't know how to write *this* book. You just say yes, commit yourself. You figure it out—you have to.

I can still see her standing with her arms crossed at the edge of the Atlantic Ocean, her eyes never leaving my small bobbing frame, and I know that I can trace every decent thing about myself back to her devotion, and the way she'd lock my hand inside of hers each morning as we stepped into the path of oncoming cars.

NO MENTOR HERE

Alison VanVolkenburgh, *Indifference is the least*, ink, 2010. Reprinted courtesy of the artist.

PAISLEY REKDAL
ON NO ONE

I've never had a writing mentor.

Let me be clear: I've always had people helping me. I've had editors and publicists and colleagues and other writers. I have an agent, whatever use that is to a poet. But a mentor, in the ways that I understand this figure to exist in the literary life, has been curiously absent.

The main reason for this is, simply, that I have never trusted anyone enough to be my mentor. A mentor, that is, who offers the professional insider's details about prizes and publications, who offers collegial protection and support, who over the years provides the sustaining encouragement and occasional wine-soaked dinner necessary to develop as a writer; in other words, the kindly overseer of one's career and protein intake during the artistic lean years. A person who has a stake of his own in your developing career and who hovers between father figure, teacher, and aide-de-camp.

I use the pronoun "he" here specifically. I'm part of that odd generation of women taught by an increasingly mixed though still male-dominated teaching profession, one for whom the most visible literary giants were primarily male. I had notable female teachers—Alice Fulton, Heather McHugh, Thylias Moss among them—but somehow the offer of mentoring was then, and maybe is still now, largely a service offered by older males. The reasons for this are familiar to anyone reading this. Women were and are less likely to mentor due to significant family and career constraints of their own. Women of the previous generation had little experience in being mentored; it was likely, in fact, that their own mentors were men, and so they'd developed little idea of how to initiate or foster their own female-helmed mentor-mentee relationships. Women were, and maybe in some circles still are, seen as direct competitors with each other. And perhaps there is something harder to pinpoint: the lack of confidence certain women suffered about their ability, their right, to offer guidance to a younger and equally ambitious generation of writers.

It takes stamina and high self-esteem to make yourself into somebody's mentor. Not only do you have to believe you know more than the person you are mentoring, but you have to believe that what you have to offer—the insights, the editorial connections, the flashy list of email addresses—essentially, your own professional status—is worth something to a younger writer. For this reason alone, I don't fault the women writers I studied with for not stepping in with advice, for not attending our readings or offering to hook us up with contacts. I was happy just to sit with them for three hours each week, learning how to write.

And it wasn't as if offers of mentorship weren't being made. Offers were being made, and on a somewhat regular basis since I began writing seriously in college. These offers were always from older male writers and, yes, several of these offers carried with them the faint whiff of sexual attraction, sometimes even predation. There was, for instance, the writer in Ireland who was drying out but liked to have me down shots of whisky during his office hours, who said he liked my poems and offered to take me to literary parties around Dublin to meet "important" people. There was the famous male poet at a conference, who took me aside to praise my work and then spent the rest of an hour telling me about the beautiful whores he met in Asia. There was the novelist who directed my graduate program who, when I asked for advice on how to choose between the two agents interested in representing me (one of only three times in my entire life I have ever asked anyone explicitly for mentoring help), looked me up and down, smiled, and asked: "Do you photograph as good as you look?"

And then there was the poet I studied with as an undergraduate, a wildly talented man who was also a brilliant teacher of prosody. He gave me the first piece of praise that I actually wanted to believe—and that I respected—when I read it. At the back of a sheaf of my poems, he'd written a long letter discussing my various successes and failings with meter, and then ended it with this: "You have a ways to go. But you are much farther along than I could have dreamed of being at your age."

The hope this sentence offered, coupled with the clear-eyed assessments of my current abilities, seemed like writing well could be—would be—a realizable ambition for me. The letter made me almost light-headed with relief. It was better than praise. He was not only allowing that I might attain what he had but also subtly encouraging me to try to best him at it.

It was one of the most generous things anyone could have offered me.

And then, a few months later, when I'd moved to Ireland, I received a letter from him. I don't know how he got the address, whether I'd given it to him or my parents had forwarded it on, but one day a couple of handwritten pages came in the mail, and I didn't know what to do with them. The letter said nothing inappropriate. It made no insinuations, didn't attempt to provoke or sexually court me in any way, but still I felt it was odd. I didn't know what answering it would mean, what a friendship between two professional unequals would entail. I was twenty years old; he was somewhere in his forties. I didn't feel harassed, but I also didn't feel powerful enough yet to answer him. And so I never sent back a reply. My silence was meant to make clear to myself, if not to him, what my position would be in the world among writers: I wanted people to help my work, not me. Frankly, I didn't even want there to be a me.

Over the years, I have continued to receive a smattering of letters and offers of professional attention that hover between the intellectually interested and baldly flirtatious. More established, sometimes famous, male writers asking to see poems or books. Asking me to send them work. And true to my then-twenty-year-old's sense of decorum, I have never responded to any of them. About this decision, I have been both right and wrong. Were some of these men more willing to help me because they thought I was pretty? Yes. Did I ever feel unsafe with them or worry that I was at their professional mercy? No. Was it unfortunate that my experience of mentorship to date had relied occasionally upon my appearance as well as on my writing talent? Absolutely. Should I have thus rejected outright all these offers of help? No.

Because to dismiss outright all offers of professional help based on the desire to be seen as competing and existing in a meritocracy, to insist that I be treated solely as a collection of poems, to be essentially un-selfed, is unrealistic. In the end, you seek a mentor to help ensure your work finds an audience, the widest one it can. Let me be clear: I am not suggesting that I should have sexually compromised myself. But the fact is, my looks were my looks. They were there, and one day they would not be.

I couldn't hold off taking advice from those who offered help in order to make me feel perfectly comfortable. You engage in a mentoring relationship for professional, not only personal, reasons. In retrospect, I think I was too fastidious—or just naïve—about certain emotional entanglements of mentorship. The envy I have felt—still feel—for people with mentors who have helped get them jobs and awards and certain high-profile publications is, I realize, an envy entirely of my own making. I, too, could likely have benefited more directly in these ways and not had to scrap for every little thing in my career. But this is what I have denied myself. In my search for the perfect mentor, I overlooked a number of people who certainly would have been good enough. I didn't want to understand that mentorship at its heart may be practical, but it is also messy. It is, if both writers are meant to benefit from it, an unfolding work.

Also, the fact is, the question of my "appearance" had already been a significant factor in my professional life. I am not simply talking about the problems (and benefits) of female attractiveness, but about the fact of my being mixed race and passing (or not passing) for whatever race the audience of the moment wants me to be. To say that I didn't want an older male writer to mentor me because I was afraid of being objectified misses the point. I was always already being objectified. And I had also been doing a little of this back. Because the reality is that I, too, was looking for a very specific physical body to mentor me: not a man, but a woman, and a woman I hadn't yet come across, on the page or in the classroom, a woman I couldn't even yet imagine.

And I was ruthless in my rejection of potential mentors. In graduate school for medieval studies, there were only two female professors teaching in the institute, one of them a young, ambitious, and as-yet untenured scholar of Avicenna, the other a fifty-five-year-old art historian who had been relegated to also being the institute's "secretary." Unfairly, I despised this woman. I nicknamed her "Trembles" for the way she cowered in class, stammering and unsure, overpraising the male students while casting a nervous eye at her female ones. "Trembles" was the product of years of professional bullying, I now realize, which was why—at fifty-five years of age and with twenty-five years of teaching in the same institution—she remained untenured and permanently saddled with secretaryship. But back then I didn't care about the generational struggles she represented and had weathered; I wanted someone I could look up to without reservation. Someone I could be or admire.

Had I been paying attention, perhaps I might have spent a bit more time focusing on that Avicenna scholar, but by then my attention had shifted to the literary world where, still seething from my institutional time with poor "Trembles," whom I wrote off as a feminist betrayal, I went on to dismiss a long parade of teachers for various personal failings. This one was too lazy, that one too grasping, this one competed with her students, that one got high before class. This was true, but why did this necessarily make them useless as fonts of information about writing? Why didn't I press them for names of other writers to read, journals to submit to? Why hadn't I asked them some of the many questions I'd privately collected about strategizing how to assemble a collection of poems into a book? How, even, to publish said poems as a book? Why was I so interested in perfection, when what I really needed was someone simply "good enough"?

Added to these mentoring "sins" was one I knew was worse, and certainly more personally painful, than all the others. Were I to list all the casually or implicitly racist remarks about other writers (and even myself) that I'd either overheard in the hallways or outside the classroom or during the wine-soaked dinners at writing conferences over the years, this essay would go on for pages. The worst part of the racism of the liberal artist or academic, however, is that it is largely hidden, unleashed just when the possible mentor figure has earned your trust, when you are likeliest to accept him or her as your professional advisor. This, too, is one of the reasons I think that, over the years, I've resisted mentorship. In the end, it's too disheartening to hear the writer you admire privately suggest that so-and-so got his job or prize due to affirmative action or white liberal guilt. It is physically painful to then consider whether your silence afterwards is the basest form of cowardice or the more practical attempt to keep the fact of your own biracial identity a secret in order to protect yourself, to ensure that this decorated writer or colleague will not—if he or she has not already done so—say the exact same thing about you.

As I write this, I see that I have two competing arguments in my thoughts about mentors. One is that the personal traits and failings—the person—of the mentor doesn't matter so much as the information this mentor has to offer. The other is that the mentor as person is all that matters. I have a harder time defending the second argument, considering my conflicted feelings about the relationship between identity and art, and yet in all honesty this is the argument that most emotionally engages me. I am aware of the criticisms, fair and unfair, of identity-based writing. I have absorbed, consciously and through the slow osmosis of cultural self-hatred, the blunt "truisms" about what constitutes Poetry. The assurances drilled into me as a young writer—implicitly and explicitly—that issues of race and gender and sexuality and politics must never enter into poems, or enter either primarily as self-conscious parody of these subjects or as examinations of form which might rescue their inherently reductivist sentimentality, are ones that most people reading this are probably familiar with. And these assurances were not only drilled into me in the uber-pale midwest college town where I went to graduate school, but even by my Chinese American mother, who has spent her life teaching and promoting multiculturalism in the Seattle school district, and who told me after my first book on biracial identity was published that one day I, too, might write something "universal." As I've matured in my writing career, I see that one of the most important questions I have wanted to ask and have answered, the one part of my writing life I have never quite grasped myself, was how to balance this continued expectation that writing should primarily constitute an act of formal experiment and innovation, one that both utilizes and transcends personal experience, all the while consciously ignoring three-quarters of what has defined my human experience in the world.

And who, really, can answer that?

When I think of that word *mentor*, all these problems and conundrums bubble up. And yet another memory, too, swims up to me: one of a night three years ago in Denver, giving an off-site reading at the Associated Writing Programs conference in support of Kundiman / Cave Canem and finding David Mura sitting right in front of me in the audience.

David Mura is a writer I have had a lot of arguments with. Not in person, as that night was the first time we had ever officially "met," but in the classrooms where I've taught him, and in my thoughts after finishing one of his books. He's infuriated, inspired, and intrigued me. His work has forced me to reexamine the terms in which race and ethnicity and gender do—or don't—get written into a poem. A Japanese American Nissei male, David Mura is someone with whom, in many ways, I don't have a lot in common but whose presence, I realized, as I watched him watching me from his little table in the front row of that packed reading, had been undeniably powerful to me.

Powerful in the ways that the presences of Maxine Hong Kingston or Frank Chin or Lois Ann Yamanaka or Myung Mi Kim or Theresa Hak Kyung Cha or Li Young Lee or Carlos Bulosan would have been had they also been in that room, impossible as that thought is. Though I have attended plenty of AWPs, have met and listened to dozens of writers I admire, that night in Denver was the first time I had ever felt electrified by the presence of another writer. I was now standing and reading my work in front of someone who I knew had made his own similar forays into the literary world, running up against problems that—if they were never the same as mine—certainly tread a very familiar path. However much I disagreed with or admired or fought against his work, David Mura had cracked open the subject matters and genres in which I myself was now working; he had made a connection into the literary world that made it possible for me to make my own. I was, quite literally, on the verge of tears leaving the bar after that reading. I realized that over the years, I had been denying myself not only the information that would have made my writing career easier to manage, but the ability to express gratitude to those whose work was written, if even in part, for those like me.

And that is what I now understand the acceptance of mentoring to be on the part of the mentored writer: a sign of gratitude. In its way, a debt of honor. I understood, suddenly, the true meaning of what I had denied myself and others, and since then have had to take comfort in the knowledge that, even if I'd never admitted this debt of mentorship consciously to myself, I had at least taken advantage of a deep engagement with the work of Mura and others over the course of my life. In that sense, I had long been mentored by writers who were also, conveniently, absent enough to let me experiment with my own language: to help me write as me. To bring me, in that sense, into being.

Perhaps this is the kind of epiphany only a writing conference whose social hub is a bar can inspire. And yet, it was there. I stumbled out of the Denver nightclub, blinking and breathless. A piece of David Mura, a scrap of Heather McHugh, snippets clipped from the Irish poet, a perfectly metered line from the prosodist, and more and more and others trailed after me. My own little poetic Frankenstein. Aesthetically incoherent, maybe, disordered in appearance, and professionally not useful, but something.

A something, for better or worse, that has become my more than good enough.

CHRISTINE HUME
ON SOME TEACHERS

My first teacher told me the stories about Vietnam I craved from my father, and he hounded me sexually.

My second teacher barely made it on the plane from Boston to NYC every week for class. She was a good parent that way, rewilding herself in the spirit of her son. She believed in disobedience and rebellion, and sometimes not showing up.

My next told me to let red wine alchemize discrete poems into a manuscript. He instructed me about which bottles to drink as I spread my poems on the floor and which bottles to drink as I arranged them—collected them from the floor in a meaningful order.

My sixth teacher told the workshop to go ahead and meet without her. She had a dentist appointment or she would rather be in Paris. Later, because she was angry at another member of my committee, she could not speak during my dissertation defense, she explained in an email.

The one she was angry with—that one had already changed the world for me. He was a mentor. He spoke through texts and as them.

As any woman will tell you, Emily Dickinson claimed that she never had a mother.

It's not that Athena never had a mother, but her father would like us to think so. Athena—a patriarchal displacement of the trinity goddess Athene-Metis-Medusa who predated her—sprang full-grown from the head of Zeus.

She was a thought that materialized, allergic to interiority, and she knew how to throw out her own thoughts through the mouths of others. Twice, she cloaked herself in the voice of Mentor, Odysseus's trusted friend. Through Mentor's voice, she instructed Telemachus to search for his father and to stand up to the suitors, a counsel that made everything happen, and happen right. Another time, she spoke through Mentor to safeguard Odysseus's homecoming.

What would the mouth of a mentor say?

The first time the word *mentor* appears, it's personified, an abstraction in period costume. But Mentor is most powerful as a disguise, as ventriloquism, as karaoke, as vocal transvestism, as vocoder.

Zeus swallowed his first wife, whose advice he badly needed. She was a fly when he swallowed her, and from her perch in his brain, she spoke. If I listen, *men*, from the Indo-European, means "to think." Mentor is a cognate of mind. Metis, a fly on the mental, coming for you and turning away.

TIBOR FISCHER

ON A MENTOR MISSED

In 1986 I rolled up my towel and took the elevator to the top floor of the Holiday Inn on Sunset Boulevard. I was in Los Angeles making a documentary for the BBC about the Hungarian Revolution of 1956, and I had come to quiz the cinematographer Vilmos Zsigmond about his revolutionary anecdotes. Our appointment was canceled at the last minute so I had a whole day free in LA, and as I had been working quite hard (really), I just wanted to slob out by the pool.

Three BBC producers already basking there immediately gave me their justifications for lolling by the pool. There were also three dancers sunbathing topless (at this location and stage of western civilization, definitely wild). However, as we were joined by several Chippendales disporting themselves, relations between the BBC and the topless dancers of LA didn't strengthen. I went to bed a little swarthier, but uneasy. Something didn't feel right, as if I had forgotten something, a piece of luggage, someone's birthday . . . although I couldn't work out what it was. And I didn't work out what it was until some ten years later.

A writer's mentors tend to be books, very often written by authors who are dead or distant (although it's a curious thing, when there are 7 billion of us on the planet, how often you bump into people you don't expect to bump into). That, as a writer, I later came into contact with other writers, is hardly surprising: but it is a strangely small world. I once ended up having a conversation with a favorite rock star on a broken-down train as we tried to get fresh air by jamming open a door that refused to be jammed open.

A home with books was certainly the most powerful factor in my becoming a writer. As far as I can remember, I always liked the idea of writing. However, it was after a talk by Isaac Asimov on a rare visit to London (I was twelve and obsessed with sci-fi, having just read the Robot stories) that I made the decision that I had to be a writer. My father mentioned to Asimov, as he was signing a book for me, that I had aspirations, and Asimov added the line, "Give me a run for the money." It was an act of extraordinary kindness that fired me up for a long time.

Shortly afterwards I read *A Clockwork Orange* with a lot of enthusiasm, partly because I wasn't supposed to be reading it. I met Anthony Burgess briefly, a decade later when I was working on a television chat show. I was amazed that Burgess was bothering to do a four-minute interview (this was the birth of satellite television and our audience was so small as to be undetectable). But then I had little idea of the preposterous amount of shit you have to eat as a writer and how remarkably hard it is to make any money. I was too junior and intimidated to do more than to offer Burgess some peanuts and eavesdrop in the hope of some *bons mots*. There weren't any—I don't think Burgess was thrilled about being there.

When I was sixteen I stayed with an American school friend who had returned to the United States, and although I had an enjoyable trip because I discovered that (at that stage of western civilization) many American girls were intrigued by a British accent, the highlight of my stay was buying a copy of Tom Robbins's *Even Cowgirls Get the Blues*, which had just been published. I had already read his first novel, *Another Roadside Attraction*, which was available in the U.K. and which I had liked, but this was the book that showed me conclusively that there were no rules, that you could do *anything* in a novel. (Underneath all its pyrotechnics *A Clockwork Orange* is a very straightforward story.) It was like a flying saucer landing in my garden, the pilot getting out and saying, "Come for a ride."

I took Tom Robbins out for an Indian meal a few years ago. I wish I could have gotten a message back to my sixteen-year-old self: one day you'll get to complain about publishers with Tom Robbins. Writers' rankings are always bobbing up and down, you can argue about that, but there's absolutely no question that for many years Robbins was the coolest novelist on earth, and that desire to hang out with the cool kids never leaves you. I also thanked him for publishing a short story in *Playboy*, "The Purpose of the Moon." At that stage in western civilization much fruitier material than *Playboy* was available on any corner but it was great to get a new story by a favorite author and to be able to look everyone in the eye and say with complete sincerity, "I only bought it for the articles."

Tom explained to me that he had had difficulty writing "The Purpose of the Moon" and that he didn't consider it his best work. Yet it's one of my favorite short stories and one that my hard-to-please creative writing students consistently go for. It was confirmation that the ease or difficulty of writing is something that has little bearing on its quality and that writers usually aren't the best judges of their work. (See what Voltaire and Cervantes thought their finest hour was—it's not *Candide* or *Don Quixote*.)

As you get older, it's less and less likely that you'll be bowled over by a writer or really instructed by one. I came to Sándor Márai late (despite the fact that a Márai book was on the shelf in my childhood home) when an English friend recommended him. How, I thought, could Márai be that good if *I* hadn't read him? I picked up the terribly-titled-in-translation *Memoir of Hungary 1944–48* and immediately realized that Márai was one of the great writers of the last century and pretty much the greatest Hungarian prose writer. I rationed myself to a couple of pages a day to make the book last longer. I was very angry with my Hungarian coterie for not making me read Márai years earlier.

Márai left Hungary in 1948 after the Communist takeover and was largely erased from Hungarian intellectual life. Though he was widely translated in Europe in the thirties, his first novel to be translated into English appeared only in 2001. *Embers* was quite successful and led to a rediscovery of Márai in Europe and his acclamation in the Anglo-Saxon world.

To return to 1986: while I was luxuriating in the pool on Sunset Boulevard, Márai was down the road in San Diego in not very salubrious circumstances. Old, poor, ill, alone, apparently forgotten, Márai committed suicide in 1989 (ironically just before Hungary was to wipe away the Communist system and republish his books).

It would have been a short train ride down to San Diego, along the coast. I would have loved to grill Márai on many subjects. I like to think he would have been pleased or at least not too annoyed to have a visitor ask him out to lunch. Márai was just down the road from me, and that was what had made me uneasy. I had forgotten to go to see him, although it would be fifteen years before I realized what I had forgotten. A mentor missed is a terrible thing.

TONY HOAGLAND

ON REJECTING YOUR MENTORS

Maybe I was lucky; in my early twenties, when I desperately wanted a literary mentor, a teacher, or a poetry father figure, I couldn't find one. In college, and afterwards, I repeatedly sought the attention of elder writers (they were usually men) who would tell me everything they knew about poetry. I kept knocking on doors, like a beggar in winter, but I wasn't an impressive apprentice, and no one wanted to take me in. By the time I finally might have merited some attention from my betters, I had mostly outgrown the need for a mentor. I had acquired a valuable disbelief in outside help, and a corresponding faith in my ability to learn on my own.

Even so, it doesn't mean that some figures have not been more meaningful than others. I know one thing is true: there has been no influential teacher from whom I didn't have to break away. Consciously or unconsciously, it became at some point necessary for me to reject them, to step outside the perimeter of their approval or disapproval. Patronage always forms some dependence, dependence always forms some sense of subordinacy, subordinacy always creates some resentment, which requires a small explosion, the way a spacecraft jettisons and then pulls away from its booster rocket.

In at least one case, my rejection of a mentor, and my exodus away, was caused by an aesthetic disagreement. My poetic mode shifted away from the style of my old patron. I had shown my work to him for years, but now his comments kept trying to revise my poems back into their previous form. I felt injured and misunderstood, and I found I had to turn a cold shoulder to his opinion. Even his unspoken judgment was harmful. I stopped answering his letters.

In the mid-seventies I was in the undergraduate program of the University of Iowa Writers' Workshop. My teachers had famous names; they were resident or visiting luminosities. They were good poets, but (with one exception) they were bland, careless, and unmotivated as teachers: disengaged, methodical, protective of their own time and energy, stingy with their acumen. At that time, when I felt thirsty enough to drink an ocean of craft wisdom, they shared their knowledge and experience in quantities that could be administered with an eyedropper.

But that was the seventies, when running a workshop consisted pretty much of providing a place, a time, and permission to write. I think the poets of my own generation, whelped in the lazy, groovy workshops of the seventies, determined that if we were ever given the chance to teach, we would be more rigorous and more energetic than the teachers who had served us. As a consequence, I believe my generation is wealthy with extraordinary, rigorous, and generous teachers.

The poets I feel closest to, the ones towards whom I feel the deepest fealty and gratitude, are those I know through their printed work, their books. I feel towards them as I would towards aunts and uncles, cousins and great-grandparents; I respect their generosity and ongoing benevolence; I revere what they have taught me about craft as well as human nature. Ours is an ongoing relation that shows no sign of running dry or becoming conditional. Their work has been my grow light and my aquifer; and I suppose that this is what ancestry and lineage must be about. O'Hara, Auden, Cavafy, Moore, and many, many others. Could it be that I am just more comfortable with non-living teachers?

Now I've had the chance to see plenty of my former students have their own complicated reaction-formations, and move instinctively away from me and my influence. A granite silence, for example, emanates from the direction of former student X. Or sometimes, I sense a kind of irritability in the air between myself and a once-favorite student, an allergic reaction to the old status quo.

At such times, I am sorry to report that my feelings are wounded, as the feelings of my former teachers probably were injured by my distancing/separation from them. But I try to remember and recognize that these former students are just taking the distance they require to move freely, without being shadowed by some person who thinks he knows more than they do. They are trying to move to deeper water, where they can swim for themselves.

It's an undeniably strange business. For some artistic temperaments, estrangement itself is a necessary condition. Isolation is sometimes a useful kind of landscape, and some species of the truth can only be discovered by spending extended time there. Many artists are intentional orphans. It may not be a cozy destiny, full of potluck dinners and quality family time, but radical news requires radical commitment. And part of the commitment to the life of art is believing your own story.

We live between the underworld and the overworld, between the center and the periphery, between the social and the solitary, and that is how we evolve, too, by moving backwards and forwards as we negotiate the contradictory needs of being nourished and being independent. It would be foolish not to be grateful for the remarkable help we have received, and ungrateful not to try to practice that generosity towards younger artists.

A certain passage in Auden's great poem "Easter" has always seemed to me a beautifully expressed code for such leaving and remembering:

> . . . So I remember all those whose death
> is necessary condition of the season's setting forth
> . . . and recent particulars come to mind:
> the death by cancer of a once hated master;
> a friend's analysis of his own failure,
> listened to at intervals throughout the winter
> at different hours and in different rooms . . .

Of whom was Auden thinking? I feel I know, though he will not tell me.

INTERVENTIONS

Pat Perry, *Trespassers*, ink on paper, 2014. Reprinted courtesy of the artist.

STEPHEN ELLIOTT

ON SURROUNDING YOURSELF WITH THE PEOPLE YOU MOST WISH TO BECOME

I didn't have a mentor, not at first, when it mattered. I was *influenced*. Influenced by Jack Kerouac and Charles Bukowski and Michelle Tea. We repeat our childhood, I think, and as a child I did not like adults and they did not like me. I was a ward of the state, locked up and shuttled through a network of innocuous institutions. I didn't have a mentor in my life when, at sixteen, I decided to quit doing drugs. The adults came after. It was after getting clean that a kind family finally took me in.

Writing was like that for me, too. I was a history major as an undergrad, then I did a one-year film degree. I wrote three books before I sold any of them. And it was right around this time that I was awarded a Stegner Fellowship to Stanford University. At Stanford I met Tobias Wolff who was kind of a mentor. I love Tobias and strive to be like him, not just as a writer but as a person. I can't actually do either but the goal is worthwhile. Toby took me under his wing, as did many of the other faculty at Stanford.

They were exceedingly kind, the program was generous. Because I had never studied writing I had so much more to gain than any of the other fellows. The other fellows at the time had all done advanced degrees in creative writing, and I felt like I was inhaling their years of study.

But still, *mentor* doesn't strike me as the right term. I sold my first books, two of them that I'd submitted un-agented to MacAdam/Cage, for 18,000 dollars apiece, at almost exactly the same time I was awarded the fellowship.

I love the way Tobias Wolff writes, and I imitated, as much as I could, his spare, polished style. A kind word from him was inspiration for a week . . .

You see what I'm getting at? There is something wrong with me. When I was in eighth grade I slept on the streets for a year. My father moved and didn't leave me his new address. My friend's parents all knew I was homeless but nobody took me in. My favorite teachers would buy me lunch. I mean, the entire neighborhood knew I was sleeping on top of the convenience store a block away from the grammar school. How is that possible?

I have fantastic taste in people I look up to, starting with Louie who introduced me to riverboat gambling and heroin, and continuing with Dave Eggers and Po Bronson. I look up to people who are curious and good and stay engaged with the world while so many other people get tired of making the effort. And I've somehow become very close with some amazing people, despite the inconsistency of my moods and affection. The teachers that took me under their wing when I quit drugs and decided I needed to graduate from high school in two years, after failing the first two years, were the best around. Something stopped me from connecting with them earlier. I was in the group-home school at the time, and I saw the neighborhood kids loping by our three-story red-brick building on their way to the normal high school across the street, and I thought, They're no better than me. That was the idea that turned me around.

When I talk to kids in detention centers I talk about how once they do something for themselves others will join them. I tell them I didn't have to pay for college thanks to the scholarships available for wards of the state. I tell them about the 18,000 dollars I got for each book and the free Nikes from the Nike employee store. And in my heart I know it's not true. I know there are children in every institution that the adults will try to save, instinctively reaching their arms into the water to grab a drowning child. And I know there are other kids they won't try to save. I know that all of this happens on some level below the surface of what we can understand and that people who do volunteer work with children are the best people in the world.

Here's something funny, though. I'm lucky. In the moments when I've been ready to let someone in, a saint has always arrived in my life. I'm surrounded by the people I wish most to become. But to call someone a mentor, that implies something else. It implies someone saw a spark in you and wrapped their hands around it before you even knew a flame. Or maybe it means something else and I'm just defining it wrong.

JOSIP NOVAKOVICH

ON TERRENCE MALICK

I learned mostly from reading books and that's where I got the desire to write stories. My mentors were primarily Beckett, Maupassant, Dostoyevsky, and Tolstoy. I didn't have a particular live mentor, although I was influenced by several people at various stages of my development and decay. Growing up in a totalitarian socialist regime, with Tito pictures and police everywhere, I developed early on a strong distaste for personality cults, leaders, and teachers, and I gravitated toward those who seemed to be at odds with the system, who had enough strength and courage to seek their own ways. A sculptor in my home town, Nikola Kechanin, influenced me with his rather forceful way of dealing with the materials of stone, bronze, paper, and pencil, but most of all with his courage to stand up in a large Communist assembly and declare that atheism is folly, that there is a God, and that we should tremble in front of him and do the right things. I was religious at the time. I liked to draw, not because of him, but his presence enhanced my ambition, and I might have become a painter if I had followed my early impulses.

An anatomy professor at the University of Novi Sad School of Medicine impressed me with his clear and clinical way of thinking, but I have not become a doctor.

I listened to several philosophy and theology professors at Vassar and Yale, and I was usually disappointed—I wanted to hear a great lecturer, *Slavoj-Žižek* style, but instead I heard lots of incoherent mumbling without charisma.

In Austin, Texas, when I studied creative writing, I developed a friendship with a man with a charismatic mind and relentless curiosity and wonder, a genuinely philosophical mind. I met Terry Malick one cold and stormy night, with a friend of mine, who was friends with Terry's wife at the time; as we walked in the streets, totally soaked in the storm, she said, "I have very interesting friends who live right around the block, let's visit them and warm up with some tea." And we did.

Terry looked like Aristotle, with a tall balding forehead, strong black and graying beard, and a dignified manner. Terry immediately took a interest in my background, former Yugoslavia, small town, etc., and wanted to find out a lot about it, so he asked me to meet him for coffee the following day. He found it entertaining and fascinating that I had grown up without a TV set, that I used the telephone for the first time at the age of seventeen, that my home in Daruvar had a deepwater well with a spindle, and that I used to spend at least three hours a day walking with friends and discussing things. Terry and I became fast friends.

It was great to have a friendship with an older wise man, taking walks and drinking lots of coffee. What I enjoyed most about it was that it was in a certain way a trip back to Croatia for me. In Croatia, I had friends with whom I could talk for hours while walking, a sort of peripatetic school of philosophy—even though it was no school and lots of ideas came and went and so did time; time kind of warped in its own way through dialogue. When I got to the States, I was surprised to find out that people didn't seem to treasure walking and talking—that it was not the way to communicate, and conversations were usually short and practically oriented. Of course, I may have had bad luck in college where people had busy schedules. And here, this man talked just as though he were from the Old World, and he claimed that he was, that he had Assyrian roots.

We had coffee at least three times a week for almost two years. We'd meet at Les Amis (where *Slacker* was mostly filmed afterward, and now the place does not exist any more), and then we'd take a walk along a creek. Usually he'd ask me what I had read the night before, and if I said, Nothing, he'd reply, "Aren't you afraid your mind will dry up without a fresh flow of ideas and information? You can't rely only on impressions."

I don't.

The world is way too amazing not to pay attention to it, and not to study it.

A waitress once asked him what kind of work he did, and he replied, "I am an aging student."

"You look like a professor."

"Being a student is much better," he said. "I don't want to become a professor when I grow up."

He apparently read most of his free time, and any subject that came up, he'd research in the *Encyclopedia Britannica*, etymological dictionaries, and university archives, and some evenings, he'd go to the observatory to study astronomy and astrophysics.

For at least half a year I didn't know what he did for a living—my friend who introduced us said he'd done some work for movies but that he hated to talk about it, and his wife said, "Don't ask me what he does; for all I know he could be a pornographer, and I wouldn't know, as he never lets me know what he's working on and he has a separate studio, and I don't even know where it is." A friend of mine, Eric, said, "Who is that august-looking man you spend so much time with? What's his name?" I said, "I don't know what he does; his name is Terry Malick." "You mean Terrence?" he said. "He is one of the most famous film directors in the world." "Really?" I said. I had never heard of him as a director, and I had given up on movies for a while anyhow. I'd expected Terry to be a philosopher or a writer more than a filmmaker.

I think I was learning more from him when I didn't know that he was a big director. But the fact that I knew didn't change our relationship much. He'd usually wince a bit if the conversation took a practical turn, about how one makes it in business of writing. He advised against business and fame and argued for writing, pure and simple. At the time he wrote screenplays under pseudonyms to make a living, as though deliberately avoiding fame and credit in the business. On one occasion, we went to the library and he checked out a few books. The checkout librarian looked shocked when she read his card. She said, "Are you *the* Terrence Malick?"

"No, ma'am, just a coincidence."

When we walked out, I said, "Look what you've done. You could have made her day. She has a miserable job, but you need to stay private even if you deprive a saint like that, and a librarian is a saint."

"You know, you have a good point," he said. "I love librarians."

"But not enough."

"Not enough," he laughed.

Terry's critique was usually, "You know, this is interesting and strong, but your conversation is better. You write as though you were in a fight with one of your hands tied behind your back, and that is not how you talk. Why are you afraid of the page? You seem desperate to have plot and afraid to be speaking your mind."

"Well, it's fiction," I'd say. "It's not a forum for thought." How would I express my opinions and philosophize and keep the story going in a suspenseful way?

"Don't worry about suspense. I don't have a prescription but don't be afraid. Your stories would be more powerful if you did express your thoughts without restraint and artifice."

"Yes, but with lots of thinking, the story often stops."

"Sometimes, without enough thinking it stops. Put the thoughts in dialogue if they don't seem to fit in the narrative. What's wrong with having thoughtful characters? Plato could evolve the most complex philosophy in dialogue, and some of his dialogue is quite dramatic."

I don't remember if these were his exact words, but he was making strong arguments against cutting out ideas.

This was in the age of minimalism, death of the author ideology—the writer was supposed to be invisible, and the story would take care of itself through sheer power of well-chosen details, a few lines of dialogue, etc. Any kind of thinking, Thomas-Bernhard style, seemed eccentric. I didn't yet know the freedom in writing personal essays, where without pressure for plot, I am free to think.

Terry seemed to like my story about a sculptor, my first mentor, who excommunicates himself from the Communist party and instead of making sculptures ends up making tombstones. Terry hated anything businesslike in conversation—he advised me to avoid commerce, not to seek fame but only good stories; nevertheless, he suggested that I send the sculptor story to his friend who edited the *Atlantic*. Mr. Whitworth responded that he loved the story and would probably take it if I rewrote it in the third-person so it would not sound like a memoir. I said okay, but just then the *Paris Review* wanted to take the story, and I thought, what the hell, that's good enough, they don't worry about point of view and neither do I. At the end of my stay in Austin, I was broke, and I didn't know how to make it to Yaddo for my first writers' colony residency, and Terry and my friend Carlos Castro Perelman, a physicist from Colombia, bought me airfare to Albany.

I think it's partly thanks to Terry that I sought a way to bring the conversation into my fiction. Before meeting him, I thought my dialogue sucked, and I relied on narration, description, etc., and he thought I needed more dialogue, more natural dialogue, like what we were having. For a long time afterward, I was embarrassed by my dialogue, even when friends and editors occasionally said, "You know, your story has some problems but the dialogue is fantastic." Maybe talking to Terry gave me courage to begin to rely on dialogue, and sometimes I do that to the point of fault, losing the labored artfulness of descriptions, which I savored in my first fictions. It is hard to know how much I learned from whom, but Terry's friendship was uplifting and encouraging for my writing for sure.

Anyway, we exchanged a few letters afterward, typewritten, but he moved and so did I, so I am not sure who exactly dropped the ball and lost track, but we have not been in touch. I learned more from his insistence on freedom of speech in writing than from my creative writing teachers anywhere.

MAAZA MENGISTE
ON BREYTEN BREYTENBACH

I was completing my first novel, *Beneath the Lion's Gaze,* set during a Marxist-backed revolution that began in Ethiopia in 1974. What I knew of the history was personal, the estimated 500,000 killed pared down to the three who were in my family. I wasn't sure what it meant to write fiction about a national tragedy. I didn't know how those three lives could be contained in what has been called the *artful lie.* Wasn't this revolution the terrain of nonfiction? I asked my professor, the South African poet Breyten Breytenbach. Isn't there an obligation to honor the dead by speaking of them exactly as they existed?

Breyten had been jailed for several years in South Africa, beginning in 1975, for his anti-apartheid activities. He had written extensively about his experiences through poetry and memoir, as well as essays, plays, and short stories. It seemed to me that he had found the voice through which to speak those moments, whereas I had been able to confront mine only in silence, trapped by my own misgivings and questions. I felt I had no language to address those ghosts that hovered across every page I tried to write. I had no way to approach them, and it seemed that it was my own fault. This was not a story to be rendered through creative writing. There were too many sharp edges. The wounds, as I witnessed when I asked family and friends to speak of their experiences, were still too raw. Only solid facts, undiluted by the craft of storytelling, seemed sturdy enough to carry the weight of this history.

What Breyten said to me was this: I could write this story. I was capable. And that sometimes, fiction tells a truth that history cannot.

But what did I really know of the cost of Ethiopia's revolution? What did I know of the way communities change under a Marxist- or Communist-backed regime? What did I know of the effects of ration cards and literacy programs on families, of nationalized properties and new value systems, of the many ways that life can continue to go on, despite it all? I didn't know enough. But I would need to learn as best as I could. In my trips to Ethiopia, I had found that present-day changes sometimes pressed too closely against the past, nearly stamped it out. I wanted to try to observe a small part of revolutionary history by walking into it, and hoped that imagination could do the rest. I would travel to Cuba. I would be a foreigner. I would be an outsider. My observations would be peripheral and brief. All of this would be inadequate, but I hoped that it would reveal something unexpected. Some way for me to look back at those three lost lives and find the words to speak of them.

It was in a tiny, sundrenched café in Havana that I met a man whose father will never forget Ethiopia. "I know your country," R., the son of a former Cuban soldier stationed in Ethiopia in the late 1970s, told me as we sat down and ordered sweet coffee. "You eat like this," and he motioned with his hands. "Your city is beautiful," he continued. "Your music," he added as he smiled.

R.'s father fought next to Ethiopians in the border wars with Somalia and Eritrea. He had been a young man, then, sent on behalf of the Cuban government in a show of support and solidarity. On his return to Cuba, R.'s father told his stories so many times that his son could repeat specific details of geography and culture by heart. "Three wars," he told me later in a quiet moment, holding three fingers up to my face. "My father had to fight in three wars: Angola, Ethiopia, Mozambique. All he got was a black-and-white television," he said, unable to wipe the bitterness from his voice. In the tiny café I watched him wade through unspoken memories. I thought back to something else another Cuban man had told me, a statement that I now began to understand. "Our blood," he had said, "is soaked in your land. Your people and mine share more than history."

I heard something of my own quest in R.'s voice. In his family, too, history had stepped in and left silence. Three wars had been boiled down to a black-and-white television set and given to a young man who had repeated only good memories to his son. The TV, the anecdotes, the small facts of Ethiopian food and music—all of it hinting at a truth that tells a more complex story than the history R. had learned at school. Sitting in that café, on that hot summer day, I heard the way stories can rewrite the erased facts of history. I saw the way remembrance and retelling can gather around a silenced life and give it form.

Breyten's words came back to me: R.'s stories told a truth that history cannot. But what does history tell that cannot be encompassed by our stories? As R. recounted another incident from his father's life, I went back to those three wars experienced by a man who had been no more than a boy. I went back to those nearly 500,000 lives lost during my country's revolution. I saw moments too overwhelming to comprehend except through the personal and intimate. How to quantify what is lost when we lose 500,000? How to stand before the thought of three different wars and really understand what was seen and felt and lived? Only fiction allows us the breathing room to take it all in, in increments. It rests in pauses and silences. It offers us a mercy that history cannot. History is ruthless and full of noise; it must be reduced for us to bear the burdens of its many truths.

Through Breyten, I saw that fiction tells a truth that history cannot. Through R., I began to understand that fiction offers a solace when history is too much. As writers we like to say that imagination moves faster than awareness, but I realize, too, that awareness is shaped by imagination. There is no other way to understand what is contained in a certain moment in history—those 500,000 gone, those three wars fought—without first imagining the individual stories unfolding at its center.

There were three and now there are none.

Here is an elderly man sitting in front of an outdated black-and-white television set, talking to his son.

Havana, Cuba. Photograph by Maaza Mengiste.

ALISSA NUTTING

ON KATE BERNHEIMER

I compare my pre–Kate Bernheimer life to Brendan Fraser's newly thawed character in *Encino Man:* I had no grasp of the world. I frequently misinterpreted very basic aspects of modern life. I had a prehistoric sense of aggression that did not serve me well.

When I decided to get an MFA, I figured I needed to start flying mainstream. "We are going to clean the freak right out of you," I thought. My mind had always been a duplex of sorts—one side was set up like a stage, completely regular, a show home safe for public view. The other was brimming with snakes, windup chatter teeth, Victorian drawings of medical abnormalities: everything that would cause an average taxpayer to gasp. "Alissa the person can live on this bizarre side surrounded by ceramic unicorns. Alissa the writer will live over there where it's acceptable. She will reside on a beige couch with accent pillows and keep her nails trimmed."

But it was hard to avoid cross-contamination. I'd be sitting on Side Normal and snakes would pour though the vents; I'd turn on the faucet and chatter teeth would come out in the water. "These damn snakes," I thought. I was angry, about a lot of things. Mainly about what happened when I tried to write straight realism: it was really, really bad.

Other points of fury included the type of person I thought writers were supposed to be: competitive, cutthroat, vaguely prickish, and superior. I like tiny animals, luxe fleece blankets, and hugging, and I didn't want to stop hugging, or do/say things that might make others want to stop hugging me. I was mad about how the value of a writer was supposedly measured through sales and advances. Sure, I loved a lot of popular writers and books, but I *really* loved a lot of small weird books too. I knew what these books had done for me, the ways they'd been necessary to my survival.

By the second year of my MFA, I felt so defeated when I took Kate's workshop and turned in my first story: I'd tried to write something that could really happen, but ended up taking the A train to Wackyville once again. It involved werewolves and a boy who sat on chocolate bars nude to melt them with his body heat.

I was prepared and eager to hear how I could help make it less strange, but her comments shocked me. "Whatever you're doing," she wrote, "don't stop." There it was in writing: complete permission.

Kate is like one of those infamous rainforest tree frogs, except instead of secreting poison she emanates a Valium-generosity substrate. She is infinitely kind, accepting, and giving, and she is a writer: these are her ways of being in the world, and they are a conscious choice. Watching her benevolent manner, I knew instinctively that this was the type of writer and person I wanted to be, and that different aspects of my self needn't lead separate lives. Kate wears many hats—novelist, editor, short story writer, children's author—and she lets her utmost passion, fairy tales, inform every part of her creative work. What a relief it was to see how I could focus on my obsessions instead of bury them. What a relief to cover my beige couch with snakes.

JON PAUL FIORENTINO
ON ROBERT KROETSCH

Tonight I did a reading. The de Sève Cinema amphitheater was more than half full. I always count the audience. (It calms my nerves.) Tonight there were fifty-eight people in the room. There were people I loved, people I wanted to impress. I read from new work—a comedic text—and I struggled. I flubbed lines, failed to convey the rhythm of the prose, apologized to the audience, and did pretty much everything else you aren't supposed to do when you present your work. When I was done with the new stuff, I felt relief and regained my composure. Then I read some selections from a text I had been reading all day: "Towards an Essay: The Upstate New York Journals" from Robert Kroetsch's *The Lovely Treachery of Words*. I wasn't ready to read *Seed Catalogue* (my favorite). I needed to share with the audience a sense of the man.

The journal is not that long. It documents a time in the 1970s when he was teaching. Some of the entries are matter-of-fact. Most contain gems: his brief encounter with Basil Bunting and the secrets Bunting revealed about his own poetry and about the title of a certain T. S. Eliot text; the image of Gwendolyn MacEwen at the 1969 Governor General's Literary Awards ceremony sitting alongside her young Greek lover; George Bowering with his green velvet suit and extravagant silk shirt—so many small ruminations, striking in their intellectual acuity. I read a passage in which Kroetsch describes finding out that he was to receive the Governor General's Award for his novel *The Studhorse Man*. He proceeded to recall how twenty years earlier he had received his first-ever acceptance letter for a story (to be published in *The Montrealer*). Then I read my own "Civic Poem," which is inspired by and dedicated to him. When the reading was over, I exited the theater without looking anyone in the eye. I ran to my office and cried.

I found out via text message this morning, June 22, 2011, that Robert had died in a car accident. I broke down instantly.

Never has anyone been so encouraging, kind, and inspiring to me as Robert Kroetsch was. It was enough that his books taught me so much, but the fact that he took a particular interest in me and my writing was astonishing. I am aware of the fact that he had similar relationships with countless other writers. If you were a reader or a writer, he had time for you. We met about eleven years ago. In Winnipeg. I remember sitting across from him at the restaurant in McNally Robinson. I was in awe. I had some poems I wanted him to look at and, to my surprise, he had brought me some poems of his to look at, too. I remember thinking, "Why on earth would he want my opinion on new poems?" I had just started volunteering for *Matrix* magazine in Montreal, and he asked if I might like to publish them. The poems were exquisite, of course. And being the young, hyper-ambitious guy that I was, I insisted that he let me interview him as well. And he said yes.

He always said yes. In 2007 he said yes to lending his name to my fledgling literary press, Snare Books. The Robert Kroetsch Award for Innovative Poetry was established. My favorite annual email was the one he would write after reading the latest winner. His enthusiasm for new poetry, for new ways of poetry, was awe-inspiring. As our friendship grew and our conversations became more sophisticated, he kept telling me: "It's your turn to talk." (And I tried. And I'm trying.) But it always provided more pleasure, more bliss, to listen to him.

In the upstate journals, Kroetsch writes about Charles Olson's passing, observing that he "is only his books." The elegance of Kroestch. The staggering peculiarities of his language. The way he changed our language. The imperceptible ease with which he articulated so much wisdom. He was always fascinated with the poem he "could never complete." But the truth is, he was the complete poet. The complete writer. He approached language and life with a sense of rigorous play. Now he is only his books. I will visit him there for the rest of my life. You will, too.

NATHAN DEUEL

ON WILLIAM T. VOLLMANN

Allow me to share a few facts about a guy I remain sheepish to call a mentor, a great producer of books and legends, a guy who fought or at least appeared to fight alongside the mujahideen and in at least one public reading is said to have held a gun to his head.

At times it's been a strange, perplexing, and unhelpful situation, to know William T. Vollmann to the extent that I do, and I suppose that amount is negligible and yet it's not nothing. I assure you, to have hung out with a guy like that, and as my life has mirrored his in some ways—we both attended the same small college, spent time in Southeast Asia, got married, fathered daughters, wrote, followed the story of our time to more and more dangerous places—and even as mine was admittedly a very pale and underwhelming imitation, indeed, even as I spent a great deal of time and energy thinking about who Vollmann is and how any of us might look to him for direction, I was still surprised to find a letter from him in my mailbox this summer. Months earlier I had sent him a letter accompanying a copy of my first book, which detailed five years I spent living in and traveling to Saudi Arabia, Yemen, Iraq, Turkey, and Lebanon, and in that letter I'd asked him to tell me what he thought of my attempt to write as an American and father and husband and writer. Hoping to increase the odds he'd actually respond, I included a self-addressed stamped envelope, and on a letter slipped into that smaller envelope I'd written, "I, William T. Vollmann, have the following thoughts about Nathan Deuel's book," thinking this would not only be a clear indication of how I hoped he might respond, but humorous enough to disarm any awkwardness. How often, after all, do we attempt to contact the people who have in part made us who we are? (Or, perhaps, made us who we are not?) And yet how likely was it, I reckoned, that not only would he never write me back, he might just as likely rip up or slot me even lower on whatever low or likely very not high spot I had previously held, if I held one at all. (Picture Vollmann. Picture Vollmann getting my letter.) So with the letter, not only would he know or be reminded of my name, but he would associate that name perhaps more so not with grace or excellence or bravery but with weakness, supplication, and some mix of self-acknowledged doubt and regret. I'd written a book! I'd written a book. I'd written this book? Then I checked my mailbox on a warm day in summer and discovered not only my own unsure handwriting on a small but familiar envelope but, more importantly, a postmark from Sacramento, long-time home to the man himself. I ripped it open, and saw the line of my own writing "I, William T. Vollmann, have the following thoughts about Nathan Deuel's book." And underneath, his unmistakable scrawl.

Why on earth did he bother to write me back? It was the summer of 2014: William T. Vollmann was a fellow father and citizen of California. He was the object of fan groups, anthologies, past and future prizes of note. With all we did not have in common and also the little we maybe did, it was unmistakably true that this man had taken the time to write me a four-page letter.

1. We first met at tiny Deep Springs College, an all-male institution in the middle of the desert of California. In the summer of 1997, Vollmann entered my dorm room and asked to see a book that had been written by our eccentric founder. I found the slim volume on my shelf and handed it over. Vollmann looked rather bizarre himself: giant glasses, work shirt tucked into ill-fitting jeans, stubble. Who the hell was he? A friend of mine at this very small college (just thirteen admitted per year) explained: Vollmann was the alum who'd written all those stories about smoking crack with prostitutes in San Francisco. I wondered about him one night not long after, as I killed a cow (my then-assignment at the self-sustaining school was in the slaughterhouse) and I took one of the best steaks into the desert and cooked it over a fire.

2. Then I dropped out of college and moved to Cambodia. One night, I gave a prostitute five dollars, but it was for nothing more than sitting next to me in a karaoke parlor. Another night, running down a dark sidewalk in Phnom Penh, I recklessly leapt over a hammock. A woman in the gloom began to scream and, turning back, I realized that there was a baby in that hammock. I had recklessly jumped over a baby.

3. I met a woman I wanted to marry. We moved to Indonesia and lived in the master bedroom of a house owned by an Islamic scholar. We'd displaced the scholar's second wife, who moved into a smaller room down the hall. She woke up early to comb her long black hair in the kitchen. Most mornings, she'd fire up the karaoke machine in the living room and belt out Air Supply. Mice cavorted in our communal rice jar. I walked everywhere, arriving covered in sweat. My wife dissuaded me from getting a pair of giant glasses. I got malaria and shivered under sweat-soaked sheets. Rats tumbled around in the roof over our heads.

4. I started going to Russia. One day, the same year Russian security services would detain my journalist wife, who was reporting in the troubled southern republic of Dagestan, I found myself sitting next to Vollmann. We ordered absinthe together and I can't now recall and mostly doubt that anything of import or note was said. He spent most of his time in Russia interviewing poor people. He later wrote a book about poor people. I got it from the library and read it while half-submerged in a pool in Florida.

5. My family and I lived for five years in the Middle East, where I often found myself in the position of staying at home with our very small daughter, while my wife put on a battle helmet or boarded a helicopter or in general did something badass in a place like Baghdad or Syria. I regretted the situation—her reporting in dangerous places and our daughter caught between that bravery and my own uncertain situation at the keyboard. I suppose you could say, and I have, that the book I sent Vollmann contains all I know or can say about what happened over there.

6. Now we're in California. Vollmann's latest (not final?) book concerns a man not unlike Vollmann who is dying. My wife interviews him on NPR. He says he's not dying. He says that when he does die he hopes it's in the arms of a lover.

In part his letter read,

> My feeling is that you sell yourself short . . . you write yourself into your wife's
> shadow. You idealize your wife and child in a very loving and humanly admira-
> ble way; any good family man would want to do the same. But the camera eye
> of a writer, I would claim, is meant to perceive all tones and shades—not just
> the admirable ones. So, are you prepared to create round characters, or must
> they be flat ones?
>
> All humans are a mix of good and bad. One need not be monstrous to ask,
> "What don't you like about your family?" But to the extent that one writes
> about one's relationships, one runs the risk of self-censorship, which always
> shows. My feeling is that you set yourself a very difficult task, maybe an impos-
> sible one. Can you or should you turn the same neutral, nuanced gaze upon
> your family as you might upon an Iraqi politician? You and your family wouldn't
> like that. . . . This is not meant to demean or discourage you; I am only telling
> you what I think because you asked me.

It seemed significant that it was my handwriting that began this letter, and
that it was Bill's that concluded it. He was only writing because I asked him.
The task, he said, is impossible. And maybe that's the deal: mentors demand
of you that which you might not or cannot demand of yourself. Mentors ask
questions of you that you couldn't form on your own. You could spend a lifetime writing up a decent answer.

PETER TRACHTENBERG
ON JAMES MCCOURT

B ecause he lives mostly in Washington, D.C., and I live mostly in a lot of
other places, for the past twenty years my relationship with Jimmy
McCourt has mostly been conducted over the phone. But whenever we
speak—and even now, when I'm only writing about him and don't have his
voice on the other end of the telephone to use as an *aide-mémoire*—I have a
clear picture of him sitting in profile with his eyes closed and his hands stee-
pled on his chest. It's the pose of someone listening to music. Jimmy is deeply
musical, physiologically musical, the way some performers are said to be, as if
he possessed extra sense organs dedicated to music's reception and delecta-
tion. *Mawrdew Czgowchwz*, his best-known novel is a group portrait of a super-
naturally talented opera diva (with a vocal range that goes beyond the soprano
to *oltrano*) and her devotees, characters he returned to more than thirty years
later in *Now Voyagers*. And even when he's writing about an ageless Hollywood
actress or an aging drag queen traveling across Europe with the ashes of sisters
who died in the AIDS epidemic, there's music in his prose.

But Jimmy isn't listening to music. He's listening to someone talking. It
might be one of the strange and brilliant people who gravitate to him—his
friends have included Susan Sontag, Fran Lebowitz, and Veronica Geng. It
might be me. He listens to conversation with the same gravity and generosity,
the same hollowing-out of the self, with which some other people listen to
music. To call it critical listening would be only half-right, since implicit in
most criticism is a sense that the object of attention is somehow deficient—or,

say, improvable. Until not that long ago, this was how I read every manuscript students put before me, holding a pencil in my hand to tick off each flaw with a little mark in the margin—not an x or a checkmark, just a tap of the pencil point for me to refer to later. I noted the good parts, too, but there were never as many of those. I know that one can listen to music the same way, and certainly to conversation, only the pencil is invisible. Jimmy listens without a pencil. It's largely thanks to his example that I now undertake my first reading of a manuscript without a pencil. The practice is still new enough to me that it feels as if I were reading without pants on.

At the center of what Jimmy taught me about writing—and I've never formally studied with him—is that poised, receptive listening. The practice is particularly useful for a writer whose best works are symphonic arrangements of human voices. It also shows up in his mimicry, which can be both side-splitting and shamanic. I once told Jimmy about going to see the trans performer Joey Arias, who was doing her Billie Holiday act. Arias looks nothing like Billie—for one thing, she's white, with the long, mobile features of a Picasso—but her voice is an uncanny simulacrum of hers, that creamy, satiny, glide with something broken at its center. When I told Jimmy about it, he was amused. "Oh, anybody can do Billie. You just have to use your head voice. *I* can do Billie." And he proceeded to do her, maybe not as astonishingly as Arias, but with impressive fidelity.

On the page, however, all of McCourt's characters are recognizable as aspects of himself, chips off his old block. He ingests everyone he listens to and incorporates their voices into his. That's the paradox of his work, and it may be the single most valuable thing I learned from him. Writing isn't about pretending to be someone else. (That's acting, and acting of a particular kind.) It's about taking in the other and making it part of yourself. An additional part of this performance, the part that keeps it from being cannibalistic, is that the other remains alive inside you. This is what I imagine Whitman meant by "I contain multitudes." McCourt does too.

GEORGE SINGLETON

ON FRED CHAPPELL

Fred Chappell taught me how to wake up, sit down, and write. From 1984 to 1986—the years I studied in Greensboro—Fred wrote short stories, a novel, a number of poems, critical essays, book reviews, and a goddamn libret-to. He won the Bollingen Prize and published two poetry collections. This, of course, occurred before the Internet, so at the time no one could google "Fred Chappell achievements" and learn about his output and accolades. He never mentioned any of the aforementioned, in or outside of class.

Fred stared at the blackboard at the beginning of each workshop, chalk in hand. I imagine that, like a good sculptor conjuring which image lives beneath the marble's surface, Fred waited for the correct quotation to spill out of his brain. Sometimes multiple quatrains or paragraphs emerged, often in French or Italian. He'd say the words out loud, never explain why such quotations would be important to any of us, then say, "Okay. I trust y'all have read the work for today," and so on.

Of course we'd read the work. Here's why:

On one particular occasion—and I still have nightmares about this—Fred wrote down, I don't know, maybe one of Pound's cantos on the board, sat down, and began the class. This was on the second floor of the McIver Building, the same floor that Randall Jarrell once haunted. Outside, a groundskeeper, wearing a hardhat, stood on an extension ladder leaned up against a tree. He held a chainsaw and trimmed limbs back. Each time Fred began a comment, the poor guy outside revved his saw.

Fred ceased talking. The chainsaw idled. Fred picked up where he left off. Back at this point MFA students were required to take poetry and fiction workshops, rightly, and this might've been the day Fred told me, "Do not ever write poetry again. Stick with prose."

The man outside revved his chainsaw hard, interrupting Fred again. This happened more than a few times. Finally, Fred got up out of his chair—he looked like a cross between a heavy-lidded middleweight ex-boxer and a slightly bored badger wearing a cardigan sweater—and approached the louvered window. He cranked that metal handle down, shoved the pane outward, and stuck his head out the window.

Fred's face couldn't have been more than five feet from our intruder. Would Fred recite *The Wasteland* to him? Would he go for Baudelaire or James Joyce or Schopenhauer or David Hume, maybe his friend George Garrett? Would he recite Joyce Kilmer or Frost, maybe say something about *Deliverance,* or go for Diogenes and/or Juvenal?

"I hope you fall out that tree and cut your dick off," Fred bellowed. "We're trying to learn something in here, buddy."

He laughed. The anti-arborist descended his ladder. Fred returned to his desk.

My friend Dale Ray Phillips—who took classes with Fred Chappell before I did—likes to say, "The dogs may bark, but the caravan rolls on." It's, perhaps roughly, an ancient, wise, Persian proverb, and I don't doubt that Fred might have scrawled it on the blackboard, probably in the original Farsi, one day.

That's what Fred Chappell taught me and others. Sit down and get your work done. While everyone else bitches and moans about not receiving MacArthur Foundation or National Endowment for the Arts grants, Guggenheims, Pulitzers, the National Book Award—while everyone else sits around bars and coffee shops blurting out "How can [insert any of 1,000 names here] get published and I can't? My shit's ten times better!"—find a quiet room at a quiet hour. Damn the hangover, hives, influenza, headache, gout, torn cartilage, bunions, open wounds, and write like all hell.

JAY PARINI

ON GORE VIDAL

My friendship with Gore Vidal, the novelist and essayist who became a hugely important mentor, goes back to the 1980s, when I was living in Atrani, a village on the Amalfi coast of Italy, not so far below Naples. My wife and I had young children at the time, and we lived in a small villa overlooking the sea. One can't imagine a more seductive setting. From our rooftop terrace we looked up through a lemon grove to a huge house on five stories that clung to a cliff just below the Villa Cimbrone, a well-known palace.

I wondered about this house and asked the tobacconist in Amalfi if he knew who lived in the big white house. I guessed some Italian duke or duchess. He said, "It belongs to Gore Vidal, the American writer."

He explained that Vidal had been living here for a long time, since the early seventies. He took his exercise by walking into town, and almost every afternoon he would buy a newspaper before going to the adjacent bar for a glass of wine. I decided to leave a note for Vidal, explaining that I was an American writer and so forth, and giving him my address. I said that I admired his work and hoped to meet him one day.

That very afternoon, Vidal banged on our door. "Come for dinner!" he said, when I opened the door. He was a sharply handsome man, tall, with an easy manner that surprised me.

We soon found a babysitter and joined him that evening at La Rondinaia, his villa in Ravello—an amazing piece of architecture that clung to the cliffs like a swallow's nest. I had rarely seen such a view as from the balcony of his study, with Salerno in the distance.

Gore and his partner, Howard Austen, soon became our close friends. Vidal and I had a lot in common, and I spent a huge amount of time with him, often returning to the coast to stay with him at the villa. We liked to talk about American history and politics, of course, and there never seemed any end to the conversation. I moved back to the United States, and so the friendship continued mostly by telephone; but we made sure to meet up at least once or twice a year.

Once, when I was staying with him in the summer for a week or so, I was working on a long piece of fiction. I remember sitting by his pool with my manuscript in hand. Gore came out and sat beside me. I asked him, quite innocently, whether I could get away with perhaps twenty or thirty pages in a story where two characters discussed the philosophy of Kierkegaard. Gore squinted in the sun, scratched his forehead, and said, "You can do that. But only if these two characters are sitting in a railway car, and the reader knows there is a bomb under the seat."

In some ways, that was the best piece of writing advice I've ever had. You can do anything if there is an appropriate dramatic context. But you must put that bomb under the seat.

I've now had decades of conversation with Gore, who was one of my best friends. Even in his late eighties, I sought him out to discuss ideas, to complain about things, to ask for advice. We traveled together in various parts of the world, and he read my work—the books—in rough draft and comments. I have always been grateful to him for doing this, and I feel lucky to have had his counsel over such a lengthy time.

He was a kind and generous man—traits not always apparent in television or radio interviews, where he cultivated a spiky persona. (Everyone of a certain age recalls his infamous debates with William F. Buckley during the 1968 presidential conventions. They tore at each other like a pair of wildcats.)

Vidal's wit was real, and it flowed in conversation. But there was a kind of quiet steady generosity of spirit that strikes me as the essential aspect of his character. Only his friends understand this, and it's always unpleasant when I hear him described as "bitchy" or "cynical." He was neither of these, not when he was trying to be helpful to a friend. And he had a genuine interest in younger writers—not something in ample supply in the competitive world of American letters.

FRANK X. GASPAR

ON DONALD DRURY

Well, leave it to the Greeks: a humble, aged man, wise in his own right, gives advice to another man—and through him a god speaks, making the transaction divine, and therefore something beautiful. Actually it was the goddess Athena who spoke through Mentor, especially when Odysseus returned from the war. (Leave it to the Greeks not to shrink from the feminine in the divine.) But this is going to be about a man named Donald Drury. I doubt anyone has ever heard of him, but he was a mentor, certainly, and he was humble and unassuming, and there was no doubt about the divine spark in him.

I never thought about it until just now, but I, too, was coming back from a war. Bombs were falling on Cambodia, and American mines swayed on cables in Haiphong Harbor, and my time being up, I washed ashore to a small college in California, shaken, clueless, crazy in the worst ways, living parlously for a time in a dilapidated blue Ford van with a wizard badly painted on the side. Don was an English professor. With another spin of the wheel or roll of the dice, he might have worked at a wooden desk at the New Yorker, but much to my good fortune—and the good fortune of others like me—Don worked at an open-enrollment two-year college in the lower flood plains of greater Los Angeles. Tuition was free. I got a hundred and twenty bucks a month from the GI bill. I left the navy with a little back pay. I wasn't in great shape, but I thought I could make it for a while. I had written all the time I was drifting around New York and Boston, and while I was with the navy, but I was ignorant and self-taught. I knew I needed help.

I enrolled in Don's beginning creative writing class. At first I didn't know what to make of it. Don was not one of these commanding, charismatic figures that you hear about. He would have been in his mid-fifties then, and everything about him was rather medium, including the color of his hair, which he combed straight back, quite probably the way he always had since he was a boy. He wore the then-requisite battered tweed jackets, but always with an open collar. In the classroom he was low-keyed and soft-spoken; he wasn't selling anything. Yes, he was! He was. He was selling something that was quite pure, and as I learned after a few meetings, something that was quite sufficient for the running of his own life: his absolute love of good writing. He would always walk in with a pile of books, many of them patently old and scuffed, each filigreed with tiny torn strips of paper with small notations on them. Today they would have been little post-flags, I suppose, but then they seemed like exquisite little pennants, guidons that would lead Don through rambles about everything, narrative point of view (which I had never heard of), tone, diction, dialogue, story arc, a compendium of poetic terms (*litotes*, for god's sake!) all of which came from him with the clear address of someone talking from a state of bliss.

It was infectious, at least in my case, and though I had tried to write in those young dark years when I scuttled the streets with my head bowed under the lowering sky of the Vietnam draft—and even during my time in the navy—for the first time in my life, I was a writer. I don't honestly remember exactly what other courses I took that semester—I think maybe film, political science, astronomy—and though I loved everything, I was at home with Don. A home I had been searching for for six years. He was amazingly patient, easy to talk to—and I was not easy to talk to in those days. I was edgy, scruffy, angry, and about to take shit from no one. Everyone who hadn't been in the service seemed like a sissy to me, and I could savage professors in class if I thought they were faking it or phoning it in. Don set the bar. He'd sit and show me why "Negroid, phallic smokestacks" might indicate a need on my part to look at modification, and then he'd rattle off some writers, whom I'd immediately read. If I were now to say this was like heaven to me, I'm sure Don, with his gentle yet sardonic half-smile, would push his horned-rimmed glasses up on his nose and say, "Heaven? Seriously?" But it was where I felt *right,* the possibility of getting myself right, for the first time in my life.

I moved, eventually, to a tiny shotgun apartment, furnished, all utilities paid, eighty-five dollars a month (well, it was in the nasty part of town, but even that suited me perfectly), and I turned it into a shrine for writing. I was delirious. I had a typewriter, a desk, books, and now a place to go with my writing and a mentor to show it to. I remember when my van finally died and I was hitchhiking out to campus every morning, and one day, when I was stuck halfway up Clark Avenue, a little old V-dub pulled over and picked me up. I opened the door and tossed my knapsack in and there was Don. "How are you doing?" he asked. "Great," I said. I didn't mention my dead van. I said, "I'm going to be a writer." Don was silent for a moment. A small troubled look moved over his face—really—as he navigated up the avenue. Then he said, "Well, it's going to take a lot of work, but you *might* do it." That was all I needed. No chirpy "go for it" speech. Just that little bit of possibility coming from a man who could make up villanelles in his head and rhapsodize about the most minor of minor characters in the *Iliad*. That was more than enough. I read and wrote like a mad man out of Dostoevsky (thanks, Don, for Dostoevsky). The first real story I wrote for Don wound up in a small magazine next to a piece by Charles Bukowski. I didn't know who he was until then. I believe I still have the magazine up in the attic crawlspace somewhere.

I finished my MFA at the University of California, Irvine, got a tenured job at—Long Beach City College. I was now actually working in the same department as Don, and I saw another side of him. He was politically ferocious in defense of any student or group of students he felt had been dealt a bad hand. The kids who couldn't pay for textbooks, for instance, or who lived in motels, or returning adults who were trying to piece their lives together, and especially any student he thought was getting screwed over by another professor. And he savaged the prigs and the phonies, when they dared cross him, with hilarious mailbox campaigns consisting of English sonnets, parodies of Jonathan Swift, and his poisoned dagger, the limerick. He wasn't mean, though. He was funny. And he always came down on the right side of things. He was who he was, and that was something rare: he was a good man. He retired not long after I arrived, and with a minor bit of facetious ceremony, he moved me into his office, where I sat in his old oaken chair at his old oaken desk for the next thirty-one years. There was a running joke about Don—how he was always cutting himself or banging his thumb with a hammer or some such. And there was a can (yes, they came in steel cans at one time) of desiccated Band-Aids in his top drawer, along with some elastic bands, and for some reason, a scalpel. I kept them all right there until I, too, left the college.

In the years before Don died, he continued to help me grow my mind. I love this era of my friendship with him the best, I think. He'd come by my house every so often, unannounced, though he knew I was, at that time, always home in the mid-afternoon. If he missed me, there'd be a small stack of books on the step, each festooned with the little torn gonfalons, annotated, marking the pages I should pay special attention to. If I was home, he'd always say the same thing, shyly, a finger aside his nose pushing up his glasses, "Oh, uh, I was just on my way to the barber shop, and I thought I drop these off. I hope I didn't interrupt you." And then he'd come in and we'd sit and have tea, and he would fill my house with his love for books, all books, obscure books that he found in obscure catalogues and used bookstores, unerringly picking the ones with fine writing in them, and when it was time for him to go, I'd walk him to the door, my head filled with new things, and knowing, of course, that I genuinely loved him.

Our friendship continued until his death. He enjoyed my miniscule successes. He never, never stopped giving. He not only showed me how to live a life centered on loving art but also set a mark for me as a teacher, one that I probably never reached but that at least has kept my compass pointed in a certain direction during foggy weather. Almost no one in the large world knows who Donald Drury was. He didn't publish, he didn't promote himself, he lived quietly and truly. But he helped to change a life. Don would never allow me to go on about a divine presence in mentoring, yet certainly there is something sacred about this deeply human transaction. But that's just part of what I've been trying to say.

LINEAGE III

TAYARI JONES

ON RON CARLSON

Ron Carlson taught me how to write, distilling craft lessons into pithy statements that I call "Carlsonisms." His stamp on my work is so indelible that I sometimes call myself, as his protégé, a "Carlsonite." My students are Carlsonites, once removed. Yet just as valuable as his instruction about which words to set next is his guidance on the life of an author. What follows is one of my favorites:

Being a writer is all about making mistakes and managing disappointment. Let's say you are going on a road trip. You get, say, a hundred miles down the road and you realize that you have left your wallet back home on the kitchen table. You have no choice but to go back and get it. But how's your attitude?

(A) Do you curse yourself as you make that U-turn and head back home, continue cursing until you have the wallet in hand, grumble still as you head back out, unable to relax again until you have recovered the hundred miles? Are you, for the rest of the journey, thinking about how much farther you would be if only you had not been so stupid to forget your wallet there at the beginning?

(B) Do you slap yourself on the forehead when you realize the wallet is lost and pout all the way home? Once you get home, do you pack yourself a nice lunch and set out again in good spirits?

(C) When you realize the wallet is lost, do you say, "Thank god I realized that I forgot the wallet!"? Then do you drive home with the radio blasting, singing your favorite song?

Person C is the one who is going to make it. Writing a novel is all about forgotten wallets. From a craft perspective, it could be a point-of-view error or a pacing snafu; on a professional level, it could be realizing that your first novel is in the hands of an unscrupulous publisher. You have to recover and move on.

The sooner the better.

Tayari Jones and Ron Carlson with Jones's novel *The Untelling*

RON CARLSON

ON DAVID KRANES

I took an odd tack as an undergraduate; I did everything I could to avoid majoring in English. As a sophomore I took classes in every department at the University of Utah, receiving my only college C in accounting. Geology was a contender and history, of course, which also begged the question: what are you going to do with this? I did not want to go to law school. I still walked around campus with Emily Dickinson in one pocket and Walt Whitman in the other. Then in the fall of 1968 I found myself in "American Theater" with David Kranes, and it took off the top of my head. The plays were wild and muscular and rewrote all the rules, and the professor was so utterly committed to the work, and he treated our written responses like important mail, and he wrote back—and that was important mail, and I just thought: I want to work with this guy. I don't care where it's going. Kranes was a playwright who has since written many books of fiction, and he was director of the Sundance Playwrights' Institute for years. I saw a few of his plays and I read his fiction. His dense, angular prose stirred and challenged me. It made me want to write. His prose has always sent me back to my writing table, inspired. It still does. And his work as a teacher was astonishing. He read so deeply and with such care and his measured comments were like gold. You understood you were being taken seriously. He thought that my handing him stories was a natural feature of life at the university, and his responses took my work with such engagement that I had to recommit. Reach, he seemed to say, and I reached. He was a singular force and influence in my life. In the summer of 1969, he arranged a teaching job for me in Connecticut and my career as a teacher be-gan. We began a lifelong friendship. I saw him again recently at an opening of one of his plays in Las Vegas.

I remember one night in Salt Lake after finishing one of my first stories, I called him and only then saw that it was after ten. He had two small kids! He said to bring it over, and I did, and sitting in his living room he said, "Read it to me." What a thing to say! Ever! What a gift!

ARTHUR FLOWERS

ON JOHN O. KILLENS

I am Flowers of the Delta Clan Flowers and the line of O'Killens.

Griotic tradition you often start with who you are and who you were trained by. I was trained by Babajohn Killens, the Great Griot Master of Brooklyn.

Last time I saw him was the deathwatch out in Brooklyn. First novel finally published and getting some play, I (heart broke and strung out on cocaine) had decided to leave NYC and go to LA. Ostensibly to bust Hollywood but really escaping the city, literary tail tucked firmly between my legs. Basically waiting on John to die.

Finally climbed out of a powdered funk long enough to go to Brooklyn. The brownstone on Union, a familiar pilgrimage, folk sitting around the living room on the deathwatch. I ask Ms. Grace if I can go up to see him. She give me permission and I go to the second-floor bedroom and I'm shocked to see the worn-out frame of the man I had known as such a vibrant force, damn near a skeleton, lost under voluminous covers. He pleased to see me; I had been his primary acolyte for years, so anointed by my absolute devotion, my apparent determination to learn what mystical systems call the unwritten text—the example of the master's life.

Came to NYC in the summer of '73 to get into Babajohn's workshop at Columbia and stayed in it till he died in 1986. For thirteen years I followed Babajohn Killens from school to school. Wherever he taught he always stipulated that his workshop would be "open to the community," so over the years it drew a little literary community unto him. Adero, Akua, Ashanti, Brenda, Barbara, Doris Jean, Jacqui, Joyce, Nunez, TMac, et al.—one by one my literary *companeros y companeras* drifted into the circle of young writers that gathered around Babajohn Killens and followed him from Columbia to Howard to Bronx Community to his final gig at Medgar Evers, Brooklyn.

Prestigewise, Medgar Evers was a long drop from Columbia and Babajohn's reputation had suffered. He was no longer treated as a serious writer, but for his students he was in his prime during those Medgar Evers years. Medgar Evers was not only in his own Brooklyn neighborhood but it was like this microcosm of blacks from all over the western hemisphere and all these diasporic dynamics played out there. I called it *the meeting ground* and Babajohn was its master griot. Every Saturday morning he shuffle walk the two blocks or so to campus, followed by a gaggle of literary ducklings, pacing our steps to the shuffle of the elders. These were his years of grace. Looking at him there on his deathbed, I realize every era come to an end. Barely functional, he call me over and start lecturing me. "Art," he say, "you a brilliant writer but with a little compassion you could be profound."

In my literary youth I considered myself a hordesman, trying to gather blackfolk into a conquering horde and fling them into battle. Power was my thing, in all its permutations. I aspired to be a hard man and people were just factors to be used. This was reflected in my work. When Babajohn tried to bestow compassion upon me, all I heard was "brilliant." Wasn't until years later, after I had myself been broken and had my power stripped from me, rebuilding from scratch, I heard what Babajohn was trying to tell me. I realize he was trying to make sure my legacy, as his student, would not be hard and cold but loving and warm. A literary shaman trying to keep the culture, the tribal soul, healthy.

Sounds good, don't it? But it didn't quite actually happen that way. I've told this story many times. Over the years it's been embellished. What he really told me was "Don't get lost out there in Hollywood, never let money control the work." He did tell me the compassion bit. Another place, another time. But it's the advice to compassion that I most treasure, so I strung it with the deathwatch like that because it has more mythic value that way, don't you think? More narrative punch.

Tending to Babajohn's legacy has become a major component of my literary mission. That's the way Babajohn taught me to roll: "Our struggle for liberation is indeed a long long distance race, for we are out for nothing short of winning the entire human race and we are up against a formidable foe. To win this race will require planning, pacing, discipline, and stamina, and a belief in our ability to win the long protracted struggle. . . . We must construct one hundred year plans. Two hundred year plans. We must construct institutions for generations yet unborn."

What he called being a long-distance runner. What I call the longgame.

It never cease to amaze me Babajohn don't get his due respect for being the visionary he was. Guess you want to be a visionary, can't be crying the blues because folk don't see your vision. Nonetheless, the Killens legacy has been most profound. African American literature, the voice of a culture that has since its inception felt itself under mortal siege, is fundamentally shamanistic and vitally concerned with communal health and empowerment. Its most revered figures have all been culturally engaged. Langston, Zora, Walker, Amiri, Ishmael, Toni, Wideman, Chamoiseau, et al. Creating the visions without which the people will perish and serving in its mythic heart its age-old griotic function of keeping the culture alive, vibrant, dynamic, and viable.

Back in the day Babajohn was the only one of the major black novelists who tried, systematically, to forge of himself a space where writers grow. He was the great baobab under which we shaded.

I recall once me and B. J. Ashanti all but declared war over Highjohn de Conqueror. I had been working the Highjohn voice into *De Mojo Blues*. But when I read a section in a Harlem Writers Guild workshop, Ashanti protested. *The Candy Marine*, he said, the myth of Highjohn de Conqueror, a book-length epic poem I've been working on for years. I've read it out loud in workshop. You have stolen my character. You are a thief.

I protested but he was able to prove he had read it in workshop. He had the paper trail. I had not consciously been aware of this and still protest this is not the case, but I was on shaky ground. I couldn't just give it up. It had become an integral part of my novel, my personal mythwork, a literary alterego. I was hearing the voice of the Conqueror in my head. I begged, pleaded, offered suggestions—let's both do it, try Longjohn, etc., etc.—nothing, Ashanti was charging plagiarism, not just a phrase or a passage, but a myth-based protagonist. A felony charge. The workshop commence to taking sides.

Babajohn called us out to Brooklyn. Ms. Grace fed us, we went downstairs, John had our manuscripts on the table before him, and said, "You've got to give it to Ashanti, he had it first." That was it. The highest court of appeal had ruled against me. I hung my head and apologized to Ashanti. And Ashanti said, "He can have it."

Just like that he gave it to me, and it's become the central post of my myth-work. To this day I am thankful. But it crippled our literary buddydom. He has never since let me see another work of his in play. But we didn't go to war. That would have been a cultural tragedy. We were two of Babajohn's strongest guns. Babajohn didn't play that, not amongst his legions, and he was always the final arbiter when it came to the gamemoves, we couldn't conceive of earning Babajohn's disappointment. In any shape, form or fashion. About that same time I had a short, tumultuous tenure as executive director of the Harlem Writers Guild, a storied organization that Babajohn had cofounded. After much, I realize now, unnecessary drama (I was young and full of myself), a bunch of us wanted to break off and form the New Renaissance Writers Guild. We had to trek to Brooklyn first, to get John's blessing.

I recall the time he ran as a delegate for Jesse Jackson's first presidential run, part of a radical slate taking on the black Brooklyn political machine. He asked me to be his campaign manager, which basically translated as spear carrier. We would be at these meetings, the old bulls seated around the table talking strategy, the "campaign managers" standing attendant behind them. It was primal deep. By election day I had lost about thirty pounds and the machine creamed us, we didn't get not one single delegate. But the experience is just one of many I treasure being Babajohn's chosen devotee. I realize now just how classic a mystical experience it was.

When he wasn't running as Jesse's delegate or helping Malcolm write his post-Nation manifesto, Babajohn worked hard to institutionalize a progressive black literary infrastructure—"what good vision without institutionalization, what good seeds without preparation of the ground?"—he himself trained generations of black writers in the longgame, with the expectation that they would go on to train their own—how to produce and market works, how to wield literary power, how to be a literary mob—taught us how to be "successful" writers, not only in terms of publication and such but how to be cultural influents. Ideological orchestrators.

John O. taught us that as writers and trained cultural forces we, in our works, leave a legacy for future generations, and we should be very conscious of what we want that legacy to reflect. He taught us how to use the word as nommo, reality's forge, taught us to be cultural custodians, guide and guardian of the tribal soul and destiny, shield and spear, taught us to be visionaries.

We were all politicos, literary activists who had come out of the black arts movement, for whom art was already an instrument of cultural redemption and empowerment. That's why we were drawn to John O. in the first place. Babajohn taught us the true test of any literary movement is the quality of works produced by it, the nature of the ideological instruments forged to meet its challenges. We were such fierce young politicos and had to be taught that politics can't drive a novel. Or as Babajohn used to tell us, over and over and over, "The more important what you have to say, the more obligated you are to say it well."

Babajohn paid for this knowledge in the coin of his own work. It is often more political than crafty and he is not widely read these days. His major work, *And Then We Heard the Thunder,* and his fun work, *The Cotillion,* still readable, but the others are dated. He tried to make sure we didn't suffer the same literary fate. I once read somewhere that writers are judged by their worst when they living, their best when they dead. I'm depending on that. For me and Babajohn both.

That every generation judges anew which works are important to them.

Basically what Babajohn taught us is that literature is a sacred calling; that the power of the word is not to be treated lightly. Got to come to the Word with respect. Babajohn trained us to significance and I sincerely appreciate this opportunity to give him some props. As his protégé, that's my job— tending to the legacy of Babajohn Killens, tending to his mythwork as I do his grave out at Evergreen Cemetery in Brooklyn, on the far end of Eastern Parkway. Beacon Hill #2, #13358. The stone with the open book on it. I often go there when I'm weary, when doubts and anxieties have overtaken me and I feel the need to renew my faith in the literary life. My faith in the me only I see. This writer of historical stature and significance I aspire to be. Still. In spite of all evidence to the contrary. Still.

There are times when I curse the day I met him. Hadn't been for John O. Killens I would have been a different kind of writer, some easier kind of writer. But then there are the times when I am in wonder at this life that I have lived. I love being a literary man, I love the literary life, I love being a writer. Including the dues I have paid. It is the best life I could have ever chosen. It incline me to the *cosmic* and I get to make a humble contribution to the enhancement of the human condition. To leave behind works, hopefully, of beauty and wonder, power and grace. My legacy, my gift to all the generations. To the extent that my works are pertinent to those generations, perhaps even my immortality.

What's not to love?

It was Babajohn gave that to me. To this day his precepts about being a writer live on in me, old wisdom applied to new circumstances as they arise. I been working on my current novel so long folk have taken to calling it "the phantom," but it's like I can hear Babajohn telling me, over and over, "Future generations won't have anything but your work, Art. They won't care that you were broke, tenure-/ego-starved—all they will have is the work, take your time, do it right. Give it whatever years it take, to move it from bad to good to great."

When it come to my own young Turks, Babajohn's training been a gift that keeps on giving, trying to be to my students what Babajohn was to me. At a critical moment in my aspiration to the literary life I had somebody in my life who cared. A traveler who knew the road. Giving me guidance every step of the way. From student to contender to professional, every step of the way. It is in the name of Babajohn Killens that I want/need to be that for my students. A place where writers grow.

I cannot fully express how proud I am to be one of John O. Killens's legions—what Sara Fabio in a poem once called "Killens' chillens." Knowing Babajohn as I did was a once-in-a-generation experience. There will never be another like him, or another time like the one in which he flourished, and I, unrepentant child of the sixties, feel totally blessed to have known him, to have been trained by him, to be part of his legacy—with everything I do I praise his name, Babajohn Killens, the Great Griot Master of Brooklyn.

The other great Blessing of Babajohn is my determination to conduct myself with the compassion of O. Killens in everything I do. I heard you, Babajohn. Took me a minute but I heard you.

After telling me never let money (or fame) rule the work—"never sell your name," he tell me, "that's all you got, that's all any writer has"—he ask me to put him in the easy chair next to the bed. Uneasy at the intimacy, I carefully put an arm behind his back and under his knees and I lift him up. He so feather-light I stumble and almost drop him. I place him in the chair and arrange the covers. "Call Amazing Grace," he tell me. We called her Ms. Grace, he just called her Amazing. I call her up and she smile to see him sitting there so proudly.

"I'm sitting up," he tell her.

"I see you are," she say.

"I like to know what's going on around me," he say.

"I know you do," she say.

That's the last time I saw him. That's how I remember him. Babajohn Killens. The Great Griot Master of Brooklyn. Upright. May your work serve many generations. May the Gods of Literature be good to you.

This spell is done. God's blessings on us all.

From left: Baron James Ashanti, Brenda Connor-Bey, John Killens, Doris Jean Austin, Arthur Flowers, Joan Cofer., ca. 1980. Courtesy of Arthur Flowers.

ANNIE LIONTAS

ON ARTHUR FLOWERS

He's a black hoodoo from Memphis, a Vietnam vet, a witness of the civil rights movement, a cat lover, a shed man, a music man, a woman-loving-man, a Johnny Walker, a fighter, and he is all heart. I'm an immigrant, a woman-loving-woman, a worker, a fighter, an eater, a hustler, and what he has called, on multiple occasions, "desperate." The first time we ever met, he eyed me up, I eyed him up, and it was agreed without a word: our spirits took.

Last year, Arthur Flowers officiated my marriage to my wife, Sara, accepting payment in the form of a black-label bottle. It was his first gay wedding, though I know for a fact that he has not always looked so favorably on a union between two women. Nonetheless on August 31, 2014, I believe that Arthur Flowers called down every servant of Love from the heavens to the seas, and wherever else they were hiding out, just to bless my marriage. (Author's note: it's going awesome.) He was in true *mentoh* form that balmy evening, in trim black suit, with a conch shell in one hand, an iPad in the other. His blessing was all Love, as he is always:

> when my people gather together like this in peace and love and harmony that place, that gathering place, that place is holyground . . .

> . . . this partnership, this companionship so special im willing to go mythic on you and claim this one has the potential of being one of humanities great loves, poetry, myth, and legend—an inspiration to us all. with folk of this caliber and a love of this magnitude anything is possible.

If you have never heard Arthur Flowers invoke, let me just say that you are missing something thunderous.

Six months later, when I sold my novel, Arthur was number three on the list of people I called. He responded, all cool with it, like he'd never had a doubt: "So how does it feel to be a contender?" He promised he wouldn't tell anyone for twenty-four hours, just till I told my people. Then he immediately confessed in a text message that he had gone ahead and spoiled the good news with everybody.

Can you even be mad at that? That's love overfloweth.

At Syracuse University, Arthur serves as a kind of mentor for all novelists. I'll rephrase: he does his damnedest to get all short story writers to turn into novelists. He even tries to get at the poets. I think Flowers believes that a novel lives in each of us—and he might be right.

I can't tell you how many times Arthur took me out to Alto Cinco for a compatriot lunch to talk about my novel, flying through the Syracuse streets in his low-ride like he was the one who put them there in the first place. He sits facing the restaurant's exit, a holdover, he explains, from the civil rights movement, when folk didn't want their backs to the door. "Though these days," he lets me in on the secret, "it's an affect." I'm like, "Yeah, but it wasn't always an affect." And he laughs, a glint in his eye, "Aw, it was an affect even back then." That's one of the most beautiful things about the man: the realness.

Plus he gives great hugs.

No matter how many times we hit Alto Cinco, Flowers always orders the same thing—vegan tostadas (He's a vegetarian but he is also a complex man and so has no problem pocketing bacon when it's free.) We talk James Baldwin, talk women, talk craft, trade ways to kill time—his most adorable form of procrastination being "rub the cat," 'cause, lord, he loves his cats. He hands over his personal copy of Chamoiseau's *Texaco,* introducing me to the mythic, mystical mentoh with roots in the African occult. During one of these very lunches, Arthur confronts me with the most important question I've encountered as a writer: "Whose story is this? Who does it belong to?" I realize I can't answer him, and this non-answer becomes a critical part of my novel *Let Me Explain You.*

Flowers is full of encouragement and pickups, which is the one true job of the mentor, because everyone in this game knows at all times—and we are tricking ourselves if we ever think otherwise—that this vocation is mysterious and uncharted. In our line of work, *advice* means nothing more than "educated guess" and "hopeful approximation." We are chasing something that doesn't want to be caught, aiming dim flashlights down a very dark, changing path, and, sure, we make headway, but the only thing that ever really matters is that we keep going. And Arthur Flower knows this.

The magical thing about Arthur is, he gives Alto Cinco to everybody. He shares his time, his sermons; he breaks bread with us. He wants to confirm that we are not alone in the struggle. The true magic about this hoodoo is that he never made me feel there had been dozens, scores before me, whom he had likewise lifted up. He treats every one of us like equals, never like students: because we are all of us students in the following of the Word.

We are, all of us, his literary compatriots, *companeros y companeras.*

Did my mentoh and I always see eye to eye? Of course not. We're both too hot-blooded. Early on I fought Arthur tooth and nail about outlines: it seemed to me that until I hit page 60 of a novel, I didn't have critical mass. How the hell could I plan out something when I couldn't even hear its heartbeat yet? "True," he said, "so get the heart beating, and then lay out the outline." He was right, of course, and I've been outlining ever since. My outlines, though, look nothing like Flowers's, which, I imagine, resemble a sort of sheet music. Mine are maps, hung on living room walls of my compact one-bedroom in Philly. (Author's note: Thank you to my wife for tolerating this and for letting me use your special markers.) When I'm lost, these maps tell me where to go.

Syracuse can be a devastatingly gray, frigid place, and so it needs a man like Arthur to bring warmth and heat and, okay, sometimes he gets a little intense. I have seen him cry tears that shook the room at news of a terrible loss, and I have seen him laugh so deeply that even the most surly, disaffected, miserable writer had no choice but to join in. He is not a perfect man, and, yes, he has a political agenda—every writer should. But his heart and values are right, even if he can get a little hotheaded.

Ooh, let me just say it: I like somebody with a little fire.

But it's equally true that Arthur has a wonderful vision for Syracuse. What he wants to cultivate is a Literary Mob. To that end, in 2013, Arthur generously and in unprecedented form used all of his research monies, collected over several years, to fly in Syracuse alumni as part of his course on literary success. In that seminar, we were privileged to read our Syracuse predecessors. Adam Levin, Jeff Parker, Ellen Litman, E. C. Osondu—they all came back, thirteen of them, not just because of Arthur, but for him. Sure, some of them pushed to get a few extra bucks in the process. But with that singular gathering, Flowers put something into motion that has since taken on a life of its own— we have become a roughneck mob of sorts. Thanks to Flowers and others at Syracuse, we've been able to strike out on our own, following each other out to the corners of the earth, dragging our tools behind us, not so isolated now.

My secret about Arthur Flowers is that I don't know that my work has ever really spoken to him. He is a lyricist, seeking out certain crucial, tender notes on the page, and I don't know that I give him what he wants out of literature. I don't know if I go deep enough for the man. I'll share that on one occasion, in a scroungy scrawl that looked exactly like chicken feet, he wrote, "WHAT IS THIS SHIT?" in the margins of one of my stories. Others might have been mad, but I wasn't—I know why he did it. I have a thick skin, but also: I know that, ironically, no one writes such a thing unless he respects you.

Can your mentor be a mentor if he doesn't believe in your work but believes in you? Yes.

Arthur Flowers was my professor, but he was so much more. Compatriot, mentoh, Totoro, a kind of spiritual guide with a walking stick—trying, as much as anyone else, to see the forest for the trees. He is a good man, a flawed man, and, yes, I'll just get out with it, he has offered the kind of compassion and tending I never received from my own father. Unfortunately, he also has the hoodoo habit of ghosting, and so he left my wedding reception before I had a chance to ask him to dance.

Last week, I texted Arthur Flowers:

YOU WERE IN MY DREAM LAST NIGHT, DRIVING AND—AS USUAL—TAKING CARE OF ME.

He wrote back:

I LOVE YOU TOO

Arthur Flowers officiating at the wedding of Annie Liontas and Sara Nordstrom

ACKNOWLEDGMENTS

In a sense, this is a book of gratitude. So we would be remiss in not thanking those who were of great help in seeing it into being.

Thank you to all the contributors who took the time to compose the pieces for this book as well as the visual artists who generously allowed us to showcase their work. A special thanks to Doug Unger for letting us use the title of his essay as the title of the book and for being a real inspiration for the project.

Andrew Cothren, a great writer and an MFA student at the University of Massachusetts, Amherst, was instrumental in corralling and organizing the particulars of almost seventy contributions. And Katelyn Edwards, Parker's assistant when he was director of the low-residency MFA at the University of Tampa, did a lot of the logistical heavy lifting in the early stages. Thank you both!

Thank you to Nina Puro and Nadxi Nieto of Literary Mothers for introducing us to incredible voices in the community.

Thank you also to Richard Mathews, who spent a great deal of time talking with the editors as the project came together.

And a huge thank you to the good people at the University of Massachusetts Press, particularly senior editor Clark Dougan, who enthusiastically shepherded this book through the publishing house, and the new director, Mary Dougherty, who has welcomed the anthology with open arms.

ABOUT THE CONTRIBUTORS

KEN BABSTOCK is the author of, most recently, *Methodist Hatchet,* published in April 2011 by House of Anansi and chosen by the *Globe and Mail* as one of their top one hundred books. His previous three collections were finalists for the Governor General's Award for Poetry and the Griffin Prize for Excellence in Poetry, and he has won the Trillium Book Award for Poetry and the *Atlantic Poetry Prize.* His poems have been translated into several languages and anthologized widely in Ireland, the United States, and Canada, most recently in *The Oxford Anthology of Canadian Literature in English.* He lives in Toronto.

POLINA BARSKOVA's first book of poems was published when she was still a teenager. After receiving a degree in Russian literature and classics from Saint Petersburg University, she came to the United States, where she earned a Ph.D. in Russian literature from the University of California, Berkeley. She is the author of seven books of poetry, including *The Zoo in Winter,* her first collection in English. Barskova teaches at Hampshire College.

AIMEE BENDER is the author of five books, most recently *The Color Master.* Her short fiction has been published in *Granta, GQ, Harper's,* the *Paris Review,* and elsewhere, as well as heard on *This American Life.* She lives in Los Angeles and teaches at the University of Southern California.

MEGAN MAYHEW BERGMAN lives on a small farm in Vermont and is the recipient of the 2015 George Garrett Award from the Fellowship of Southern Writers. Her first book, *Birds of a Lesser Paradise,* published by Scribner, was a Barnes and Noble Discover Great New Writers pick, an Indie Next Selection, and one of *Huffington Post's* best books of 2012. Her second book, *Almost Famous Women,* was published in January 2015.

JEDEDIAH BERRY is the award-winning author of *The Manual of Detection.* His short stories have appeared in *Conjunctions, Ninth Letter,* and *Chicago Review,* among other journals, and in anthologies such as *Best New American Voices* and *Best American Fantasy*. He teaches at the Solstice MFA program of Pine Manor College.

KEVIN CANTY's seventh book, a novel called *Everything*, was published by Nan A. Talese / Doubleday in 2010. He is also the author of three collections of short stories (*Where the Money Went, Honeymoon*, and *A Stranger in This World*) and three previous novels (*Nine below Zero, Into the Great Wide Open*, and *Winslow in Love*). His short stories have appeared in the *New Yorker, Esquire, Tin House, GQ, Glimmer Train, Story*, the *New England Review*, and elsewhere. His essays and articles have appeared in *Vogue, Details, Playboy*, the *New York Times*, and the *Oxford American*, and in many other venues. Canty's work has been translated into French, Dutch, Spanish, German, Polish, Italian, and English. He lives and writes in Missoula, Montana.

MARY CAPONEGRO is the author of *Tales from the Next Village, The Star Café, Five Doubts, The Complexities of Intimacy*, and *All Fall Down*. She has taught at Brown University, the Rhode Island School of Design, the Institute of American Indian Arts, Hobart and William Smith Colleges, and Syracuse University and, since 2002, has been the Richard B. Fisher Family Professor of Writing and Literature at Bard College. She is a recipient of the General Electric Award, the Rome Prize in Literature, the Charles Flint Kellogg Award in Arts and Letters, and the Bruno Arcudi Award.

RON CARLSON is the author of ten books of fiction and a volume of poems. He has been teaching for more than forty years and directs the graduate programs in writing at the University of California, Irvine.

BYRON CASE, an imprisoned writer from Kansas City, Missouri, is the author of *The Pariah Syntax: Notes from an Innocent Man*. The legitimacy of his 2002 murder conviction is a subject of ongoing debate. Meanwhile, his work has been published widely, in print and online, and his frequent dispatches appear on pariahblog.com.

DIANE COOK is the author of the story collection *Man v. Nature*, published by HarperCollins in October 2014. Her fiction has appeared in *Harper's, One Story, Granta, Tin House, Zoetrope, Guernica*, and elsewhere. Her nonfiction has been featured in the *New York Times Magazine* and on *This American Life*, where she worked as a radio producer for six years. Cook won the 2012 Calvino Prize for fabulist fiction. She earned an MFA from Columbia University, where she was a teaching fellow, and she lives in Oakland, California.

ERICA DAWSON is the author of two collections of poetry: *The Small Blades Hurt* (Measure Press, 2014) and *Big-Eyed Afraid* (Waywiser Press, 2007). Her poems have appeared in journals and anthologies such as *Best American Poetry 2008* and *2012*, *Barrow Street*, *Birmingham Poetry Review*, *Blackbird*, *Virginia Quarterly Review*, and *Florida Review*. She is the poetry editor of the *Tampa Review* and teaches at the University of Tampa.

TONY D'SOUZA is the author of three novels. He contributes to magazines, radio, and television and has been awarded a Guggenheim, a National Endowment for the Arts fellowship, an O. Henry Prize, and the Sue Kaufman Prize from the American Academy of Arts and Letters. He maintains the writing discipline first beaten into him by his mentor when he was nineteen years old.

NATHAN DEUEL is the author of *Friday Was the Bomb*, named one of Amazon's best books of the month. He teaches writing at the University of California, Los Angeles, and has published essays in the *New York Times Magazine*, *GQ*, *Harper's*, and the *New Republic*, among other magazines.

STEPHEN ELLIOTT is the author of seven books, including *The Adderall Diaries*. He is the founding editor of a literary website, the *Rumpus*; and his novel *Happy Baby* was recently turned into a feature film.

JON PAUL Fiorentino is the author of the novel *Stripmalling* and the poetry books *Indexical Elegies*, *The Theory of the Loser Class*, and *Hello Serotonin*. He lives in Montreal, where he teaches at Concordia University and is the editor of *Matrix* magazine.

TIBOR FISCHER, son of Hungarian refugees, was born in Stockport, England, in 1959. His first novel, *Under the Frog*, was short-listed for the Booker Prize in 1993. He is the author of four other novels, *The Thought Gang*, *The Collector Collector*, *Voyage to the End of the Room*, and *Good to Be God*, as well as a collection of short stories, *Don't Read This Book If You're Stupid*. He is a fellow of the Royal Society of Literature, and his work has been published in twenty-five languages.

ARTHUR FLOWERS is the author of various novels and works of nonfiction, including *Another Good Loving Blues* and *I See the Promised Land*, a graphic work from Tara Books in India. He is a blues-based performance poet, recipient of a National Endowment for the Arts fellowship and other awards, and webmaster of *Rootsblog*. He teaches fiction at the Syracuse University MFA program and has been executive director of various nonprofits, including the Harlem Writers Guild, New York City.

NICK FLYNN has received fellowships and awards from, among other organizations, the Guggenheim Foundation, PEN, and the Library of Congress. His poems, essays, and nonfiction have appeared in the *New Yorker* and the *Paris Review*, on the radio show *This American Life*, and many other venues. He is currently a creative writing professor at the University of Houston, where he is in residence each spring. In 2015 he published his ninth book, *My Feelings* (Graywolf Press), a collection of poems. His work has been translated into fifteen languages.

JAMES FRANCO is an actor, director, screenwriter, producer, teacher, and author. He began his career on *Freaks and Geeks* and received a Golden Globe Award for his performance in the biographical film *James Dean*. Notable film credits include *OZ The Great and Powerful*, *Spring Breakers*, Harry Osborn in the Spider-Man trilogy, *Milk*, and *127 Hours*, for which he received Academy Award, SAG, and Golden Globe nominations for Best Actor. He has directed, written, and produced several features and has been published several times in magazines and through his own books. He is currently teaching college courses at UCLA, USC, and CalArts and acting classes at Studio 4 and recently made his Broadway debut in *Of Mice and Men* to rave reviews.

MARY GAITSKILL is the author of the novels *Two Girls, Fat and Thin* and *Veronica* as well as the story collections *Bad Behavior, Because They Wanted To,* and *Don't Cry.* Her stories and essays have appeared in the *New Yorker, Harper's, Granta, Best American Short Stories, The O. Henry Prize Stories,* and elsewhere. She was awarded a Guggenheim Fellowship in 2004 and a Cullman Fellowship in 2010. She currently holds the Sidney Harmon Chair at Baruch College.

FRANK X. GASPAR is the author of five collections of poetry and two novels. Among his many awards are the Morse, Anhinga, and Brittingham prizes for poetry, multiple inclusions in *Best American Poetry,* four Pushcart Prizes, a National Endowment for the Arts fellowship, and a California Arts Council fellowship. His work has appeared widely in magazines and literary journals, including the *Nation,* the *Harvard Review,* the *Hudson Review,* the *Kenyon Review,* the *Georgia Review,* the *American Poetry Review,* the *Southern Review, Prairie Schooner,* the *Tampa Review,* and *Miramar.* He teaches in the MFA writing program at Pacific University in Oregon. His latest collection of poems, *Late Rapturous,* was published by Autumn House Press in July 2012.

ANYA GRONER teaches English at Loyola University in New Orleans. Her poems, stories, and essays appear in *Ninth Letter, Oxford American, Guernica,* the *Atlantic,* and elsewhere. More of her writing can be found at AnyaGroner.com.

TONY HOAGLAND's poetry collections include *What Narcissism Means to Me* and *Unincorporated Persons.* A new full-length collection of poems was released by Graywolf in September 2015. He teaches at the University of Houston, and his essays about poetry appear widely.

SHEILA HETI is the author of six books, including the short story collection, *The Middle Stories,* the novels *Ticknor* and *How Should a Person Be?,* and the *New York Times* bestseller *Women in Clothes,* edited with Heidi Julavits and Leanne Shapton. She lives in Toronto.

NOY HOLLAND's debut novel, *Bird,* is forthcoming from Counterpoint in fall 2015. Her collections of short fiction and novellas include *Swim for the Little One First, What Begins with Bird,* and *The Spectacle of the Body.* She has published work in the *Kenyon Review,* the *Antioch Review, Conjunctions,* the *Quarterly, Glimmer Train, Western Humanities Review,* the *Believer, NOON,* and the *New York Tyrant,* among other journals. She was a recipient of a Massachusetts Cultural Council award for artistic merit and a National Endowment for the Arts fellowship. She has taught for many years in the MFA creative writing program at the University of Massachusetts Amherst, as well as at Phillips Andover and the University of Florida. She serves on the board of directors at Fiction Collective Two.

PAM HOUSTON's most recent book is *Contents May Have Shifted,* published by Norton in 2012. She is also the author of two collections of linked short stories, *Cowboys Are My Weakness* and *Waltzing the Cat;* a novel, *Sight Hound;* and a collection of essays, *A Little More about Me.* Her stories have been selected for *Best American Short Stories,* the O. Henry Awards, the 2013 Pushcart Prize, and *Best American Short Stories of the Century.* She is the winner of the Western States Book Award, the WILLA Award for contemporary fiction, the Evil Companions Literary Award, and multiple teaching awards. Houston is a professor of English at the University of California, Davis. She also directs a literary nonprofit, Writing by Writers, and teaches in Pacific University's low-residency MFA program and at writer's conferences around the world. She lives on a Colorado ranch, 9,000 feet above sea level, near the headwaters of the Rio Grande.

CHRISTINE HUME is the author of three books, most recently *Shot* (Counterpath, 2010), and three chapbooks, *Lullaby: Speculations on the First Active Sense* (Ugly Duckling Presse, 2008), *Ventifacts* (Omnidawn, 2012), and *Hum* (Dikembe, 2014). She teaches in the interdisciplinary creative writing program at Eastern Michigan University.

Leningrad, USSR-born MIKHAIL IOSSEL is the founder and executive director of the Summer Literary Seminars International programs and professor of English at Concordia University in Montreal. He is the author of *Every Hunter Wants to Know,* a collection of stories, and co-editor (with Jeff Parker) of the anthologies *Amerika: Russian Writers View the United States* (Dalkey Archive, 2004) and *Rasskazy: New Fiction from a New Russia* (Tin House, 2010). His stories have appeared, both in English and in Russian, in numerous publications, such as *The New Yorker, The Literarian, Agni Review, The North American Review,* and others, and were translated into a number of languages and anthologized in the *Best American Short Stories* and elsewhere. He has been awarded Guggenheim and National Endowment for the Arts fellowships, among others.

TAYARI JONES is the author of three novels, including *Silver Sparrow* and *Leaving Atlanta.* She has received fellowships from the National Endowment for the Arts, the Radcliffe Institute for Advanced Study, and the United States Artists Foundation.

ROY KESEY's latest books are the short story collection *Any Deadly Thing* (Dzanc Books, 2013) and the novel *Pacazo* (Dzanc Books, 2011; Jonathan Cape, 2012). His other books include the short story collection *All Over,* the novella *Nothing in the World,* and two historical guidebooks. He has received a National Endowment for the Arts fellowship, the Paula Anderson Book Award, and the Bullfight Media Little Book Award. His short stories, essays, translations, and poems have appeared in more than a hundred magazines and anthologies, including *Best American Short Stories* and *New Sudden Fiction.*

STEFAN KIESBYE is the author of four novels. *Next Door Lived a Girl* won the Low Fidelity Press Award, and *Your House Is on Fire, Your Children All Gone* was released by Penguin in 2012. Both novels have been translated into German, Spanish, and Japanese. *Messer, Gabel, Schere, Licht* was published in 2014 by Tropen Verlag, Germany, and *Fluchtpunkt Los Angeles* by ars vivendi verlag in 2015. Stefan lives in Rohnert Park, California, with his wife, Sanaz, and their dogs, Dunkin, Nozomi, and Kurt. He teaches creative writing at Sonoma State University.

LEONID KOSTYUKOV is a prose writer, poet, and literary critic. His work has been published in Serbia, Israel, France, and the United States. He frequently presents his work to audiences across Russia and teaches literary master classes, including creative writing seminars.

MAYA LANG's debut novel, *The Sixteenth of June*, was long-listed for the 2014 Flaherty-Dunnan Prize. She was awarded a 2012 Bread Loaf–Rona Jaffe Foundation scholarship in fiction and was a finalist for *Glimmer Train*'s Short Story Award for New Writers. A first-generation daughter of Indian immigrants, she currently lives in New York.

SCOTT LAUGHLIN is co-founder and associate director of the Disquiet International Literary Program in Lisbon, Portugal. His work has appeared in the journals *Post Road*, the *San Francisco Bay Guardian*, and *Night Owl* and the book *Such Conjunctions*. He is currently enrolled in the low-residency MFA program at Converse College and teaches English at San Francisco University High School.

ADAM LEVIN is the author of *Hot Pink* and *The Instructions*. He lives in Chicago.

ANNIE LIONTAS's novel *Let Me Explain You* was selected by the ABA as an Indies Introduce 2015 Debut. She is the recent recipient of a grant from the Barbara Deming Memorial Fund, and her story "Two Planes in Love" was selected as runner-up in *BOMB Magazine*'s 2013 Fiction Prize contest. Since 2003, Annie has been dedicated to urban education, working with teachers and youth in Newark and Philadelphia. She lives with her wife in Philadelphia across the street from the best pizza jawn.

SAM LIPSYTE is the author of three novels and two short story collections. His fiction has appeared in the *New Yorker*, the *Paris Review*, *Tin House*, the *Quarterly*, *Playboy*, and *Best American Short Stories*, among other places. He lives in New York and teaches at Columbia University's School of the Arts.

Translator JAMES J. LÓPEZ is a professor of Spanish at the University of Tampa, Florida. He has written and presented extensively on contemporary Latin American literature. He has also published original fiction and literary translations.

CARMEN MARIA MACHADO is a fiction writer, critic, and essayist whose work has appeared in the *New Yorker*, the *Paris Review*, *Granta*, *AGNI*, the *Los*

Angeles Review of Books, VICE, and elsewhere, as well as on National Public Radio. She is the 2014–15 CINTAS Foundation fellow and has received the Richard Yates Short Story Prize and a residency at the Millay Colony for the Arts. She is a graduate of the Iowa Writers' Workshop and the Clarion Science Fiction and Fantasy Writers' Workshop and lives in Philadelphia with her partner.

Translator VIOLETTA MARMOR was born in Moldova and raised in New York City. She received an MFA in fiction from the Program for Poets and Writers at the University of Massachusetts Amherst. A native Russian speaker, she learned English watching reruns of '80s American sitcoms. She's currently working on a novel inspired by her war-torn childhood in the Transnistria region.

MICHAEL MARTONE was born in Fort Wayne, Indiana, where he played Little League baseball in Hamilton Park. The park was built on land owned by the Hamilton family, whose members included the famous popularizer of Greek myths, Edith, and it had once been a garbage dump. During long stretches in the outfield, Martone would toe through the sparse grass to see what scrap of junk had bubbled up from below. Tin cans and bottles, springs and rubber tires. Marbles. Old boots and shoes. Once, after a particularly bad winter filled with many thaws and freezes, a whole icebox found its way to the surface, its door a kind of hatch leading back underground. Michael Martone's father called Michael Martone "Mickey." Most people thought he was called that after the great Yankee centerfielder, Mickey Mantle, but he was really named after Martone's father's childhood friend, who died when Martone's father was Martone's age when he played Little League baseball in Hamilton Park in Fort Wayne, Indiana. It was the first time Martone's father was a pallbearer but not the last.

EDIE MEIDAV is the author of three novels, most recently *Lola, California*. She teaches in the MFA program at the University of Massachusetts, Amherst, and can be found online at lolacalifornia.com.

PETER MEINKE's work has received major awards in both poetry and fiction, and he has published more than twenty books, most recently *Lucky Bones* (University of Pittsburgh Press, 2014). He has been writer-in-residence at many colleges and universities and is the first poet laureate of Saint Petersburg, Florida.

MAAZA MENGISTE is a Fulbright scholar, a photographer, and the award-winning author of *Beneath the Lion's Gaze*, selected by the *Guardian* as one of the ten best contemporary African books. The novel was also named one of the best books of 2010 by the *Christian Science Monitor*, the *Boston Globe*, *Publishers Weekly*, and other publications. Her fiction and nonfiction writing appears in the *New Yorker*, the *Guardian*, the *New York Times*, *BBC Radio 4*, *Granta*, and *Lettre Internationale*, among other places. Her second novel, *The Shadow King*, is forthcoming.

KEVIN MOFFETT, who contributed the illustration in Mike Spry's essay, is the author of *Permanent Visitors* and *Further Interpretations of Real-Life Events*. He lives in Claremont, California.

LEE MONTGOMERY is the author of *The Things Between Us*, *Whose World Is This?*, and *Searching for Emily: Illustrated*. *The Things Between Us* received the 2007 Oregon Book Award and was a four-star critic's choice for *People* magazine. *Whose World Is This?* received the 2007 John Simmons Iowa Short Fiction Award and was also a finalist for the 2008 Ken Kesey Award in fiction. Her short fiction and nonfiction have appeared in numerous publications, most recently in the *New York Times Magazine*, *Glimmer Train*, the *Antioch Review*, the *Iowa Review*, and *Tin House*. Montgomery is also an editor who has worked for magazines and book companies, including the *Iowa Review*, the *Santa Monica Review*, and Dove Books. She was the editorial director and associate publisher at Tin House Books, an executive editor with the magazine, and the founding director of the Tin House Summer Writers' Workshop. Presently, she is a fellow at the Atheneum Masters Program in Portland and an editor for a new ebook platform for women, Shebooks.net.

SABINA MURRAY is the author of the novels *Forgery*, *A Carnivore's Inquiry*, and *Slow Burn* and two short story collections, the Pen/Faulkner Award–winning *The Caprices*, and *Tales of the New World*. She is a former Michener Fellow at the University of Texas at Austin, Bunting Fellow of the Radcliffe Institute at Harvard University, Guggenheim Fellow, Massachusetts Cultural Council Fellow, and National Endowment of the Arts Fellow. She currently teaches in the MFA Program for Poets and Writers at the University of Massachusetts Amherst.

JOSIP NOVAKOVICH teaches fiction and nonfiction writing at Concordia University in Montreal. He has published four collections of stories, three collections of essays (most recently *Shopping for a Better Country*), two books of practical criticism, and a novel that has been translated into ten languages. His honors include Whiting, Ingram Merrill, and American Book awards as well as a Guggenheim fellowship, and he was a Booker International Prize finalist in 2013.

ALISSA NUTTING's debut novel, *Tampa*, was published by Ecco/Harper-Collins in 2013. She is author of the short story collection *Unclean Jobs for Women and Girls* (Dzanc Books, 2010), which won the Starcherone Prize for Innovative Fiction, judged by Ben Marcus. Her fiction has or will appear in publications such as *The Norton Introduction to Literature, Tin House, Bomb,* and *Conduit;* her essays have appeared in *Fence,* the *New York Times, O: The Oprah Magazine,* and other venues. An assistant professor of creative writing and English literature at John Carroll University, she lives in Ohio with her husband, her daughter, and two spoiled tiny dogs.

JEFF PARKER's books include *Where Bears Roam the Streets: A Russian Journal* (Harper Collins, 2014), *The Taste of Penny* (Dzanc, 2010), and *Ovenman* (Tin House Books, 2007). With Pasha Malla he "wrote" the book of found sports poetry *Erratic Fire, Erratic Passion* (Featherproof, 2015), and with Mikhail Iossel he edited two collections of contemporary Russian writing in translation. He is the director of the Disquiet International Literary Program in Lisbon Portugal, and he teaches in the MFA program at the University of Massachusetts Amherst.

JAY PARINI is a poet, novelist, biographer, and critic. His five books of poetry include *The Art of Subtraction: New and Selected Poems.* He has written eight novels, including *Benjamin's Crossing, The Apprentice Lover, The Passages of H. M.,* and *The Last Station,* which was made into an Academy Award–nominated film starring Helen Mirren and Christopher Plummer. Parini has written biographies of John Steinbeck, Robert Frost, and William Faulkner. His nonfiction works include *Jesus: The Human Face of God, Why Poetry Matters,* and *Promised Land: Thirteen Books That Changed America.* He writes for various publications, including the *New York Times,* the *Guardian,* and the *Chronicle of Higher Education.*

PAT PERRY is an artist from Michigan who writes and makes pictures through careful and cautious observation. He works itinerantly, and is currently based in Detroit.

RICHARD POPLAK is the author of *Ja, No, Man: Growing Up White in Apart-*

heid-Era South Africa (Penguin, 2007), *The Sheikh's Batmobile: In Pursuit of American Pop-Culture in the Muslim World* (Soft Skull, 2010), and the experimental journalistic graphic novel *Kenk: A Graphic Portrait* (Pop Sandbox, 2010). His election coverage from South Africa's 2014 election, written under the nom de plume Hannibal Elector, was collected as *Until Julius Comes: Adventures in the Political Jungle* (Tafelberg, 2014). *Ja, No, Man* was long-listed for the Alan Paton Nonfiction Prize, short-listed for the University of Johannesburg Literary Award, and voted one of the top-ten books of 2007 by *Now* magazine. Poplak has won South Africa's Media-24 Best Feature Writing Award and a National Magazine Award in Canada.

PADGETT POWELL's most recent books are *The Interrogative Mood* and *You & Me* (published as *You & I* in England).

Artist WILLIAM POWHIDA earned a BFA from Syracuse University and an MFA from Hunter College. He is represented by Platform Gallery in Seattle and Charlie James Gallery in Los Angeles.

DAWN RAFFEL is the author of four books, most recently *The Secret Life of Objects*.

PAISLEY REKDAL is the author of several books of poetry and nonfiction, most recently *Animal Eye* (University of Pittsburgh Press, 2012) and *Intimate* (Tupelo Books, 2011). She currently teaches at the University of Utah.

RODRIGO REY ROSA was born in Guatemala in 1958. His novels and story collections, which have been translated into various languages, include *The Beggar's Knife* (1986); *Still Water* (1990); *Jail of Trees* (1991); *Let Them Kill Me If . . .* (1996); *No Sacred Place* (1998); *The African Shore* (1999); *Enchanted Stones* (2001); *The Train to Travancore* (2002); *Some Other Zoo* (2005); *The Stable* (2006); *Human Material* (2009); *Severina* (2011); *The Deaf* (2012); and *1986, Complete Stories* (2014). *Tail of the Dragon* (2014) is a compilation of his articles and essays. He has also translated into Spanish works by authors such as Paul Bowles, Norman Lewis, Paul Léautaud, François Augiéras, and Robert Fitterman. In 2004 he was awarded Guatemala's Miguel Ángel Asturias National Prize in Literature.

HENRY ROLLINS has written and published several books of his writing on his 2.13.61 Publications imprint. He works in television, film, voiceover, stage, and radio.

DAVY ROTHBART is the creator of *Found* magazine, a frequent contributor to *This American Life,* and the author of a book of personal essays, *My Heart Is an Idiot,* and a collection of stories, *The Lone Surfer of Montana, Kansas.* He writes regularly for *GQ* and *Grantland,* and his work has appeared in the *New Yorker,* the *New York Times,* and the *Believer.* His documentary film, *Medora,* about a resilient high school basketball team in a dwindling Indiana town, premiered at the SXSW film festival before airing recently on the acclaimed PBS series *Independent Lens.* Rothbart is also the founder of Washington to Washington, an annual hiking adventure for inner-city kids. He lives in Los Angeles and Ann Arbor, Michigan.

Artist GRAHAM ROUMIEU's illustration work has appeared in the *New York Times,* the *Wall Street Journal,* the *Guardian,* the *Atlantic, Harper's,* and a bunch of other places. He is the creator of a series of faux autobiographies of Bigfoot and some other non-Bigfoot books, including a project with Douglas Coupland titled *Highly Inappropriate Tales for Young People.*

Translator ALINA RYABOVOLOVA's translations from English to Russian include British novelist Ben Elton's *Popcorn.* She is currently a doctoral student in Communication at the University of Massachusetts Amherst.

GEORGE SAUNDERS is the author of eight books, most recently *Congratulations, by the Way: Some Thoughts on Kindness* (Random House, 2014) and *Tenth of December* (Random House, 2013), a *New York Times* bestseller that has earned him national and international awards, including the inaugural Folio Prize, the Story Prize, and the PEN/Malamud Award for Excellence in the Short Story. He has been a finalist for the National Book Award for fiction and has received fellowships from the American Academy of Arts and Letters and the MacArthur, Guggenheim, and Lannan foundations. He was recently inducted into the American Academy of Arts and Sciences. Saunders's fiction and long-form journalism regularly appear in the world's top literary publications, including the *New Yorker, Harper's,* and *GQ.*

CHRISTINE SCHUTT is the author of two short story collections and three novels. Her first novel, *Florida,* was a National Book Award finalist; her second novel, *All Souls,* a finalist for the 2009 Pulitzer Prize. A third novel, *Prosperous Friends,* was noted in the *New Yorker* as one of the best books of 2012. Among other honors, Schutt has twice won the O. Henry Short Story Prize. Schutt is the recipient of fellowships from the New York Foundation of the Arts and the Guggenheim Foundation. She is a senior editor of *NOON,* a literary annual, and lives and teaches in New York.

GEORGE SINGLETON has published six collections of stories, two novels, and a book of advice. His stories have appeared in the *Atlantic, Harper's, Playboy,* the *Georgia Review, New Stories from the South,* and elsewhere. A past Guggenheim fellow, he received the 2011 Hillsdale Award for fiction from the Fellowship of Southern Writers.

ALEKSANDR SKIDAN was born in Leningrad in 1965. His poetry collections include *Delirium, In the Re-Reading, Red Shifting,* and *Dissolution.* He is also the author of two books of essays, *Critical Mass* and *The Resistance to/of Poetry.* He has translated into Russian the poetry of Charles Olson, Susan Howe, Michael Palmer, and other contemporary American poets as well as works of theory and art criticism. In 1998 Skidan received the Turgenev Award for short prose. In 2006, he won the Andrey Bely Prize in poetry for *Red Shifting* (2006) and the Bridge Award for the best critical text on poetry. His poems have been trans-lated into many languages and published in various anthologies. In 2008 *Red Shifting* was published in the United States by Ugly Duckling Presse. A co-ed-itor of the *New Literary Observer* magazine, he lives in Saint Petersburg, Russia.

MIKE SPRY has written for the *Toronto Star,* the *National Post,* TSN, MTV, *Joyland,* and *Maisonneuve.* He is the author of the poetry collections *JACK* (Snare Books, 2008), which was shortlisted for the 2009 A. M. Klein Prize for poetry, and *Bourbon & Eventide.* He was long-listed for the 2010 Journey Prize for a story from his collection *Distillery Songs,* which was shortlisted for the 2012 ReLit Award. He lives in Montreal.

MECCA JAMILAH SULLIVAN was born and raised in Harlem, New York City. She is the author of the short story collection *Blue Talk and Love* (Riverdale Avenue Books, 2015). Her fiction has appeared in *Callaloo, Best New Writing, American Fiction, Prairie Schooner, Crab Orchard Review, TriQuarterly, Feminist Studies, Kweli, Narrative Northeast, All about Skin,* and many other venues. Her critical essays on gender and sexuality in African diaspora culture have appeared on Ebony.com and The Root.com as well in *Palimpsest, GLQ,* the *Scholar and Feminist, Ms. Magazine Online,* and the *Feminist Wire,* where she is associate editor for arts and culture. Sullivan has received the James Baldwin Memorial Playwriting Award, the Charles Johnson Fiction Award, and honors from the Bread Loaf Writers' Conference, Yaddo, Hedgebrook, the Mellon Foundation, the Social Sciences Research Council, and the National Endowment for the Arts. She earned a doctorate in English literature at the University of Pennsylvania and is assistant professor of women, gender, and sexuality studies at the University of Massachusetts Amherst. Learn more at meccajamilahsullivan.com.

ROSEMARY SULLIVAN, a poet, biographer, journalist, and author, was born in Montreal. She has published thirteen books of nonfiction, including *Villa Air-Bel: World War II, Escape and a House in Marseille, Labyrinth of Desire: Women, Passion, and Romantic Obsession, Cuba: Grace under Pressure,* and *Shadow Maker.* Her work has won the Governor General's Award, the Yad Vashem Canadian Jewish Book Prize, and the Canadian Authors Association Prize for biography. She has held Guggenheim, Camargo, and Trudeau fellowships and was the founding director of the University of Toronto's master's program in creative writing. Sullivan was appointed an officer of the Order of Canada in 2012.

PETER TRACHTENBERG is the author of *7 Tattoos* and *The Book of Calamities: Five Questions about Suffering and Its Meaning.* He is the winner of a Whiting Award, a Guggenheim fellowship, and a Nelson Algren Award for short fiction. He teaches writing at the University of Pittsburgh.

DEB OLIN UNFERTH is the author of the memoir *Revolution,* the story collection *Minor Robberies,* and the novel *Vacation.*

DOUGLAS UNGER is the author of four novels, including *Leaving the Land,* a Pulitzer finalist; *Voices from Silence,* a year's end selection of the *Washington Post Book World;* and a short fiction collection, *Looking for War and Other Stories.* He recently completed a novel set in Las Vegas, titled *Dream City.* He serves on the executive boards of Words without Borders and other arts organizations and as an editorial adviser for the Americas Series for Texas Tech University Press. He is co-founder of the creative writing international program at the University of Nevada, Las Vegas, where he teaches.

Artist ALISON VANVOLKENBURGH grew up moving between Minnetonka, Minnesota, and the island of Singapore, before settling in Boston, Massachusetts, where she currently lives and works. Having graduated from Wellesley in 2008, Alison has since received an MFA in printmaking from the University of Nebraska–Lincoln. In her work, Alison explores the ideas of perception and cognitive recognition through the use of printmaking, drawing, digital techniques, and other mixed media.

TOBIAS WOLFF's books include the memoirs *This Boy's Life* and *In Pharaoh's Army: Memories of the Lost War;* the novels *The Barracks Thief* and *Old School;* and four collections of short stories: *In the Garden of the North American Martyrs,*

Back in the World, The Night in Question, and, most recently, *Our Story Begins: New and Selected Stories.* He has also edited several anthologies, among them *Best American Short Stories, 1994; A Doctor's Visit: The Short Stories of Anton Chekhov;* and *The Vintage Book of Contemporary American Short Stories.* His work is translated widely and has received numerous awards, including the PEN/Faulkner Award, the *Los Angeles Times* Book Prize, the PEN/Malamud and the Rea awards for the short story, the Story Prize, and an Academy Award in Literature from the American Academy of Arts and Letters. He is a fellow of the American Academy of Arts and Sciences and of the American Academy of Arts and Letters. Wolff is the Ward W. and Priscilla B. Woods Professor in the Humanities at Stanford University. He lives in Stanford with his wife, Catherine. They have three children.

C. DALE YOUNG is the author of three collections of poetry: *Torn* and *The Second Person* (both published by Four Way Books, in 2011 and 2007) as well as *The Day Underneath the Day* (Northwestern University Press, 2001). He practices medicine full time, edits poetry for the *New England Review,* and teaches in the Warren Wilson College MFA program for writers.

Artist VLADIMIR ZIMAKOV is a designer and illustrator who works in a variety of techniques, including linocut, silkscreen, and letterpress among other traditional and digital media. He is the director of the Wedeman Gallery and an associate professor of art and design at Lasell College. As a designer and illustrator, he has worked with the world's leading publishing houses, such as Penguin, Random House, Faber and Faber, the Folio Society, and Vita Nova. He has illustrated books and book covers for the works of Gustav Meyrink, Nikolai Gogol, Fyodor Dostoyevsky, Alexandre Dumas, Herman Melville, and E. T. A. Hoffman among others. His work has been exhibited in numerous solo and group exhibitions in the United States and Europe.

RUI ZINK, born in Lisbon in 1961, is the author of more than twenty books, including *A Arte Suprema,* the first Portuguese graphic novel, and *Dádiva Divina,* which was awarded Portugal's prestigious Pen Club Award. He is a lecturer at Universidade Nova de Lisboa, and his work has been translated into several languages. An excerpt from his book *O Destino Turístico* appeared in *Best European Fiction 2012.*